rks, Glasgow.

ENNANT & CO,

turers of

Soda.

SULPHURIC, MURIATIC, & NITRIC ACIDS.

Sculp.t Edinburgh.

ES, JAMES LEE, NEW YORK.

DAVID
MURRAY
BALLYMENOCH
SUUM CUIQUE

Tennant's Stalk

THE STORY OF

The Tennants of the Glen

BY

Nancy Crathorne

COMPLETED BY

Katharine Elliot of Harwood

&

James Dugdale

MACMILLAN

SBN Boards 333 138201 1

First published 1973 by
MACMILLAN LONDON LIMITED
London and Basingstoke
Associated Companies in New York
Dublin Melbourne Johannesburg and Madras

Printed in Great Britain by
A. Wheaton & Company
Exeter

CONTENTS

Foreword by Katharine, Baroness Elliot of Harwood, D.B.E., LL.D. vii

Dedication ix

Acknowledgements xiii

List of illustrations xv

Prologue xvii

PART I

Chapter I First beginnings on the land: 1296–1726 3

Chapter II John Tennant 'Auld Glen': 1726–1810 12

Chapter III David Tennant and his descendants: 1734–1823 44

PART II

Chapter IV Charles Tennant of St Rollox: 1768–1838 55

Chapter V Charles Tennant—radical leader: 1768–1838 78

Chapter VI Charles Tennant—railways, waterways and rewards: 1768–1838 89

Chapter VII John Tennant of St Rollox: 1796–1878 99

PART III

Chapter VIII Sir Charles Tennant of the Glen: 1823–1906 117
Chapter IX Sir Charles Tennant, industrialist 131
Chapter X Sir Charles Tennant, politician 148
Chapter XI Sir Charles Tennant, an *avant-garde* family 164
Chapter XII Sir Charles Tennant—second marriage 198

APPENDICES

I Sir Charles Tennant's second family 219
II The Leblanc Process 222
III Tennant's Stalk 224
IV St Rollox in 1858 225
V Some Paintings in Sir Charles Tennant's Collection 230
VI The Tennant Companies 232
VII Company Positions held by Sir Charles Tennant 234

Genealogies 235
Bibliography 245
Reference notes 250
Index 258

FOREWORD

by Katharine, Baroness Elliot of Harwood,
D.B.E., LL.D.

This history of four generations of the Tennant family was begun in 1950 by my youngest sister, Nancy Crathorne. She undertook the work at the suggestion of Ernest Tennant, then a partner in the family business Charles Tennant Sons & Co. Ltd.

It was not an easy task as during the bombing raids over London in the Second World War the offices and records of the company were destroyed. Nevertheless my sister, confident that the story was worth recording, researched in family archives and diaries, and in the Mitchell library in Glasgow and the British Museum Library.

Nancy was not able to complete her work before she died in 1969 and her son James Dugdale and I have done the necessary work to finish the book.

There are two of Sir Charles Tennant's sixteen children living, Peggy Wakehurst and myself. It is 150 years since our father was born, a record of which we are both proud. It is fitting that *Tennant's Stalk* should be published in 1973 on this remarkable anniversary.

It would be appropriate for this book to be dedicated to my sister Nancy since without her research and work this history could never have been written. She wanted the book dedicated to those young men, members of the family, who gave their lives for their country in two World Wars.

This book is dedicated to the 'Lost Generation'.

These laid the world away; poured out the red
Sweet wine of youth; gave up the years to be
Of work and joy; and that unhoped serene
That men call age, and those who would have been,
Their sons, they gave, their immortality.

Rupert Brooke

Thomas Lister, D.S.O. aged 26	10th Hussars. Volunteered for the Somaliland Expedition and was killed on active service there in 1904. Eldest son of Charlotte (Tennant) Ribblesdale of Gisburne, Lancashire.

1914–1918

Charles Alan Tennant aged 27	The London Scottish, later the 3rd Dorsetshire Regiment and the 2nd Devons. Second son of William Augustus Tennant, of Orford House, Essex. Killed near Armentières, France, 1915.
Charles Grant Tennant aged 33	The 4th Seaforth Highlanders. Only son of James Tennant of Fairlieburn, Ayrshire. Killed in the Battle of Festubert, France 1915.
Edward Wyndham Tennant aged 19	The Grenadier Guards, later the Royal Flying Corps. Eldest son of (Edward) Lord Glenconner, of The Glen, Innerleithen. Killed at the Battle of the Somme, France 1916.

Henry Tennant aged 20	The 2nd Dragoon Guards, later the Royal Flying Corps. Eldest son of the Rt Hon. Harold John Tennant, of Great Maytham, Kent. Killed in France, 1917.
Hugh Tennant aged 36	The London Scottish, later the Royal Engineers. Third and youngest son of John Tennant of 19 The Boltons, London, invalided out of the army and died in 1927, from the effects of having been gassed.
John Amherst Tennant aged 26	The Bedfordshire Regiment, later attached to the First Border Regiment, second son of John Tennant, of 19 The Boltons, London. Killed in the Dardanelles, 1915.
Mark Tennant aged 24	The 4th Battalion, Seaforth Highlanders, later the Scots Guards. Seconp son of Francis John Tennant of Innes House, Morayshire. Killed in the Battle of the Somme, France, 1916.
William Galbraith Tennant aged 36	Strathcona Horse. Eldest son of John Tennant of 19 The Boltons, London. Killed in France, 1915.
Lachlan Gordon Duff aged 34	The First Battalion Gordon Highlanders. Only son of Pauline (Tennant) Gordon Duff, of Drummuir, Banffshire. Killed in France, 1914.
Charles Lister aged 28	The Middlesex Hussars. The Royal Naval Volunteer Reserve. Second son of Charlotte (Tennant) Ribblesdale, of Gisburne, Lancashire. Died of wounds received in the Dardanelles Campaign, 1915.

1939–1945

John Edward Tennant, D.S.O. M.C. Legion of Honour aged 51	Served in the First World War in the Scots Guards, then in the Royal Flying Corps. In the Second World War in the Royal Air Force which he commanded in Mesopotamia. Eldest son of Francis John Tennant, of Innes House, Elgin. Killed on duty in a flying accident in Scotland, 1941.
Michael Lindsay aged 32	The Royal Navy. Killed at sea, 1940.
Harry Lachlan Lindsay aged 32	The Royal Horse Artillery. Killed in Italy 1944. Only sons of Joan (Gordon Duff) Lindsay of Carnoustie, Aberdeenshire, and grandsons of Pauline (Tennant) Gordon Duff.

ACKNOWLEDGEMENTS

Our grateful thanks are due to many people for their help, very particularly to:

The Rt Hon. Harold Macmillan who knew Nancy and other members of the Tennant family for many years and who read the manuscript and suggested to his company that they should publish the book. *Chloë Green* who edited and shortened the text with great skill. *Professor and Mrs C. J. Fordyce* who read and corrected the manuscript and gave so much scholarly advice. *Ivor Brown* who several years ago gave Nancy the necessary encouragement to continue. *Sir James Fergusson of Kilkerran, Bart.* whose great knowledge of Scottish, and particularly Ayrshire, history helped greatly with the first part of the book. *Kenneth Rose* who lent his typescripts of the letters written to Lord Curzon by four of Sir Charles Tennant's daughters and who made many helpful suggestions. *Dr Williams*, Editor of the I.C.I. Magazine, for help on technical details. *The Hon. Julian Fane* who gave permission to use letters written by Charlotte Ribblesdale. *Mark Bonham-Carter* who lent Margot Asquith's diaries and who granted permission to quote from her letters and diaries. The late *Viscount Chandos* for permission to quote from Laura Lyttelton's letters and diaries. *Dame Margaret Wakehurst* who allowed Lucy Graham-Smith's watercolours to be reproduced. *Nan Tennant* who provided material about Laura Lyttelton. *The Hon. Henrietta Reader-Harris* who discovered a box of family letters at Glenconner and provided the photograph of John Tennant. *Sylvia Dugdale* who prepared the genealogy and painstakingly located a large number of quotations used. *Miss A. I. Lees* who started researching in Edinburgh and Glasgow in 1950 and has typed various parts of the manuscript more than once. *Daphne Brown* who has also typed and retyped parts of the book. *Professor S. G. Checkland* whose great knowledge of Sir Charles Tennant's interest in the mines of Tharsis was most valuable. *John R. Hume* of The University of Strathclyde whose researches in the City of

Glasgow archives have been invaluable and who has patiently answered many queries. The late *Major John Alexander* who allowed the 1844 painting of St Rollox to be reproduced as the jacket of this book. Many members of the Tennant family including *Lord Glenconner* and the late *Ernest Tennant*. Their respective sons *Colin* and *Julian Tennant* who have given access to material and answered many questions. *James Tennant Bailward* who has lent letters and photographs and has provided part of the genealogy. *David Tennant* and *Ranald Boyle* who helped with the genealogy. *Charles Tennant* who provided material concerning David Tennant.

We would also like to thank the authors and publishers who have given us permission to use copyright material. *W. J. Reader*, official I.C.I. historian, who gave permission to reproduce the engraving of St Rollox; *Dr Peter Reynolds* who obtained access to the Tennant Knox letter book 1800–02 from the I.C.I. Archives and Imperial Chemical Industries for permission to quote from the book; the National Library of Scotland for access to the Rosebery Papers; Longmans, Green for permission to quote from W. A. Campbell's *The Chemical Industry*, 1971.

LIST OF ILLUSTRATIONS

1. (a and b) John Tennant's tombstone
2. (a and b) Glenconner, Ochiltree
3. (a) The Revd William Tennant
   (b) John Tennant of Creoch
   (c) Captain David Tennant
   (d) Alexander Tennant
4. (a) Charles Tennant of St Rollox by Andrew Geddes
   (b) Mrs Charles Tennant by Andrew Geddes
5. The opening of the Garnkirk and Glasgow Railway
6. 195 West George Street, Glasgow
7. Robina Arrol
8. John Tennant of St Rollox
9. St Rollox in 1844
10. Four generations of the Tennant family
11. The families of Sir Charles and his brother John Tennant, 1864
12. Emma, Lady Tennant
13. Sir Charles Tennant by Sir Daniel Macnee
14. 40 Grosvenor Square
15. The Glen, Innerleithen
16. (a) Lucy Graham-Smith
    (b) Laura Lyttelton
    (c) Charlotte Ribblesdale
    (d) Margot Asquith
17. (a) Francis John Tennant
    (b) Harold John Tennant
    (c) Edward Tennant
    (d) Mr Gladstone
18. Mr Gladstone at Glen
19. Glenconner, North Berwick
20. Shooting party at Glen 1899
21. A group at Glen 1895
22. Sir Charles Tennant by J. S. Sargent
23. Marguerite, Lady Tennant, and her daughters by J. J. Shannon (detail)

24. Sir Charles Tennant practising golf
25. Marguerite, Lady Tennant
26. Tennant's Stalk
27. Sir Charles' second family in 1907

Line Illustrations

Endpapers St Rollox
figure (i) A letter from Robert Burns to John Tennant Page 39
(ii) Tennant Knox & Co. letter book of 1801 Page 54
(iii) Plan of the St Rollox works Page 77

Acknowledgements

The publishers are grateful to the Hon. Colin Tennant for Plates 4a and b, 7, 13, 20, 21 and fig (i); The Hon. Mrs J. Reader-Harris for Plate 8; to James Tennant Bailward for Plate 18, to Dame Margaret Wakehurst for Plates 17a, b, c, d; to the Hon. J. and the Hon. D. Dugdale for Plate 23; to the Hon. James Dugdale for Plate 22; to Glasgow University Library for Plate 5; to Charles Tennant & Co. Ltd of Glasgow for Plate 9; to I.C.I. archives for the endpapers and fig (ii). The photographs for Plates 1a and b and 2a and b were taken by Mrs S. Barnes, and all unacknowledged Plates are from photographs in the possession of the Hon. James Dugdale.

Prologue

THIS is the story of a family. In the seventeenth century its members were crofters on the soil of Ayrshire; others, in the eighteenth century, played a large part in Glasgow's industrial revolution; in the nineteenth century they sailed on the crest of the wave of world expansion; and in the twentieth century they fought for their country's survival and modernised their businesses to keep pace with the competitive world.

In 1742 only a thin column of peat smoke curled to the sky from the chimney of the Tennants' Ayrshire cottage. In 1842 smoke from industrial power belched from 'Tennant's Stalk', a chimney which stood 435 feet 6 inches high in the St Rollox works of Charles Tennant and Company. At that time it was the largest chemical works in the world. 'The Stalk' towered above the turbulent city, casting a murky shroud over the cathedral of St Mungo where the city's motto: 'Let Glasgow flourish by the Preaching of the Word' had been proclaimed for centuries. For eighty years 'The Stalk' was Glasgow's most prominent landmark until it was struck by lightning in 1922. Fumes had already weakened its walls and it had to be felled to the ground with high explosives.

'The Stalk' and all it stood for arose through the vision and energy of one member in three consecutive generations of the same family, who creatively contributed to the industrial revolution which drew men to the cities in the hope that their lives would be transformed and alleviated by the magic of scientific discoveries. It was a time when political ideas of liberty and *laissez-faire* thrived on the expansionist creed of free trade, when Great Britain became the sovereign creditor country and Queen Victoria reigned 'By the Grace of God of the United Kingdom of Great Britain and Ireland, Queen, Defender of the Faith, Empress of India'.

Glasgow's first historian in 1736 gives an idyllic picture of his town: 'The city is surrounded with Corn-fields, Kitchen & Flower Gardens, and beautiful Orchyards, abounding with Fruits of all Sorts, which by Reason of the open & large Streets, send forth a pleasant and odoriferous Smell.'(1) Little over a century later many 'Stalks' serrated Glasgow's skyline and emitted odours of more questionable fragrance over the Royal Burgh. In 1700 it housed approximately 12,500 people. This rose to 80,000 in 1800 and today it is a capital of industry and international trade with over one million inhabitants.

Part I

CHAPTER ONE

First beginnings on the land 1296-1726

In 1296 when unlettered barons spent much of their surplus energy being bad neighbours and despoiling each other's lands and when serfs formed a large part of the population, variations of the name of Tennant first appear on the parish registers. 'William Tennant of Crestone of County of Linlescu' is to be found, having a seal showing a large dog added to his name 'S. Will'i Tenaunt'. The following century, in 1309, Thomas Tenaunt was one of the witnesses in the enquiry concerning the Knights Templars. Another John Tenant was one of the garrison of Edinburgh Castle in 1339–40. In 1366 John Tennand was one of the Burgesses of Stirling who attacked the cruives (coups made of wickerwork left in rivers to catch salmon) and fishings of the Abbey of Cambuskenneth. In the fifteenth century the Tennant family is recorded as having settled around Ayr as bonnet lairds (so named because they could not afford hats like the landowners) or yeomen farmers, and it is these Ayrshire Tennants of Maybole and Ochiltree with whom this book is concerned.

We first hear of them in the sixteenth century when James V was burning those men suspected of Lutheran tendencies in a vain effort to check the spread of heretical opinions. But Europe was at last emerging from the Middle Ages. Learning was becoming more widespread and the Church was being reformed. The young Mary Queen of Scots, who desired that the old order should continue, fell before the reforming rigours of John Knox. In 1556 when Ayrshire had become almost wholly Protestant, the famous divine preached in the parish of Ochiltree. Eight years later he returned to marry his second wife, the tender Margaret Stewart, the younger daughter of Andrew, Lord Stewart of Ochiltree. She was of the blood royal through her forebear Robert, Duke of Albany. In a letter to Cecil in March 1564 Randolph, the English ambassador to the Scottish Court, comments on Queen Mary's angry reaction to the news: 'whereat the Queen stormeth wonderfully, for that she is of the blood and name.'[(1)]

Religious faction, with all its attendant persecution, lowered over the Scottish scene, animating men's minds and hearts and playing havoc with their lives. Witch-hunting haunted the public imagination and ended many a blameless woman's life. Smallpox, dysentery, malaria, measles and influenza, which was known as the 'new acquaintance', all went unchecked. By 1649 revolution and war had swept the country. King Charles had been beheaded and the Stewart dynasty had fallen. It was a century of woe for Scotland.

John Tennant was born in 1635 and lived and reared his family at Blairston Mill in the parish of Maybole, close to the border with the parish of Alloway. On the brae above the river Doon in Alloway Old Kirkyard his tombstone testifies on its west face:

J. T. M. C.
This is y[e] buriall
place of Iohn
Tennent late Miller in Blair-
stown Mill who died Apr[l] 7th 1728 ag[d]
93 As also his spouse Iean Mctaggart
who died Feb[r]y 12: 1723, aged 54
And their offspring As Also CHA
RLES JOHN ARCH . . .
Passenger we here who lye
oun it is just that Man should dye
And bless God who so freely gave
the Faith which triumphs ore y[e] grave
When glorious Jesus Christ shall come
To give the Worldly endless Doom
we . . .

Three and a half centuries of wind and rain have swept away the poet's closing lines. On the reverse of the stone are carved, below, a smith's tools and a horse with panniers commemorating the work at Blairston Mill; above, an hourglass, a skull and a crown, symbols of time, death and immortality. Sir James Fergusson wrote that, 'The stone is the most interesting I know in these parts. The horse has a particular charm in its sturdy build and the delicacy of the carving of its head. The skull and hourglass are common motifs hereabouts . . . the crown is rarer. It is a royal crown, quite like the one among the Honours, but I am certain its significance is spiritual.'(2)

John lived through eight reigns, those of Charles I, the Commonwealth, Charles II, James II, William and Mary, Anne, George I and George II. When he died in 'That faith which triumphs o'er the grave', his eldest son John, according to custom, bid the whole population of the village to the funeral. After the 'coffining' and 'lykewakis' (the watch kept at night over a corpse), invitations were sent by special messenger 'Bidding to the Burial . . . the morn 'gin 10 hours'. There was no religious service at funerals lest the flavour of popery might taint the burial, which was a civil act. Neighbours and friends gathered at the appointed hour, for it was discourtesy to the dead not to attend funerals, and foolish not to partake of the good fare always provided. Food was served by the family on boards in the late miller's barn, where a long prayer was said before and after the 'service', as the meal was called. The most active young man was honoured by being appointed server. When the guests were seated, they were served with a drink of ale, then a dram drunk with a piece of shortbread, which in turn was washed down with the aid of one more dram, or a drink of some other kind of liquor reinforced by currant bread, and yet another dram of spirits or wine, followed by a ballast of loaves and cheese, ending with pipes and tobacco, snuff and mourning conviviality. Thus was the service celebrated. The miller's 'corp', preceded by the bell-ringing beadle, was not consigned to the grave until evening, after which the guests returned to complete their carousal and finally to totter unsteadily home.

It was considered a disgrace for a man to be found wanting in hospitality after he had been gathered to his fathers, or to 'come on the parish' for such an important event as his burial. John had prudently saved money to avoid this stigma falling upon his family. Nor did he wish to embarrass his children's slender purse, for the expense of the funerals sometimes ruined families for years.

His eldest son John became a blacksmith at nearby Brigend of Doon (now called Doonside), but his life was a tragic one because five of his sons died young. The miller's second son William married Agnes Reid and farmed the Mains Farm also at Brigend of Doon. This farm no longer exists, but the slender cobbled crescent of the Auld Brig o' Doon still spans the trout- and salmon-filled river and Brown Carrick Hill still dominates the distant view. It was this bridge that Robert Burns immortalised in his poem 'Tam O' Shanter'.

The years of the new century from 1700 to 1707 were known as 'the seven lean years' or 'the hungry years'. Bitter winters and barren summers succeeded each other; crops did not ripen and harvests remained ungathered. Farmers were ruined, the land was peopled by over a million starving beggars and many died of hunger.

The land was so poor that the good fields were divided, sometimes by yearly allocations after the death of the proprietor, to ensure that each tenant had a strip of good 'tack'. Naturally these strips were intermixed and there might be between four and eight tenants to one field. This infamous patchwork, known as the 'Run Rig' system, existed in all parts of Scotland. It gave the tenants no security of tenure and where there was no tradition of good neighbourliness there was of course undisguised jealousy.

It was to this inheritance that William Tennant, 'an admirable specimen of the douce, staid, pawky type of Ayrshire farmer'(3) bravely turned his hand to cultivate the Mains Farm in the parish of Maybole. It lay in a trough of land surrounded by the Carrick Hills, hills of rough moors and peat mosses upon which the clouds rained regularly. As the saying went: 'If you can see Arran clear, that's a sign of rain; if you can't see it, it's probably raining already.' Here he lived and worked hard and was much respected by his neighbours; but he did not live long enough to see the end of the stagnant years, or to reap the benefits of the increase in trade and industrial activity of the last half of the century.

William and his wife Agnes lived in a damp, two-roomed, whinstone cottage with an earthen floor and low ceilings. The 'fire room', misty and reeking of smoke from the fire in the centre, had nothing but a hole in the thatched roof to serve as a chimney and this did little to clear the air. Two tiny glass windows set in a three-foot-thick wall looked out on to the sombre countryside. The dunghill steamed at the door.

Their first child Sarah was born in 1724, only two years after an old grandmother became the last witch to be executed in Scotland. John was born two years later and five more followed with clockwork regularity. Despite the recurring famine and disease in the district all Agnes' children survived. They were lucky to do so, for doctors were scarce and midwives generally unskilled. Typhus and tuberculosis were believed to have been sent by the Divine Will of God, and vaccination for the rampant fever, smallpox, was as yet unknown.

Living conditions for William and his large family were hard and the margin between health and hunger was precarious. According to custom he held his land at the unpredictable will of his landlord and his earnings were subject to the vicissitudes of the climate and the primitive farming methods of his generation. The life of the family was confined to the extent of the farm, for stage coaches and carts were almost unknown. Their literature was the Bible, possibly a volume of Rutherford's Lectures and a Confession of Faith, with the aroma of peat smoke emanating from the well-thumbed pages. In the evening twilight Agnes, in her bonnet and plaid, would sit by her distaff and spin the flax that William grew to help clothe his family; or she would knit and weave homespun cloth for their use. They made their own pleasures and entertainments, centring them mostly on the natural events of births, marriages and deaths. These convivial gatherings were often frowned upon by the killjoy ecclesiastics.

Though the Mains Farm was humble, and family manners rough and ready, there were love, happiness, vitality, work and warmth of heart in abundance. Through the wet west-country winters the regular rhythm of each day followed the sun. Up by four in the morning, William was out on his land until seven or eight in the evening. At harvest time he would not be seen trudging home from the fields until ten o'clock at night. An hour's break sufficed for meals and, 'bonnet laird' though he was, he would not take more than one or two handfuls of boiled beans for the meal known as the 'twal hour'.

In the evening the family gathered round the table and all the workers on the farm were welcome to the communal meal. It was eaten out of one large dish which may not have been washed often in days when hygiene was unknown. 'The mair dirt, the less hurt', 'Muck makes luck' were the sayings of a superstitious nation. Most comforting was the belief that 'If the butter has no hair in it the cow will not thrive'. Each person carried a horn spoon, there being no knives or forks. The family's diet consisted of oatmeal porridge with milk and home-brewed ale, 'broth made of cabbage left overnight and oat bannock', kail and beans, cake and sowans, sometimes beef or mutton salted in winter. Tea had been newly imported but was sold at the prohibitive price of 25 *s.* to 30 *s.* a pound, and the new potato plants were regarded as 'the device of the devil'. This austere diet was supplemented by a little milk and butter from the Ayrshire reared cattle. In this respect they were perhaps better off than other parts of the country.

The Mains Farm, which William rented for nearly fifty years, was divided into the customary 'infield' and 'outfield'. Draining, manuring and the rotation of crops were still unknown as means to increase production. The 'outfield' land therefore remained as barren pasture. The 'infield' land lay around William's cottage and was cared for and roughly enclosed. Like other farmers of his time, he would crop it without intermission—one year oats and one year barley—until it tired into sterility.

> If land be three years out and three years in
> Will keep in good heart till the de'il grow blin'.
> [till the devil grows blind]

By day the poultry pecked about on the 'infield' land and when night fell Agnes gathered them and put them by the fire with the comforting belief that protective warmth would encourage them to lay more eggs.

William always waited until Candlemas, 2 February, before starting to plough his undrained land in preparation for sowing the earliest oats in April. The difficulty of working the soil lay not only in the primitive, unwieldy wooden plough of the time, but also in the need for good relations with neighbours, for a team of four ploughmen and four or six oxen were needed to drag it through the earth. Even so, it was only able lightly to turn the topsoil of half an acre a day. William was too poor to own enough oxen to work his plough, so he depended upon the loan of beasts from his fellow farmers. When the corn was finally ready for threshing the dull thump of the heavy hand flail would be heard thudding upon the ground, followed by a shower of grain as it was thrown into the air for winnowing. Later it was ground by being bruised on a 'knocking stone'. To avoid this laborious process of winnowing a mechanical fanner had been introduced from Holland, but pious prejudice prevented its use. It was thought that it smacked of evil by defying the Scripture which ordained that artificial wind took 'the power out o' the hands o' the Almighty' and so contravened the laws of God. It was also thought morally wrong to glean the fields of all fallen corn because birds had a divine right to be fed as well as human beings.

Like other owners of cattle, William had few means of procuring straw and meadow hay for wintering. This was the only known feed and it was rationed at the fancy of the landlord. When spring came it was a common sight to see beasts, after having been bled to enable them to acquire flesh more readily, scarcely able to rise to their feet without assistance. Those that did not die had to be carried into the fields of common pasture, a custom that was known as 'the lifting'.

Although it was a struggle to feed his family of seven, William found that it was always just possible. To educate them was more difficult. When Sarah and John were born there were no schools in many Ayrshire parishes, and where they did exist knowledge was instilled by means of the tawse upon the skin rather than by the impact of mind upon mind.

> This new moral suasion is all a humbug,
> There's nothing persuades like a cuff on the lug.[4]

By the time the younger children were born the elements of education were taught in a humble school held in the Kirk of Alloway, which had ceased to be used as a place of worship half a century earlier. When the children grew up the Minister was still the monitor of manners and rode his parishioners on the tight rein of the Reformed Church. The hard-seated 'cutty stool' was the punishment he ordered for 'Drunkenness, profane language, slander, fornication, adultery and general neglect of Church Ordinances' or 'profanation of the Sabbath by beating and blooding one another'. (In church the 'cutty stool' was a three-legged stool mounted on a platform between the precentor and the first row of pews in full view of the congregation. Pews were not always fixed; people brought their own stools and there were sometimes brawls when they fought for seats.)

William's eldest son John was a successful farmer and fathered sixteen children. Robert became a cloth merchant and, later, Deacon Convenor of the Trades in Ayr. David was a classics master and rector of the Burgh School in Ayr, while James went to seek his fortune in the West Indies. One of the daughters, Jean, became a mantua-maker, or dressmaker, in Kilmarnock.

William's life at the Mains Farm had been one of unremitting toil and poverty. He died at the age of forty-nine on 19 November 1744. Two years later Agnes, herself only forty-six, followed him to the grave.

CHAPTER TWO

John Tennant 'Auld Glen' 1726-1810

JOHN TENNANT was the only son of William sufficiently intrepid to embark upon a life on the land. When still in his teens he branched out for himself. With his father's help he rented the nearby farm of Laigh Corton, lying eastwards near Mount Oliphant in the neighbouring parish of Ayr. Thus he became the successful tenant farmer of some of the best land in the parish and the near neighbour of the Burness family. (The poet Burns' name was spelt Burnes or Burness until he changed it to Burns in April 1786.) When his father died John persuaded his grief-stricken mother to bring his younger brothers and sisters to live with him. So Agnes lived for two years surrounded by her devoted family until she died on a wild December night in 1746. John and his twenty-two-year old sister Sarah were left to bring up their brothers and sisters, the youngest of whom was just six years old. This they did extremely well and were helped by many kind neighbours and friends.

At this time, 1730, Ayrshire was ringing with the exploits of one, Jamie Macrae, who had returned to his native soil after forty-three years' absence in India. Jamie's mother, Bell Macrae, a washerwoman first in Ochiltree and later in Ayr, had been a lifelong friend and neighbour of William Tennant and his family. When her husband died Jamie's cousin-by-marriage, Hugh M'Guire, had helped him to earn a precarious living as a messenger boy and to acquire some education in the town. But life at home had proved too restricted for Jamie and he had managed to secure a berth in one of the coastal vessels trading at the Ayrshire ports. He rose to be the captain of the East India Company's ship *Cassandra*, in which he distinguished himself in a fight with two heavily armed pirate vessels. The last time his mother had seen him he was setting sail to seek his fortune in the East Indies. When age had prevented her from supporting herself she had gone to live in Ayr with her niece and namesake Bell and her husband, the same Hugh M'Guire. In their care she eventually died.

Now at fifty-six Jamie was home again as the Honourable James Macrae, retired Governor of the Madras Presidency, the most important of the East India Company's possessions. He was a very rich man. When he arrived in Ayr after a twelve months' voyage he was deeply moved by the story of how Hugh and Bell M'Guire had cared for his mother so lovingly during her old age. He poured out his gratitude on their children, one son and three daughters who had skelped (hurried) to school barefoot with John Tennant and his brothers. The eldest daughter Elizabeth had helped as a maid in the Tennant household. The story goes that William, 13th Earl of Glencairn, who owned a large estate and little money and whose ancestor had helped to rob Mary Queen of Scots of her kingdom at the Battle of Langside, met the newly returned Governor Macrae in Edinburgh. Macrae, it seems, suggested that if the Earl would marry Elizabeth he would ensure a handsome dowry for her. The Earl was willing but wished to see the lass before making a final decision. The two men set out for Alloway and when they rode forward to Mains of Brigend of Doon the nineteen-year-old girl was outside going about her usual work. Glencairn was pleased with her appearance and Elizabeth, when told of their errand, agreed 'with sma' persuasion'. She was sent away to be educated for her future high position and thus John Tennant lost his first early companion.

In 1744 Elizabeth became the Countess of Glencairn with Governor Macrae's 'consent and bounty'. Her dowry consisted of the whole Barony of Ochiltree, the house and estate which had cost him £25,000 in 1737, as well as diamonds to the value of £45,000, altogether a very sumptuous 'down sitting'.(1)

Weddings and burials have long been events for sociability in Scotland; indeed an English officer pronounced 'a Scots funeral to be merrier than an English wedding'.(2) Drink flowed at christenings; at funerals consumption was increased; but at weddings alcoholic rejoicing knew no bounds. Judging from a contemporary opinion it might have been possible at this time of first emancipation from the rigours of the Reformed Church to hear the ghost-voice of John Knox projecting itself into the wedding festivities:

> Considering that the great abuse that is committed at Wedding dinners, and in particular by promiscuous dancing betwixt young men and young women, which is most abominable, not to be practised in a land of light, and condemned in former time of Presbytery and not only unnecessary but sensual, being only an inlet of lust and provocation to uncleanness through the corruptions of men and women in this loose and degenerate age, wherein the devil seems to be raging by a spirit of uncleanness and profanity, making such practices an occasion to the flesh, and thereby drawing men and women to dishonour God, ruine their own Souls, and cast reproach upon holy ways of religion.

Four years after Elizabeth M'Guire had become the Countess of Glencairn John Tennant married Jean, daughter of James McClure of St Quivox parish. Heedless of the proverb:

> He's a fule who marries at Yule,
> For when the bairn's to bear, the corn's to shear.(3)

they were married on Christmas Eve and were the toast of the district.

Life was so precarious in those days that when a woman married she spun her winding-sheet, for she was well aware of the dangers of child-bearing and disease. Ague was the dread sickness that dogged people who lived on undrained land and it did not yield to the only known prescription, 'A little ox-dung drunk with half a scruple of masterwort'. The young couple's first child, William, died in infancy. The next two, James and Jean, lived; but the young mother, loved and needed by her husband and young children, died at the age of twenty-seven.

The following year on 23 August 1757 John remarried, choosing his first wife's nineteen-year-old second cousin Margaret, daughter of John McClure, a farmer in Netherton of Alloway. This second marriage was blessed with a family of six sons and seven daughters, born at regular two-yearly intervals between 1758 and 1782. In 1762, with characteristic directness and economy of time, he made one omnibus entry in the Ayr parish register for the birth of his first five children by his first two wives. In his typical Ayrshire home a peat fire glowed and young life pulsated with the rough and tumble, love and quarrels of a happy family. The children grew up strong, energetic, well able to help their father till the soil, care for their precious horses, keep the cattle from straying over the unfenced fields and milk the cows.

Hay and harvest times were always long and hard. Each year the golden fields were filled with young people working on their home farms, or with casual workers—sometimes from as far as Ireland—who were hired for the season. Each couple was assigned a 'rig', or ridge, and the sickles' slash left a line of flattened grain as they vied with each other to be the first to finish their 'rig'. When harvesting was over on Laigh Corton farm many Harvest Homes made the rafters ring with music, song and dance. No revelry was complete without the much loved Hugh M'Guire and his violin. Governor Macrae's generosity had freed him from financial worries, but he still delighted in gaiety and continued to play his fiddle at social gatherings till time stiffened his fingers.

John was a leader in the agrarian revolution. It progressed slowly owing to farmers' inborn dislike of change, but in spite of this by the end of the century land which had been leased at two and three shillings an acre in 1750 rose by eight and tenfold in price. There were seasonal setbacks such as the Great Frost of 1740 and there were the disturbances of the '45 Rebellion. Nevertheless the country continued to prosper. Union with England brought English methods of cultivating the soil, even though everything which came from the south was wholeheartedly disliked by the Scots. 'Thou Eunuch of language,' wrote Robert Burns, 'Thou Englishman . . . thou servile echo of fashionable barbarisms. . . . Thou marriage-maker between vowels and consonants, on the Gretna Green of caprice . . . thou arch-heretic in pronunciation.'

Enterprising landlords used new agricultural implements and introduced the rotation of crops. Farmers took up the new ideas of fallowing and making hay and they began to grow clover and rye-grass. They took to cultivating cabbages and turnips in the open fields, and potatoes in such numbers that they were rapidly becoming a staple food. The fear of famine receded and farmers managed by a small margin to keep starvation at bay. In 1723, to add impetus to these beginnings, forty-two peers and 260 commoners formed the influential Society for Improving the Knowledge of Agriculture.(4) It was the first of its kind in Europe and during the thirty years of its working life it succeeded in sowing the seeds of better husbandry to the lasting benefit of the impoverished countryside.

In 1727 the linen trade, which was to be of dominating importance in the fortunes of the Tennant family, received a state subsidy of £2650 spread over three years. Premiums were paid to the growers of lint and hemp, and prizes were given to housewives producing the best linen cloth, which they laid out on the grassland making the familiar patchwork of bleach-fields. The natural coloured linen sometimes took several months to whiten in the unreliable rays of the sun. These monetary inducements stimulated the industry and increased it rapidly.

John's neighbour and lifelong friend was William Burnes, who was working as a gardener at Doonholm, close to Blairston Mill. He was a man who rarely made friends but his eldest son, the poet Robert, wrote of him: 'I have met with few who understood men, their manners and their ways to equal him.' The poet's birth was attended by a violent storm and on the following day the thirty-four-year-old figure of John was seen, windswept and drenched, jogging bareback on his pony to obey William's summons to the christening in the kitchen of the home-made 'clay biggin' (a clay 'building'—a humble cottage built of biggish stones, held together with a clay mortar). The entry in the old parochial register of the Parish of Ayr states that: 'Robert Burnes lawful son of William Burnes, in Alloway, and Agnes Brown, his spouse, was born on 25th January 1759, and baptised on the 26th by the Revd. Dr. William Dalrymple, witness Jno. Tennant and James Young.'

Like John Tennant, William Burnes was engaged in cultivating the soil, for he was a gardener, nurseryman and farmer. Both men held revered positions as head of a family. They each possessed an active mind trained by reading and the rough rudiments of education received in their youth. They shared a love of learning and a desire to enlarge what little they had, and to educate their children. Like true Scots they were mind-conscious, not class-conscious. Their children attended a one-class school and this tuition was supplemented at their father's hand by the light of a 'ruffie' (split roots of fir found in the peat moss, 'lit for set purposes', and 'family worship') or a tallow candle after the hard work of the day was over. Only a few treasured, well worn books were owned by the two families, the antithesis of the unread library which later inspired Burns' couplet:

Through and through th' inspired leaves
ye maggots make your windings;
But O, respect his lordship's taste
and spare the golden bindings!

When William Burnes decided to have a schoolmaster of his own choosing near home, his sons Robert and Gilbert were six and five years old; James, Jean and William Tennant were eleven, nine and seven respectively. He unfolded his scheme to four of the most intelligent of his neighbours and won their support. John Tennant's fourth brother David, who was a master at the Burgh School at Ayr, recommended one of his pupils, John Murdoch, as 'a lad o' pairts', for the position of dominie. On a cold March morning William Burnes set out to meet the nineteen-year-old student from Ayr.

In a letter from Hart Street, Bloomsbury Square, London, written on 22 February 1799, Murdoch describes this memorable meeting, and its subsequent outcome:

> In 1765, about the middle of March, Mr. W. Burnes came to Ayr, and sent to the school where I was improving in writing, desiring that I would come and speak with him at a certain inn, and bring my writing book with me. This was immediately complied with. Having examined my writing, he was very pleased with it and told me he had received very satisfactory information of Mr. Tennant, the master of the English School, concerning my improvement in English and in his method of teaching. In the month of May following, I was engaged by Mr. Burnes, and four of his neighbours, to teach, and accordingly began to teach the little school of Alloway. My five employers undertook to board me by turns.(5)

The terms of his engagement were that 'Besides his keep he was guaranteed a salary of about 6d a day . . . Some six weeks after the meeting at the Inn Murdoch walked out to Alloway, bringing with him some clean shirts, a spelling-book, Fisher's *English Grammer*, Masson's *Collection of Prose and Verse* [Mr Masson kept a school in Edinburgh on the most modern lines for the children of the gentry at 5 *s.* a term], a New Testament, and a new seven-thonged leather tawse.' He brought with him too a breath of the big world. And so John Tennant's children sat beside Robert and Gilbert

Burnes in a room in the village and were instructed by their pedantic, but likeable teacher.

> Hustling his pupils through what they still lacked of the 'elements', he soon had them busy paraphrasing, turning verse into prose, 'substituting synonyms' and 'supplying ellipses'. Masson's enterprising *Collection* contained elegant extracts from a dozen or so of the greatest writers from Shakespeare—dead—to Henry Mackenzie—much alive—and selected letters, 'Moral and Entertaining' from Mrs. Elizabeth Rowe. Murdoch made the boys learn many passages by heart . . . He also tried, according to promise, to make them sing the Sternhold and Hopkins version of the Psalms . . . The Dominie had nothing against thrashing as an aid to learning . . .[(6)]

Mr Murdoch's teaching was the most satisfactorily consistent education the children ever received. Unfortunately it was brought to an end after two years by his departure to Dumfries.

An episode of about 1767–8 illustrates the way in which the lives of the Burnes children and the Tennants must have been interwoven by friendship and a community of interests. One day a highland bullock wandered from John Tennant's pastures and was lost to the family who searched vainly after the straying beast. A day or two later a woman walked into the kirk to pray and was greeted by a bellow from behind a pew above which rose a pair of huge horns. She fled in horror, terror-struck at having been actually face to face with the Devil himself. She raised the alarm that Old Nick had taken up his habitation in the kirk. This proved too tempting for James Tennant, then a boy of thirteen, who immediately visited Alloway church and recognised the missing bullock half-mad with fear and hunger unable to extract itself from the church furniture. He sought for help and was present when the bullock finally emerged with the loss of a horn which he took home. Robert Burns, then aged eight, his imagination stirred by James' story of the terrible drama of the kirk being invaded by 'Clootie', immortalised the scene when he wrote 'Tam o'Shanter':

A winnock-bunker in the east [window recess]
There sat Auld Nick in shape o'beast
A Towzie tyke, black grim and large, [shaggy dog]
To gie them music was his charge
He screwed the pipes and gart them skirl, [made them scream]
Till roof and rafters a' did dirl. [vibrate—shake?]

The horn was called 'The Clootie Horn' and the 'Auld Nick Horn', and was long used by the family as a bolting-tube for giving medicine to cattle. (In 1896 it came into the possession of John Tennant's great-grandson, Sir Charles Tennant, by whom it was lent to the Burns Exhibition in that year. It remains a family possession, and is at Glen.) Many years later the town crier in Ochiltree needed a horn for making village proclamations and for waking people in the early morning, clocks being rare; so the Auld Alloway Clootie Horn was fitted with a silver mouthpiece and used by him for years to call the villagers to their daily work.

Lady Glencairn, who now owned three-quarters of the parish, was the ministering angel of Ochiltree. She was a gracious, lovable character, full of benevolence for her fellows and public spirit towards her parish. Her family life was sad, for she outlived five of her six children. Her first son William was born in 1748, followed the next year by James. James grew up to be a delightful and accomplished young man who became the friend and benefactor of Robert Burns. Lady Glencairn never forgot the school companion of her childhood days and in 1769 she asked John Tennant if he would become factor over her Ochiltree estate. Although this honour would entail a change of house, district, status and to some extent of work, John did not hesitate to accept the responsibility of this office.

After nearly twenty-five years' fruitful tenancy of Laigh Corton farm he moved to the farmhouse of Glenconner, in the parish of Ochiltree, and became tenant of the surrounding farmland. 'Auld Ochiltree's the core o' Kyle'; it lay on a gentle slope facing the sunrise in hilly country, encircled by the gleaming rivers of Lugar, Kyle, and Burnock Water.

> Behind yon hills where Lugar flows
> 'Mang moors and mosses monie, o,

Burns wrote of his native land.

The flitting was done in springless carts with iron-hooped wheels which had superseded sledges and pack-horses. The eight children and their mother, great with child and carrying in her arms the baby, Charles, the future chemist and founder of St Rollox Chemical Works, piled into these carts with their household goods and trekked along the green tracks. They were followed by their animals and small black cattle, and the menfolk on horseback brought up the rear. The little cavalcade travelled eastward over the moors and mosses of the hills until they reached the whitewashed house with a thatched roof which was to be their new home. It must have looked very large to them. Unprotected by trees and naked to the winds, it was built on a hill two miles south-west of Ochiltree. The grey stone barn with its large weather-rounded stones built in a semicircle at one end served as byre and storage house and it stands to this day. Traces of the small walled-up windows in Glenconner can still be seen today, and keep alive the remembrance of the factor's house of long ago. Today a second storey has been added; trees and shrubs have grown up round the house, green and protecting. Due east John looked across the Burnock Water burbling along the glen, 'the little Water' which divided the farms of Glenconner and Barquharrie, 'the knoll of standing stone', out towards the parishes of Cumnock and Auchinleck. To the north lay Catrine and Mauchline with Auchenbay between; to the west beyond the Coila Water (now the district of Kyle, personified under the name of Coila), the parishes of Stair and Coylton, and to the south New Cumnock and Dalmellington, a landscape without the dark pyramids which now mark the coalmines. As John surveyed his undrained, almost unenclosed land he stood undaunted.

Remote Ayrshire was still in the age of feudalism, country folk lived at the mercy of the seasons and the whim of landlords when Burns wrote in 1786:

> Our laird gets in his racked rents [extortionate]
> His coals, his kain an' a' his stents, [assigned work, rent paid in kind]
> Poor tenant bodies, scant o' cash
> How they maun thole a factor's snash, [must bear, cheek, sauce]
> I own it's past my comprehension.

From 1769–80 John filled the post of factor on the largest estate in the district; protected against the hurts of fortune by Governor Macrae's money, he achieved greater security, renown, and respect than he or his family had ever known before.

Lady Glencairn's generous heart matched her purse and the increasing prosperity of Ochiltree was certainly due to her beneficence. Her humble origins gave her an insight into the needs of the poor to whom, after the care of her family, she dedicated all her thought and time. Her lands were divided into small farms, and the first receipt to be signed by her new factor for one of her tenants runs:

> Ochiltree, Feb. 25th, 1769. Received from John Duncan in Palmerstone, Ten pounds fourteen shillings and sixpence stg:, which, with eleven shillings stg: of cess, and John Sampson's receipt for his meal, pays his rent of Palmerston and Barebelly croft, Seventeen hundred and Sixtyeight, which I, as factor for the Earl of Glencairn, hereby discharge.
>
> J. Tennant.[7]

His last receipt is dated 'Glenconner, Jany 21st. 1780'.

In 1772 Mr Murdoch was again in Ayrshire, where he became master of the First English School at the Academy School of Ayr. He revisited his old friends and received a great welcome from his former pupils. He was the first cultivated man the two families had ever known. He belonged to the left wing of the Whig Party and he had travelled, which fact alone would single him out as remarkable from among their other friends and acquaintances. The writings of Rousseau had imbued him with the revolutionary ideas of Liberty, Equality and Fraternity; and he upheld the rights of the poor, the duties of the rich, and the beauty of life in its simple natural form. He believed that 'in France alone did the world of fashion pay due homage to learning'. He must have voiced many of these new ideas to Robert Burns and John Tennant the younger when in 1776 the two young men spent three weeks with Murdoch in his lodgings in Ayr to 'revise their English grammar'. The two friends shared a room, and John complained that his bedfellow would keep him awake for hours 'o' nights' repeating verses of his own composition. Murdoch gave the boys Pope's works to read. Robert was introduced to the French language, and provided with a French dictionary, a French grammar and Fénélon's *Aventures de Télémaque*. 'The bright-witted youth soon got to read French easily', and his tutor 'did everything in his power for his improvement'.(8)

On 14 February of this same year a misfortune befell Mr Murdoch which was a blow to his friends and to the future education of his pupils; for it silenced the only voice bringing new ideas from the outside world.

The Reverend Dr William Dalrymple, who baptised Robert Burns, the loved, renowned, and much respected minister of Ayr, younger son of the Sheriff Clerk, thought fit to censure Murdoch, the liberal-minded admirer of France and all things French, for his weakness for strong ale, toddy, whisky, and French brandy. In reply the angry young tutor, when slightly in his cups in the house of Mrs Tennant, innkeeper in Ayr, and of the weaver, Patrick Auld, so far forgot himself as to accuse Dr Dalrymple of being 'revengeful as Hell and false as the Devil'; further that he was 'a liar, or a damned liar', and 'he, the said John Murdoch, also called Dr Dalrymple a hypocrite'. This outburst enraged the citizens of Ayr, who called for revenge. A petition was filed and the young master was arraigned before the magistrates who decided that he should be deprived of his post for his 'unworthy, base, reproachful and wicked expressions'. The following February 1777 Murdoch wrote to the members of the Kirk Session of Ayr: 'The sentence that the honourable the Magistrates and Town Council of Ayr have thought proper to pass on me obliges me to leave this place and to seek for bread elsewhere. I therefore must apply to you for a certificate in common form, knowing nothing to hinder you from granting it.' After this misfortune the 'lad o' pairts' went to 'seek for bread' in London, where it is said that he taught yet another distinguished pupil, Talleyrand, who visited London between 1794 and 1796.[(9)] Twenty-five years later Murdoch died in extreme poverty.

Seven children, five daughters and two sons, were born to John and Margaret at Glenconner. All were baptised by the Rev. George Reid. (He was a relative of Agnes Reid, wife of William Tennant of Brigend of Doon. The minister whom Lady Glencairn appointed to succeed him was David Grant, whom Robert Burns pilloried in verse, and it was only through the mediation of John Tennant that they afterwards became friends.) From early youth the whole family worked hard on the land. They 'guddled' for fish in the burns, plunging their arms elbow high in the stream, tickling the fish with nimble fingers, then flicking them on to the grassy bank. They took their pleasures from the countryside, roaming to find the ripest blackberries, the 'plumpest hag-berries', the most succulent hazel-nuts. When November's 'surly blast makes fields and forest bare', they would watch their elders launch the smooth curling-stone on the shining ice. Fired by their father's love of learning they attended the parochial school at Ochiltree and were taught by William Simson, native of Creoch, Ochiltree, who was 'a splendid specimen of that formerly large class of teachers who had been compelled by physical defect to forsake the plough-stilt and to take in hand the birchen rod'.[(10)] They were grounded in reading, writing and arithmetic, in Latin, logic and the classics; reams of prose and verse had to be stored in their memories, for teaching was to a great extent the training of memory by rote.

Eight years after John came to live at Glenconner, William Burnes followed him eastwards, and once again became his neighbour as tenant of Lochlea Farm, Tarbolton, where in 1777 he 'fee'd his two eldest sons as ploughmen at the market rate which had lately risen to £7 a year'. It was then that the eighteen-year-old Robert became friends with the schoolmaster whom he made known to the world as the Winsome Willie of the poem entitled 'Epistle to Willie Simson'.

In 1780 John ceased to act as factor to the Glencairn estates but he continued to live in the farmhouse of Glenconner, to rent and farm the surrounding lands and to rear the most enterprising family ever known in Ochiltree. As a parting present and token of gratitude Lord Glencairn and his wife presented their faithful factor with a large silver watch which he carried in his homespun waistcoat pocket till he died.

'Auld Glen' or 'Glenconner', as John came to be called, was a rugged personality, standing out from his fellows as a crag juts from a level landscape. He was a patriarch in his home and a highly esteemed member of the community. Farming stood high in honour among occupations; and as a farmer he was his own master, receiving no state subsidy and suffering no interference.

His success was in great contrast to the struggles of his friend William Burnes, who was hard put to it to make ends meet and feed and clothe his six children. In 1784 this old friend died, having expressed a wish to be buried in Alloway's Old Kirkyard. Hearses were unknown in those days, and fifteen miles was too far to carry his mortal remains. 'They'll be wae and dowie at the Lochlea the day,' Glenconner said to his second son James, 'Tak' the pownie and gang ower and help at the funeral.'[11] So James rode the seven or eight miles to Lochlea on a crisp February morning. On arrival he found a gathering of faithful friends and the usual villagers anxious not to miss the cakes, scones and tea, ale, tobacco and snuff, and ready to enjoy the general excitement of a funeral. The two ponies were saddled and placed in tandem.

The first was Auld Glen's, led by the poet, the second belonged to the family and was led by Gilbert. A pole was fastened into position on each side and extended from the first pony's stirrup-irons to those of the rear pony. The coffin was then laid across the two poles between the ponies. This accomplished, the procession of male mourners moved off and melted into the landscape.

Glenconner's great heart was soon to ache for deeper loss than that of his old friend William Burnes. One month later, on 2 March, his wife died, aged forty-six, leaving twelve children whose ages ranged from two to thirty years.

Shortly afterwards Robert and Gilbert Burnes moved from Lochlea to the farm of Mossgiel, ten minutes' walk north of Mauchline. The friendship between John Tennant and William Burnes was continued in their sons, James Tennant and Robert the poet, who was five years younger than James. Now that Robert had to shoulder the responsibility of being head of his family, according to custom he came to be known by the name of his farm. He needed good friends and he found them in the Tennant family. Mr Ramsay of Ochtertyre wrote of him: 'I have been in company of many men of genius, some of them poets, but never witnessed such flashes of intellectual brightness as from him—the impulse of the moment, sparks of celestial fire.' He also spoke of 'the electric emotions of his powerful mind'. With black hair framing his face, his pen flowing with poetry, his heart overflowing with 'that eternal propensity I always had to fall in love', he wrote:

> She is a woman, therefore may be woo'd;
> She is a woman, therefore may be won.

There is no wonder that more were won than the neighbours thought necessary and one Lizzie Paton had been the pregnant reason for Robert's public punishment on the cutty stool in Mauchline Kirk. That humiliation gave rise to the illness mentioned in the following letter to 'Mr. John Tennant, Junr, Glenconner, Parish Of Ochiltree', written from Mossgiel on 13 September 1784:

My dear Sir,

My unlucky illness on friday last did not do me a greater disservice than in disappointing me of the pleasure I had promised myself in spending an hour with you.—I got so much better on saturday as to be able to ride home, but I am still in a kind of slow fever, and I trouble you with this small letter rather to relieve a little the langor of my spirits than anything particular I have to tell you.—I have been inform'd by Mr. Robt Paterson how affairs went among you on friday night, tho' bye the bye I am apt to suspect his information in some particulars. He tells me you used all the powers of your eloquence, first on my friend Miss R(onald?) and next on Miss C——, to have the liberty of escorting them home, but all to no purpose; and I assure you that Mr. Paterson plumes himself not a little that he has been able to foil so formidable an antagonist.—In short, as Mr. Robt. is very sanguine in all his projects, he seems fully assured of carrying his point; and I declare I never saw a man more intoxicated with success in my life. —However to do the gentleman justice his passion is but the raptures of a Lover in Romance, not the rant of a dramatic Hero.—Her sweet, sonsy face, which [you & (deleted)] I have so often admir'd, he knows no more about it but only as it helps him to distinguish her from another person; and tho' he talks of her being 'a grand cracker' to speak in Mr. Paterson's own style, yet he seems to have little idea of her engaging frank, honest-hearted manner; and for good sense and education they are rather against him, as being so much superior to his own, they entangle him in a thousand difficulties; but, like a true Merchant he has stated it in the Ledgers of his fancy thus:

Stock, Dr. to cash, by Mrs. Paterson's Portion 300£

We talk of air & manner, of beauty & wit, and lord knows what unmeaning nonsense; but—there is solid charms for you—Who would not be in raptures with a woman that will make him 300£ richer (?)—And then to have a woman to lye with when one pleases, without running any risk of the cursed expence of bastards and all the other concomitants of that species of Smuggling—These are solid views of matrimony—

But I forget that tho' I am cheating my languid

moments with this nonsensical letter I am putting your patience to penance, so I conclude with wishing to see you, tho' when or where I know not—

I am, my Dr. Sir, yours Sincerely,
(Robt Burns)[12]

Elsewhere he wrote: 'Love is the Alpha and Omega of human enjoyment. All the pleasures, all the happiness of my humble compeers, flow immediately and directly from this delicious source. It is that spark of celestial fire which lights up the wintry hut of Poverty, and makes the cheerless mansion warm, comfortable and gay.—It is the emanation of Divinity that preserves the Sons and Daughters of rustic labour from degenerating into the brutes with which they daily hold converse.—Without it, life to the poor inmates of the cottage would be a damning gift.'

Life undoubtedly had its pleasures for the six young bachelors who were stimulated by Robert into forming The Tarbolton Bachelors' Club with the poet as their president.[13] Their constitution stated: 'Every man proper for a member of this society must have a frank, open, honest heart; above anything dirty or mean; and must be a professed lover of one or more of the female sex.' Nevertheless this convivial debating society did not offer the security Robert needed, for he was courting Alison Begbie with a serious view to marriage. In 1782 he sought the safer, wider brotherhood of freemasonry by joining the St James's Lodge, Tarbolton. With the wizardry of his personality, and 'a greyhound speed of wit' he outshone his fellow members at their meetings in the back room of Mr Manson's public house. He wrote of himself: 'My reputation for bookish knowledge, a certain wild, logical talent, and a strength of thought something like the rudiments of good sense, made me generally a welcome guest; so 'tis no great wonder that always where two or three were met together, there was I in the midst of them.'

On 8 August, probably in the same year, 1786, Burns as Deputy Master records in the Minute Book: 'This night the Lodge met, and James Tennant from Ochiltree having been recommended was admitted accordingly.'

More meetings than ever before were held under Burns' Deputy Mastership. Rules were laid down as to the sobriety of members attending meetings, thus testifying to the dram-drinking nature of their gatherings and the popularity of the 'small beer' and new whisky. Fundamentally the Lodge represented:

> A company of men, worthy, and circumspect, gathered together in order to promote charity, friendship, civility, and good neighbourhood; it is enacted that no member of this Lodge shall speak slightingly, detractingly, or calumniously of any of his brethren behind their backs, so as to damage them in their progressions or reputations, without any certain grounds; and any member committing such an offence must humble himself by asking on his knees the pardon of such person or persons as his folly or malice hath aggrieved. Obstinate refusal to comply with the findings of the Brethren assembled shall be met by expulsion from the Lodge, with every mark of ignominy and disgrace that is consistent with justice and Freemasonry.

The St James's Lodge represented a strongly-knit group of men loyally adhering to the tenets of their Lodge.

The year before James became a freemason there had been great rejoicing among the Tennants when they celebrated a double family wedding. John, aged twenty-five, had been ardently courting Margaret Colville who now became his bride; and Agnes, who was just twenty-one, married George Reid, a farmer and nephew of their loved neighbour, the Reverend George Reid of Barquharrie, now in the sixtieth year of his ministry in the parish. At Auld Glen's hospitable home there was much rejoicing among the family and wedding guests. Glenconner was also the scene of happy rivalry between young men from neighbouring farms when they came for the customary trials of strength in wrestling, running and jumping—all contests in which Burns delighted and excelled.

The years had their round of delights. In April crowds came to nearby Mauchline for the well-known race week when youths from the neighbourhood and further afield raced both barefoot and shod. In July cattle poured into the town for the famous market; with August came the most impressive gathering of all, the vast open-air communion services 'when the population swelled in a day to fourteen times its normal thousand, and the surplus thirteen thousand camped promiscuously out of doors (largely in the churchyard) there to indulge in orgies of piety, love and drink'. Sport and conviviality were not the only pleasures; in 1784–5 James and the poet started a large singing class in Ochiltree which they both attended with great enthusiasm. They were also to be seen and heard singing in the front seat of the loft in Ochiltree Church on Sunday. It was in this year that Robert asked James to assist Johnie Simson, a struggling dancing-master in Ochiltree, by taking him round the parish and introducing him to possible patrons. This help was given and resulted, so tradition goes, in the largest dancing class ever held in Ochiltree.

The Ayrshire people of this time may have been rugged and hard-working, but they had a warmth of heart and delighted in creating their own simple pleasures. Their countryside was still one of pastureland, crops and a patchwork of bleach-fields. Their dwellings were still white-washed cottages with stone-framed, sashless, small-paned windows. In Ochiltree women still dipped their pails and 'stoups' deep into Gallowlea Well, which never dried up and which was the home of a giant trout that fed daily from their hands. The age-old rhythm continued and the encroachment of industry was still only a distant threat.

Superstitions held sway and people were still in the thrall of the occult. Devils, ghosts, fairies, witches, warlocks, spankies, elf-candles, dead lights, wraiths, apparitions, contraips, bogles, brownies, kelpies, all haunted their lives. 'I wonder how folk can see these things in the dark; I've never been able to see them in braid daylight!'[14] said Auld Glen to a timorous lady who vowed she had seen an apparition on the night of Hallowe'en.

Scotland was rich in rhymesters in those days. Pedlars hawked new ballads from door to door, exchanging them for

1. *a*, *b*. This 1728 tombstone beside Alloway Auld Kirk, Ayrshire, marks the burial place of John Tennant (1634–1728), his wife and sons. On the reverse side are carved a smith's tools and a horse with panniers, commemorating the work at Blairston Mill, and above them an hourglass, a skull and a crown, symbols of time, death and immortality. It is the most interesting stone in the Kirkyard and is situated close to the tomb of Robert Burns's parents.

2. *a, b.* Modern photographs of the farm of Glenconner, Ochiltree, Ayrshire, where John Tennant (1726–1810) and his large family lived and where Robert Burns came to recite his poems. John was given the name 'Auld Glen' and was described by Burns as 'the ace and wale of honest men'. Only the foundations of the house are original but the barn *(below)* is as it was in the eighteenth century.

a penny. Burns, unsure of himself when a young man, was strangely humble about his talents. Although he was always quick to admire the poetry of others, he was reluctant to publish his own. It was five years after he began to write poetry seriously that he felt able to write to Mrs Graham of Fintry: 'But I will indulge the flattering faith that my Poetry will considerably outlive my Poverty.' He was in the habit of walking over to Glenconner to read his poems to Auld Glen and his family, and one July evening he went over with a party of friends to read the unpublished manuscript of 'Poems Chiefly in the Scottish Dialect'. The band of friends rounded the grey stone barn at the entrance to Glenconner and, to the sound of gay greetings, they entered the house. The scene was set in the peat-reeked, low-ceilinged kitchen lit by a warm glow from the tallow candles. Auld Glen sat surrounded by his family bearing his half century of life with patriarchal dignity and unimpaired vitality. The poet read his verses himself to the delight of the assembled company. When the reading was over and family prayers said, the family retired to bed. The honoured guests occupied all the spare space in the house so that the lassies had to seek lodging with Agnes at Barquharrie. Here they spent the night; but not in sleep, for they had slipped Burns' manuscript unseen beneath one of their cloaks and taken it with them. They read and reread the poems with rapture far into the night. As the poet prepared to return to Mossgiel he promised to send Auld Glen any further verses he should write. Not content with this, his host begged him not to send them but to bring them over and read them himself. For many years the family spoke of that unforgettable evening.

When at last Burns' first volume of poems appeared in print its success was immediate and his fame spread like wildfire. Glenconner brought it to the notice of Lady Glencairn and to Mr Dalziel, her eldest son's factor at Finlayston. As a result of this Lord Glencairn took the poet under his wing. Two important introductions followed; one to William Creech, 'a little, upright, pert, tart, tripping wight', the owner of a publishing and bookselling business; the other provided the *entrée* to Edinburgh literary circles.[15] Creech became Burns' literary agent and was later Lord Provost of Edinburgh. Burns showed his gratitude by presenting Auld Glen's son James with a copy of his favourite book, *Letters concerning the Religion essential to a man as it is distinct from what is merely an accession to it*, inscribed with the dedication: 'A paltry present from Robert Burns the Scotch Bard to his own friend, and his father's friend James Tennant in Glenconner, 20th Decr. 1786.' (This volume is now in the possession of The Hon. Colin Tennant, Innerleithen, Peeblesshire, great, great, great, great-grandson of John Tennant of Glenconner.)

In April of 1786 Robert wrote a rhyming epistle to James, his 'Auld comrade dear and brither sinner', mentioning nearly all the members of Auld Glen's family:

To James Tennant of Glenconner

Auld comrade dear and brither sinner
How's a' the folk about Glenconner?
How do you this blae eastlin wind [raw easterly]
That's like to blaw a body blind?
For me, my faculties are frozen,
My dearest member nearly dozen'd. [benumbed]
I've sent you here, by Johnie Simpson,
Two sage philosophers to glimpse on
Smith, wi' his sympathetic feeling,
an' Reid, to common sense appealing.[16]
Philosophers have fought and wrangled,
An' meikle Greek an' Latin mangled, [much]
Till wi' their logic-jargon tir'd
And in the depth of science mir'd,
To Common-sense they now appeal,
What wives and wabsters see and feel. [weavers]

But, hark ye, friend! I charge you strictly,
Peruse them an' return them quickly—
For now I'm grown sae cursed douce [sedate]
I pray and ponder butt the house: [i.e. in the kitchen]
My shins, my lane, I there sit roastin', [alone]
Perusing Bunyan, Brown an' Boston.[17]

Till, by an' by, if I haud on [hold]
I'll grunt a real gospel groan;
Already I begin to try it,
To cast my e'en up like a pyet [magpie]
When by the gun she tumbles o'er
Flutt'ring an' gasping in her gore:
Sae shortly you shall see me bright,
A burning an' a shining light.

My heart-warm love to guid auld Glen,
The ace an' wale of honest men: [choice]
When bending down wi' auld grey hairs
Beneath the load of years and cares
May He who made him still support him,
An' views beyond the grave comfort him:
His worthy fam'ly, far and near,
God bless them a' wi' grace and gear! [goods]

My auld schoolfellow, preacher Willie:
The manly tar, my mason-Billie: [freemason crony]
An' Auchenbay, I wish him joy—
If he's a parent,(18) lass or boy,
May he be *dad* and Meg the *Mither*
Just five and forty years thegither! [together]
An' no forgetting wabster Charlie,
I'm tauld he offers very fairly:
An' Lord, remember singing Sannock,
Wi' hale breeks, saxpence an' a bannock: [whole trousers, scone]

An' next, my auld acquaintance, Nancy,
Since she is fitted to her fancy,
An' her kind stars hae airted till her [directed to]
A good chiel wi' a pickle siller: [fellow—some money]

My kindest, best respect, I sen' it
To cousin Kate an' sister Janet;
Tell them, frae me, wi' chiels be cautious [lads]
For, feith, they'll aiblins fin' them fashious: [possibly troublesome]
To grant a heart is fairly civil,
But to grant a maidenhead's the devil;

An' lastly Jamie, for yoursel'
May guardian angels tak' a spell,

An' steer you seven miles south o' hell:
But first, before you see heaven's glory,
May ye get mony a merry story,
Monie a laugh and monie a drink,
And aye enough o' needful clink.

Now fare ye well an' joy be wi' you:
For my sake this I beg it o' you,
Assist poor Simson a' ye can,
Ye'll fin' him just an honest man:
Sae I conclude, and quat my chanter [quit]
Yours, saint or sinner,

ROB THE RANTER.

James, to whom this poem was addressed and who was Burns' particular friend in the family, was Auld Glen's second son. He was the tenant of Ochiltree Mill, where he became a successful miller as well as a farmer. A neighbour described him as 'a dungeon of wit'. He married Jean McClutchie, the first teacher at Lady Glencairn's Industrial School for Girls, and had four children. One of his grandsons, John, went into the Navy and served in the *Téméraire* at the Battle of Trafalgar.

'My auld schoolfellow, preacher Willie', Auld Glen's eldest son by his second wife, became a scholarly, evangelical clergyman and spent much of his life in India, devoting his energies to bringing secular and religious education to the Indians. Amongst other works, he wrote three volumes entitled *Indian Researches*, advocating ideas which were much in advance of his time. He never married and when he retired he returned to Glenconner where he died in 1813.

'The manly tar, my mason-Billie' was David Tennant, Auld Glen's third son by his second wife. He was a forceful little man with sparkling eyes and a thirst for adventure. He chose the hard life of a seaman in the Merchant Navy and eventually obtained command of a vessel. His right hand was shot off in an engagement during the French wars. He was offered a knighthood by George IV in recognition of his valour, but refused it. When asked by his brother why he had done so, he replied: 'Deed, Jamie, I just considered it little better than a nickname.'

Next mentioned in the poem is John 'Auchenbay', another brother who became a prosperous farmer. He it was who pioneered the method of furrow-draining so necessary in that part of Scotland. His success was such that he was able to acquire the four farms of Auchenbay, Shields, Girvan Mains and Creoch. His skill and intelligence in farming led him to be chosen to report to the House of Commons committee on the state of agriculture in Ayrshire. His wife bore him twelve children and he lived to the age of 93.

He recollected one characteristic of the poet Burns as having been particularly observed by all who enjoyed the society of his family; this was 'a peculiar propriety and felicity of expression, which, while it seemed to be a family gift, was more especially remarkable in the conversation of the poet himself'. He described Burns' manner as reserved and somewhat taciturn, except when he was engaged in conversation by his father, who seemed to take a natural paternal pride in the intellectual powers of his son, as displayed in discussion or general talk.'

One of John of Auchenbay's sidelines was whisky distilling and the transactions he conducted with Burns gave rise to the following letters:

Mr. John Tennant Auchenbay Care of Mr. John Robb
Innkeeper Ayr.
Ellisland Dec: 22nd, 1788

Dear Sir,

I yesterday tried my cask of whisky for the first time, and I assure you it does you great credit. It will bear five waters, strong; or six ordinary Toddy.—The whisky of this country is a most rascally liquor, and by consequence only drank by the most rascally part of the inhabitants.—I am persuaded, if you once get a footing here, you might do a great deal of business, both in the way of consumpt, and should you commence Distiller again, this is the native barley country.—

I am ignorant if, in your present way of dealing, you would think it worth your while to extend your business so far as this country-side.—I write you this on the account of an accident, which I must take the merit of having partly designed too.—A neighbour of mine, a John Currie, miller in Carsmill, a man who is in a word 'A good man', a 'very' good man even for a 500£ bargain, he and his wife were in my house at the time I broke open the cask.—They keep a country Publick house, & sell a great deal of foreign spirits, but all along thought that whisky would have degraded their house.—They were perfectly astonished at my whisky, both for its taste & strength, and, by their desire I write to you to know if you would supply them with liquor of an equal quality, and at what price.—Please write to me by first Post, & direct to me at Ellisland near Dumfries. If you could take a jaunt this way yourself, I have a spare spoon, knife and fork, very much at your service.

My complnts to Mrs. Tennant and all the good folks in Glenconner and Barquharrie.

I am most truly, My dear Sir, yours
Robt. Burns[19]

The 'most rascally liquor', a stranger to modern proofing, proved palatable enough to fill the public stomach, but it did not always fill Auchenbay's purse, as a letter from Burns one year later testifies:

Mr. John Tennant, Junr Auchenbay Ochiltree
parish Mauchline

My dear Sir,

I have from time to time called on the Maundersons for your money, but in vain.—They must be prosecuted, but if you please, I wish you would do it in your own name, as it would raise an odium on me, who am living in the neighbourhood.—

Direct your mandate for prosecution to Edward Hyslop, Writer, Dumfries, & I shall give him the papers. Adieu!

Robt. Burns.[20]

Dumfries,
Candlemass fair,
12 o'clock night
(Feb., 1791).

Two of Auchenbay's grandsons, John and David, emigrated to America and settled in Virginia. Today the Tennant Bryans of Richmond, Virginia are Auchenbay's direct descendants.

Following Auchenbay in the Burns poem is 'Wabster Charlie', who indeed 'offered very fairly'. He was to become the most famous of Auld Glen's sons, the inventor of bleaching powder and the founder of the famous St. Rollox chemical works. Much more will be heard of him in later chapters.

'Cousin Kate an' Sister Janet', cautioned by Burns against the pressing advances of the local lads, were Katharine, daughter of Glenconner's young brother Alexander, and Janet, Auld Glen's third daughter.

'Singing Sannock' of the poem was Alexander, Auld Glen's seventh son, who settled in Cape Town and whose grandson became Speaker of the House of Assembly there.

Burns' 'auld acquaintance Nancy', as he refers to her, was Agnes, who died after only two years of married life at the age of twenty-three, leaving two baby daughters.

Auld Glen's youngest son Robert, who eventually became a bleacher at Fintona in Ireland, was too young at the time the verses were written to merit any special attention. He was married three times and had seven children, one of whom married his first cousin Charlotte, eighth daughter of Auchenbay.

Now that he had become famous Burns decided to profit by his success and ride to Edinburgh. As he had no pony for the long journey he went to his friend George Reid at Barquharrie and borrowed a mount, promising to return the animal by carrier the day after his arrival. Early on Sunday morning, 27 November 1786, the poet started out in new buckskin breeches for what proved to be a triumphal journey. On the twenty-ninth he wrote his first letter from Edinburgh to George:

> My dear Sir,
>
> John Samson begged your pownie in such a manner, seconded by Mr. Dalrymple of Orangefield, that I hope you will forgive my not returning him by the Carrier.

I left Mr. Prentice's on Monday night. There was a most agreeable little party in the evening; a Mr. Lang, a dainty body of a clergyman; a glorious good fellow, with a still more glorious wife, Mr. and Mrs. Stodart, with whom I breakfasted along with Mr. Prentice this morning. For Mr. Prentice, no words can do him justice. Sound sterling sense and plain warm hospitality are truly his. . . .

He showed his gratitude in tangible form by sending 'his auld acquaintance Nancy' an early copy of the Edinburgh Edition of his poems. This volume is now in the possession of the Hon. Colin Tennant.

Two years later when he contemplated renting Mr Millar of Dalswinton's farm of Ellisland forty miles south from Mauchline it was to Glenconner that he turned for help in making his decision. On 7 February 1788 he wrote:

Mr. John Tennant, Glenconner.
My dear Friend,

I shall see you in eight or ten days, so shall merely make this a business letter.—I go, on my return home to take the decisive look of a farm near Dumfries; where, if you will do me the favour to accompany me, your judgemt shall determine me.—I met with an ugly accident about ten weeks ago, by the drunkenness of a Coachman; I fell and dislocated the cap of my knee, which laid me up a cripple, that I have but just lately laid aside my crutches.—I shall not have the use of my limb as formerly, for some months, perhaps years to come.

My best Compliments to all your family, and Mr. Reid. —I am at present, crazed with thought and anxiety, but particulars I refer till meeting.—

I am ever, my dearest Sir, yours

Robt. Burns.[21]

One month later on 2 March he wrote to his beloved Clarinda from Cumnock:

I have been tossed about through the country ever since I wrote to you; and am here, returning from Dumfries-shire, at an inn, the post office of the place, with just so long time as my horse eats his corn, to write to you . . . I am thinking my farming scheme will yet hold. A worthy, intelligent farmer, my father's friend and my own, has been with me on the spot: he thinks the bargain practicable. I am myself, on a more serious review of the lands, much better pleased with them.[22]

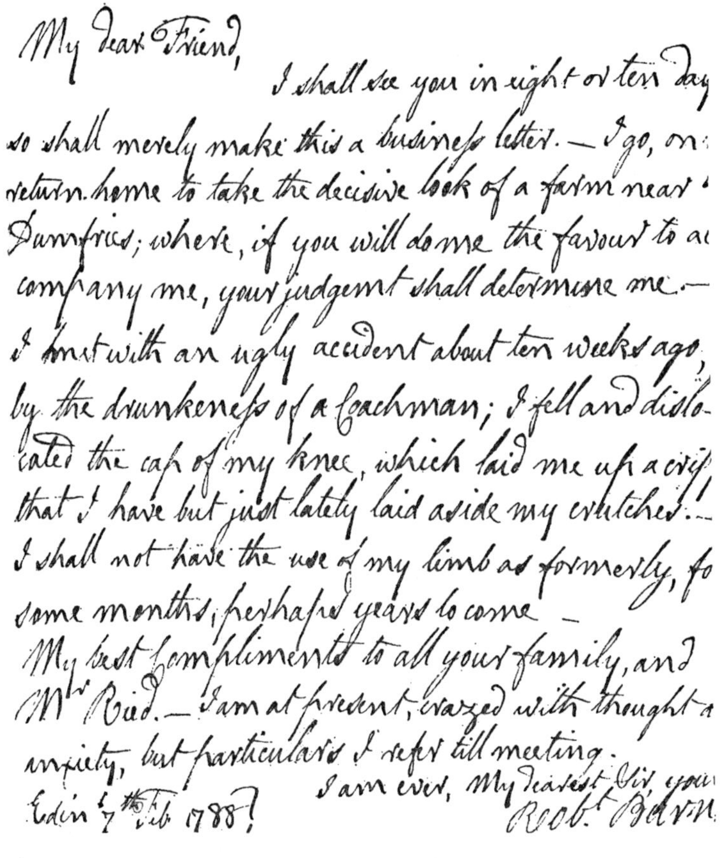

My dear Friend,
I shall see you in eight or ten day
so shall merely make this a business letter.— I go, on
return home to take the decisive look of a farm near
Dumfries; where, if you will do me the favour to ac
company me, your judgement shall determine me.—
I met with an ugly accident about ten weeks ago,
by the drunkeness of a Coachman; I fell and dislo-
cated the cap of my knee, which laid me up a cri
that I have but just lately laid aside my crutches!..
I shall not have the use of my limb as formerly, fo
some months, perhaps years to come —
My best Compliments to all your family, and
Mr Reid.— I am at present, crazed with thought a
anxiety, but particulars I refer till meeting.
I am ever, My dearest Sir, you
Edinr 7th Feb 1788. Robt Burn

Fig (i) Robert Burns' letter of 7 February, 1788 to John Tennant

The following day he writes to William Cruikshank: 'I am just returned from visiting Mr Millar's farm. The friend whom I told you I would take with me was highly pleased with the farm; and as he is, without exception, the most intelligent farmer in the country he has staggered me a good deal . . .'[23] The same day he also wrote in this vein to Robert Ainslie saying that his old friend 'was highly pleased with the bargain, and advised me to accept it'.[24] Acting immediately on John Tennant's advice, Burns wrote to: 'Mr Robt Muir, Wine Merchant, Kilmarnock, March 7th: I have partly changed my ideas, my dear Friend, since I saw you.—I took old Glenconner with me to Mr Millar's farm, and he was so pleased with it, that I have wrote an offer to Mr Millar, which, if he accepts, I shall sit down a plain farmer, the happiest of lives when a Man can live by it.'[25]

This letter shows the extent to which Burns deferred to his old friend's expert advice. Unfortunately it did not lead to prosperity, for the poet wrote in the following year that he was thinking of giving up farming to try and find employment in the Excise.

The only record of Glenconner ever having travelled far afield is in a letter from Burns to Mr Robert Gleghorn at Corstorphine, near Edinburgh:

> My Dr Sir,
>
> Give me leave to introduce the Bearer, Mr. Tennant, to your acquaintance.—He is not only one of the most respectable farmers, but also one of the most respectable men, both as to his character and connections, in Ayr-shire.—He is on a tour of pleasure thro' the East part of Scotland, or rather on a tour of information; for he is a keen Farmer, & as such, I have taken the liberty to put him under your instruction for an afternoon when he comes to your Country.[26]

Auld Glen devoted the rest of his long and honourable life to the study and practice of agriculture on the farm of Glenconner. Undoubtedly his journey to the East was motivated by a desire to study new methods of farming, for his mind was always alert to welcome innovations. He bred his own labour and his seven strong sons were a help at all seasons.

In 1787 he married his third wife, Jean McWilliam, widow

of Thomas Reid. When asked by an importunate neighbour which of his wives was his favourite he replied: 'Indeed, if the first one had lived, I would never have looked for another.[27] The shrewd and doggedly persevering old patriarch stood like a great oak, while around him the sapling offshoots of his children grew up into intrepid men and women whose lives spanned the world. He wielded increasing power and commanded ever greater respect in the parish of Ochiltree. Though his hair turned to silver, age made few inroads on the power of his mind, his body, his wit or his love of life. Auld Glen outlived his beloved patroness Lady Glencairn by nine years. The poet genius he had befriended throughout his tempestuous life died fourteen years before he did. He outlived his third wife by twelve years.

Glenconner lived to see roads superseding the green tracks of his youth. Rough though they were, a hackney coach or a post chaise could by 1788 grind its way along them to Glasgow at an average speed of three-and-a-half miles an hour. A thrifty farmer's wife could travel there three times a week by stage coach in order to sell her dairy produce for cash to the rich merchants of the town. Had she sold them in her village she would probably have been paid in kind. Auld Glen had been in the vanguard of those who worked to change the countryside from bogs and unenclosed waste land to drained and fertile pastures sheltered by belts of trees. Land which had been let for 5lb. of butter per acre in 1784 fetched 25*s*. after being drained and limed. He fought against short leases and the infamous run-rig system, and during his long life he saw many of his hopes and theories translated into reality. There had been strong prejudice against enlightened English ideas and methods of farming, but the struggle had been won. All around him Auld Glen could see that hard work now reaped its reward, whereas in earlier times it had only been possible to keep alive at a bare subsistence level.

For nearly eighty-four years Glenconner had ridden the waves of fortune and successfully tacked against the winds of misfortune. All but two of his children were living, men of Ayrshire 'loyal as her streams and hardy as her rocks'. His three wives were gathered to their fathers when at last the old patriarch joined them on 28 April 1810 and was buried in the graveyard of Ochiltree. The poet Robert Hetrick wrote:

Ye who feel for other's woe,
Who sympathise for other's pain,
Or mourn for real worth laid low,
And mingled in the dust again,
And ye who honesty revere,
As the best principle in man,
Must now lament and drap a tear
For honest, auld Glenconner gane. [gone]
A tried and trusty frien' was he,
A kind, indulgent husband too;
A better parent could not be,
And in every point of view
He was an honest man indeed,
According to great nature's plan,
For truth and honour formed the creed
Of honest auld Glenconner gane.
If ever honesty and truth
In man were mix'd with mirth and glee
With all the gaiety of youth
He bore them in the first degree.
Though turn'd the age of eighty-three,
With locks as white's the drifted snaw,
He pass'd a joke as merrily
As he had been but twenty-twa.
He saw religion in the light
That every honest man should see,
A guide to lead mankind aright
In virtue, truth and honesty.
He did mean artifice despise
That shackles up the narrow mind,
But cherished all the social joys
That dignity the human mind.
Though ye had travell'd Scotland wide,
And wal'd the people ane by ane,

And all in all their virtues tried,
Ye wadna found his match again.
His memory will lang be dear
To all who knew the godlike man,
Who all will drop the feeling tear
For honest auld Glenconner gane.[28]

CHAPTER THREE

David Tennant and his descendants 1734-1823

THE STORY of Agnes and William's firstborn son John now gives place to that of their fifth son and seventh child, David, who was born in April 1734 at the Mains Farm, Brigend of Doon in the Parish of Maybole, half a mile north of his grandfather's farm of Blairston Mill, between Ayr and Maybole.

When David was six years old he walked daily to Alloway Kirk where his father paid for him to attend the school and learn reading and a little writing. Although he only attended this school for one year he proved himself a promising pupil. There is no trace of his ever having gone to school in Ayr during his life at Brigend. In those days education had no visual aids, no gentle persuasion in its methods; children were sent to school to learn, sometimes at considerable monetary sacrifice on their parents' part. Disobedience and recalcitrance were met by sharp applications of the tawse. The pupils attending Alloway Kirk were periodically examined by the Revd Dr William Dalrymple, who rode out from Ayr to bring the prestige of his revered personality to bear upon their moral improvement.

When David was ten years old the happy home life at the Mains Farm ended abruptly with the death of his father. As told in the last chapter, his eighteen-year-old brother John became head of the family and took the fatherless children and their mother to live with him at his farm in Laigh Corton where good friends and neighbours helped David to continue his learning. At the age of twenty he showed enough aptitude to be appointed Latin teacher at the Burgh School of Ayr, a school that had been a venerated seat of learning since 1233. He stepped into a strong tradition of classical teaching, the knowledge of Latin being held to open the gates to all learning and to qualify for all manner of occupations at home and abroad. The teacher's aim was 'to make the bairnis perfyte Latine grammarians—so that they could understand, read, and write Latine, and think in it as if it were a second mother tongue'.(1)

But there was also a recreational side to school life. On Shrove Tuesday scholars carrying a fighting cock under their arm might be seen hurrying over the Auld Brig along 'that poor narrow footpath of a street where twa wheelbarrows tremble when they meet' towards the school. Cock fighting was probably held in many schools and enjoyed equally by the masters and the pupils. The masters stood to gain most. The boys paid them hush-money, or cock-money as it was called, in order to bring their birds into the school with impunity. Birds known as 'fugies' that refused to give battle provided the masters with their next meal.(2)

The records of 1784, when the Burgh School acquired its present name of 'Ayr Academy', show that a wide range of useful subjects was taught:

Arithmetic. Book-keeping. Geography with the use of globes. Euclid's Elements. Trigonometry, Plane & Spherical. Mensuration and other practical Branches of Mathematicks. Gunnery and Fortification. Natural Philosophy, in which will be included: Astronomy etc., for the illustration of which by Experiments a complete Apparatus of Instruments is provided.	Taught by Mr. Meickleham and his assistants.

Latin and Greek	Taught by Mr. David Tenant
Writing and Drawing	Taught by Mr. Robt. Taylor
English, French, Italian, etc.	Taught by proper Masters—Natives of England and France.[3]

David's time was fully occupied by his duties. The school was so enlarged during the following year that it was laid down that 'Mr Tennant should have an assistant'.[4] He taught from seven o'clock in the morning during the summer, and began one hour later in winter ending at six o'clock in the evening. Intervals from one to two o'clock were allowed for the midday meal, and from four to five o'clock for tea; the day ended with an evening class in Natural Philosophy, which included Astronomy.

David was a keen disciplinarian although not as brutal as most of his colleagues. One of his pupils, Charles Dalrymple Gairdner, recorded: 'The teacher of Latin, Mr Tennant, was a severe disciplinarian, but I must give him credit of being, in my estimation, quite conscientious when he administered the lash. The punishment was, in general, very sharp, and if any one of us seemed to writhe under it he sent us to our seats with these comfortable words: "It is all for your own good, and you may tell the rest how sore it is." '[5]

David Tennant's low salary when he first started to teach at the Burgh School does not seem to have deterred him from matrimony. Through his friendship with the second son of the Reverend Dr William Dalrymple he came to know the five children of James Dalrymple (son of Charles Dalrymple of Langlands, Kilmarnock, 1650–1720), Sheriff Clerk of the County of Ayr, and he lost no time in courting and carrying off the youngest daughter Katherine, who was six years his senior. He married into a much respected family of more ancient lineage than his, for the Dalrymples traced their descent from Adam de Dalrymple who had lived in the reign of Alexander III, and died in 1300. The name is said to derive from the Gaelic 'Dal-a-Chruimpuill', the place of the crooked pool, which accurately described the site of the Parish Church of Dalrymple, built on a bend in the river Doon on

) The Revd. William Tennant, L.L.D. 758–1813), 'My auld schoolfellow preacher illie', was a scholarly evangelical clergyman.

(b) John Tennant of Creoch (1760–1853), 'Auchenbay I wish him joy' was a very successful farmer.

Captain David Tennant (1762–1839), e Manly tar my mason-Billie', served in the rchant Navy.

(d) Alexander Tennant (1772–1814), 'Remember Singing Sannock', went to Cape Town. A grandson was Speaker of the House of Assembly.

3. Some of the sons of 'Auld Glen' mentioned in Burns' 'Epistle to James Tennant'.

4. *a, b.* Mr. and Mrs. Charles Tennant of St Rollox by Andrew Geddes. Charles Tennant (1768–1838) was granted the patent for bleaching powder and founded the St Rollox Chemical Works in 1799. Within thirty years his works had become the largest in the world. Margaret Wilson married Charles in 1795 and outlived him by five years. They had eight children.

the south-west border of Kyle. On 11 November 1763, David and Katharine's first child, Margaret, was born and she was baptised by her uncle that very day. A son William came two years later. David continued to teach for many years and later became Rector of Ayr Academy, retiring when he was sixty-two. He died in 1823 at the age of eighty-nine and was buried in the New Carlton Cemetery in Edinburgh.

The Revd William Dalrymple, inducted to the First Charge of Ayr in 1756, having been ordained and inducted to the second charge ten years earlier, attended the Directors of the school on their many visits of inspection, and there is no doubt David must have suffered considerably through two wanton attacks made on the saintly cleric. One was made by his former pupil Murdoch, who left Ayr ignominiously in 1778; the other by Burns in his poem 'The Twa Herds—or The Holy Tulzie' ('The Two Herds or The Holy Brawl'), a satire on the Auld Lichts and the New Lichts, in which he wrote 'Dalrymple has been lang our fae'. This was an unmerited attack for the gentle William was one of the first to recognise Burns' poetic gifts, and he was held in such high esteem by William Burnes that the poet said his father 'Was so much pleased with that strain of preaching and benevolent conduct that he embraced his religious opinions.'

D'rymple mild, D'rymple mild
Though your heart's like a child
And your life's like the new driven snaw
Yet that wanna save ye
Auld Satan maun hae ye
For preaching that three's ane and twa.

In all his sermons and writings the minister showed a Christian magnanimity which was not always shared by his calvinistic contemporaries. He held the opinion that no truly penitent sinner was beyond the reach of pardon; that human passions are not criminal, only their use and direction could make them so. Burns' passionate libertine nature accepted these theories with alacrity, and a few days before his life's end he is said to have soliloquised thus:

> When I was a lad about 18 living in my father's house at Mauchline he used to send me often into Ayr to collect payment of accounts from his customers for the produce of his farm. Among these was Dr. Dalrymple, one of the Ministers of Ayr. Having called upon him on this errand, as I was leaving he said to me, 'Young man, are you the author of some lines I have got here?' And having brought them out of his desk he put them into my hand [they are said to have been scribbled on the back of an account Burns had absently handed in to his customer]. Not being at that time a poet confessed, I tried to evade an answer and said, 'where did you get them?' He replied, 'No matter, did you write them?' Being brought to my confession he said, 'Young man, if you are the author of these lines let me tell you that you are possessed of a very uncommon genius, and if you improve it rightly are destined to rise to great distinction; and let me advise you to take care that you do it all justice, particularly that you do not allow it be cramped with the popular theology of the day,' and Mr. Dalrymple followed up this remark with a long dissertation on religion.

The poet then describes the feeling of delight produced in him by this first experience of outside appreciation. 'I did not know whether I was on my head or my feet as I walked, and after leaving the Minister with astonishment and thinking of the meaning of what he had said to me as I was on my way home, I said to myself, "the Minister kens better than me, and if there be any truth in these things what is the use of my trying to keep my passions under restraint", and so from that day I threw off all restraint and went headlong.'[(6)]

The Minister's generosity became proverbial. It is curious that this blameless, absent-minded man should have been the cause of controversy during his life, but he ministered to his flock at a time when conflict was rife between the Presbyterians who were loyal to the House of Hanover and the Episcopalian dissenters who were aristocrats and Jacobite in their adherence. Doctrinal disputes and the stern church discipline of the time were constant sources of difficulty for him. And there was the added irritant of unruly young elements during his services.

The Auld Kirk in Ayr is of unusual design. Three great galleries rise above the seats in the body of the Church. The gallery on the right of the pulpit was reserved for sailors visiting the port; that on the left was the Traders' Loft, reserved for members of the Incorporated Trades, such as Dyers, Hammermen, Shoemakers, Fleshers, and Squaremen. Facing the pulpit was the Merchants' Loft, which was filled with members of the Merchants' Guild. The gentry and the townsfolk filled the seats in the body of the kirk. Each gallery had a keeper to see that no unauthorised person occupied any of the seats. Sometimes a vivacious troublemaker slipped past the keeper's eye, as is shown by this complaint sent to the Town Council in 1779: 'by sitters in the back part of the Merchants' Loft and below it, showing that a great number of idle boys and girls are allowed every Sunday not only to come into the Church yard where they play and make a noise, but even into the Church, particularly into the back seat of the Merchants' Loft, and there they played or ran up and down the stairs in troops and kept the door continually clinking', and there would be 'a great disturbance publickly to the great offence of the congregation after they were convened'. The poor minister, ill-armed against such a mob, required all his powers to control the congregation among whom his wife, Susannah, sat faithfully every Sabbath in the seat she had been accustomed to occupy when she listened to her father, the Revd John Hunter, her husband's predecessor. The University of St Andrews conferred upon William its Doctorate of Divinity in 1779 and in 1781 he was elected Moderator of the General Assembly of the Church of Scotland. With honour he ended his godly life in a fine Georgian house at Mount Charles near Alloway, probably let or lent to him by his rich sister-in-law Macrae Dalrymple.

As can be seen by the genealogical tree, the Tennant and Dalrymple families were further related during the eighteenth century. Yet another family link was forged with

Robert Burns through his friendship with two of the Sheriff-Clerk's grandsons, one Robert Aiken, who became a prosperous lawyer and secured 145 subscribers for Burns' Kilmarnock Edition, nearly one-fourth of the total number of patrons. Outside the poet's intimate circle 'Orator Bob' (Robert Aiken is mentioned thus in 'The Kirk's Alarm—a Ballad') was one of the first to recognise the unusual merit of Burns' verses; 'My first poetic Patron', 'My Chief Patron' he called him and dedicated 'The Cottar's Saturday Night' to:

My lov'd, My honor'd much respected friend.
No mercenary bard this homage pays;
With honest pride I scorn each selfish end;
My dearest need, a friend's esteem and praise:
To you I sing, in simple Scottish lays,
The lovely train in life's sequested scene;
The native feelings strong, the guileless ways:
What Aiken in a cottage would have been;
Ah! tho' his worth unknown, far happier there I ween!

Robert Aiken's son, Andrew, received this poetically expressed advice when he set out to become British Consul in Riga:

The fear o' Hell's a hangman's whip
To haud the wretch in order,
But where ye feel your honour grip
Let that ay be your border.

The Sheriff-Clerk's eldest son Charles married Macrae Maguire, the fiddler Hugh Maguire's youngest daughter and favourite niece of Governor Macrae who gave her a dowry of £100,000 and bequeathed to her his principal estate of Monkton, which he had renamed Orangefield, in honour of King William III, when it became his property in 1736. (Prestwick Airport is now on this estate, and what is left of the Governor's original house was part of the control buildings until replaced by new Terminal Buildings in 1964.)

Charles and Macrae Dalrymple of Orangefield enjoyed considerable ease of living, coupled with the doubtful pleasure of having one profligate son James. Sad to relate, this young man squandered his estate, 'wasted his substance in the hunting field', was declared a bankrupt in 1791, and 'executed a disposition of the Barony of Orangefield' to trustees who included his uncle the Reverend Dr William Dalrymple and his cousin Robert Aiken. Then he removed to Edinburgh where he died five years later. He could, however, lay claim to being the second family friend of Burns who described him as:

> The owner of a pleasant spot
> Near sandy wilds I last did note,
> A Heart too warm, a pulse too hot
> At times o'er-ran;
> But large in every feature wrote,
> Appear'd the man.

Part II

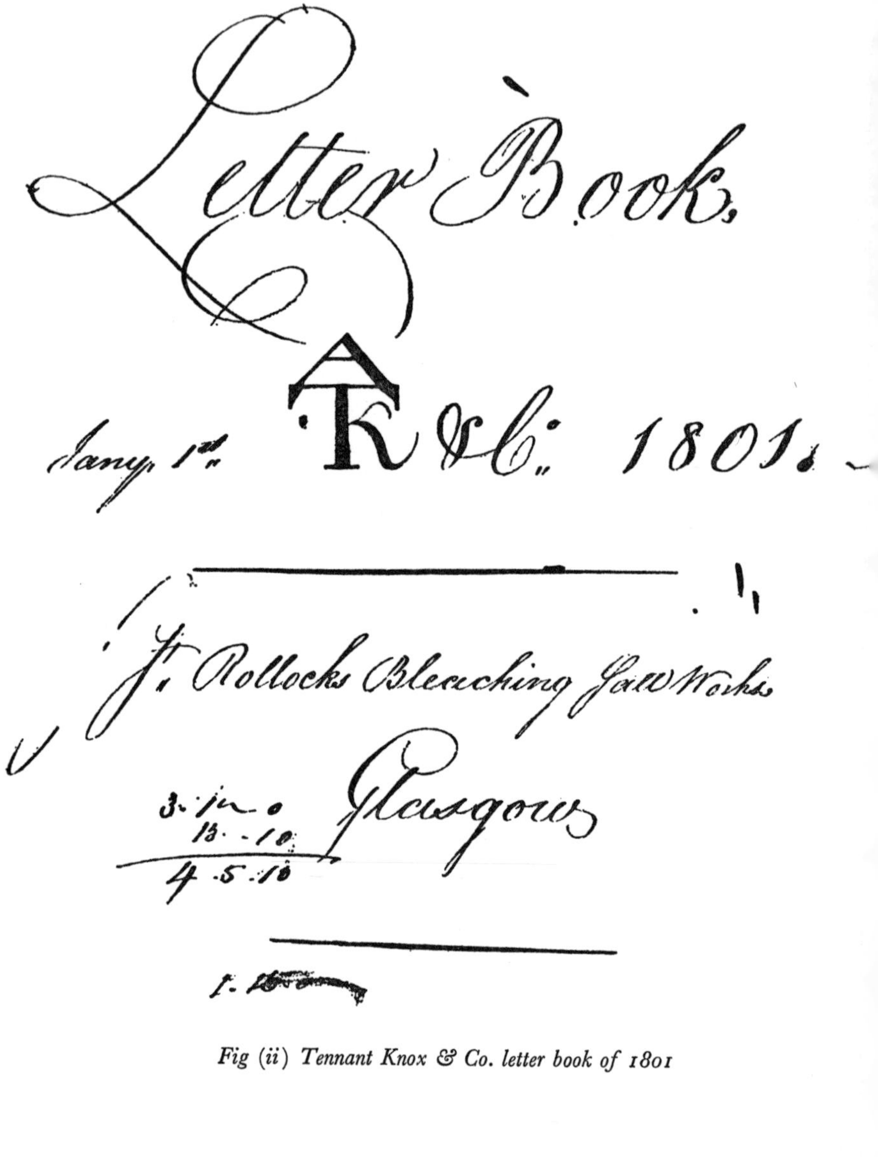

Letter Book.

Jany 1st TK & Co: 1801.

J. Rollocks Bleaching Salt Works

Glasgow

Fig (ii) Tennant Knox & Co. letter book of 1801

CHAPTER FOUR

Charles Tennant of St Rollox
1768-1838

CHARLES TENNANT, the 'Wabster Charlie' of Burns' poem, was ninth in Auld Glen's family of sixteen. His first journey was made as a baby in his mother's arms in a springless cart when the family moved from Laigh Corton farm to Glenconner. It was a humble beginning for one who was to become the founder of a great chemical industry and a keen liberal reformer who would ally himself with some of the most progressive thinkers of his time.

He was taught his lessons at home and at the Ochiltree Parish school, after which his father apprenticed him to a master handloom weaver in Kilbarchan, some thirty-five miles north of Glenconner. Handloom weavers were much in demand in the last fifteen years of the century and were considered the aristocrats of labour. They were well paid and highly skilled, for their craft demanded a long apprenticeship and considerable intelligence. Almost every village in the country had its cottage weaving industry. Most farmers grew a small quantity of flax for their wives to spin. This, together with imported cotton, provided the material for the many newly-established cotton mills. Weaving was developing into Scotland's first industry, the counterpart of the woollen industry in England.

Weavers were to be envied at the end of the eighteenth century. 'Four days did the weaver work,—for then four days was a week, as far as working went,—and such a week to a skillful workman brought 40/-'. (This was nine times as much as the average weaver was to earn by 1815). 'Sunday, Monday and Tuesday were, of course, jubilee. Lawn frills gorged freely from under the wrists of his fine blue, gilt-buttoned coat. He dusted his head with white flour on Sunday, smirked, and wore a cane. Walked in clean slippers on Monday–Tuesday heard him talking war bravado, quote Volney and get drunk. Weaving commenced gradually on Wednesday.'[1]

Charles Tennant was lucky to learn the weaver's craft during this period of prosperity. There was no hint then of the unemployment and misery which was to be brought about twenty years later when Cartwright's power looms were installed all over the country. Just as Charles was quick to become a proficient weaver, he was quick to see the shortcomings of the newly-mechanised industry. The expansion of the cotton mills had far outstripped the development of bleaching methods and, although they were an improvement on the primitive processes of the early part of the century, they were not efficient enough to prevent pyramids of unbleached bales of cotton from piling up in the warehouses.

Charles and his contemporaries realised the opportunities that would be open to them if they could solve the problems that caused this bottleneck. They saw that the increased demand for fine cloth could only be met by new methods of bleaching which could keep pace with the accelerated speed of weaving. Charles decided to leave Kilbarchan in order to study methods of bleaching at Wellmeadow, Paisley. This led him in about 1788 to start a bleachfield of his own at Darnley in the parish of Eastwood, in partnership with a friend, Mr Cochrane of Paisley. Although by this time it was a paying proposition to specialise in bleaching, capital and knowledge were required in order to be successful, and the initial outlay of Charles and his partner's must have been large.

As each day dawned Charles could be seen striding over his Darnley bleachfield, watering can in hand, spraying the whitening strips of cloth laid out on the ground. His appearance was arresting. His head was domed, yet his brow was broad; his hooded, deep-set eyes lay under ample, dark brows. His features were regular, his mouth and chin square and determined. He wore prominent side whiskers. Despite his appearance he was unexpectedly hesitant and nervous. He had inherited his father's indomitable capacity for work, and the zeal he showed by rising day after day long before the usual business hours caught the attention of a discerning neighbour.

Mr William Wilson of Hurlet, factor to Lord Glasgow at Hawkhead, had lived a long and active life, and retained the habit of rising early. As he watched Charles from a window in his large house, the initial irritation he had felt at the arrival of a bleachfield so near his home melted into admiration at its owners' enterprise.[2] Although Mr Wilson was a prominent member of a social circle from which tradesmen or dealers were excluded, his curiosity eventually overcame his class consciousness and led him to invite the good-looking Mr Tennant into his house. This invitation proved to be a turning-point in Charles's life; not only did he gain old Mr Wilson's confidence and friendship, but he captured the heart of the daughter of the house and, after a respectable interval, 'Charles Tennant, Bleacher, in this parish (Eastwood, Renfrewshire) and Margaret Wilson in the Abbey Parish of Paisley were booked (in order to Marriage) 17th Octr; 1795.' Their marriage lasted for forty-three years and Margaret bore him nine children.

Having acquired his bleachfield, Charles began to apply his mind to the use of chemicals in quickening the process of bleaching. Much had already been achieved during the century to improve on the two-thousand-year-old methods of bleaching. In the past, generations of housewives had boiled their homespun linen either in water or a weak alkali. This process was known as 'bucking'. Next the linen was spread on the 'green' or in a corner of the kailyard to whiten in the sun's intermittent rays. This was called 'crofting'. Then it would be washed by wooden scoops with water baled from trenches and finally the linen was immersed in sour milk 'souring', and the whole operation repeated as often as necessary. It was a lengthy process and extended over a period of six, seven and even eighteen months.

A great advance was made by Dr Francis Home of Edinburgh, who conducted a series of experiments the results of which he published in 1756. The importance of these in their practical application to the bleaching process was the introduction of sulphuric acid (vitriol) as a substitute for sour milk. 'The milk sours are very dear and often difficult to be got; but the vitriol is cheap [this was because Dr Roebuck's newly introduced lead chamber process greatly reduced the cost of making sulphuric acid], may be easily procured, and at any time . . . From both experience and reason, I must then give it as my opinion, that it would be for the advantage of our linen manufacture, to use vitriol in place of milk sours.'(3)

Dr Home succeeded in making bleachers interested in the chemistry of their subject and their prejudices against using such a powerful agent as vitriol were largely overcome. In following his advice they were now able to complete the process of bleaching in only four months. He thus helped to pave the way for the tremendous chemical advances that came about towards the end of the century.

In 1774 the Swedish chemist Scheele in experimenting with the action of hydrochloric acid on manganese unleashed 'a raging fury, poisonous, choking, burning, which would corrode through almost any metal in an hour, which could eat through fabrics in a matter of seconds; this was the gaseous untamed element Chlorine'.(4) Shortly afterwards Scheele discovered that the gas had the power to destroy vegetable colours, but it was Comte Claude Louis Berthollet in 1786 who first conclusively demonstrated the practical use of chlorine as a bleaching agent. In the same year Berthollet showed James Watt the results of his experiments. Watt returned to Glasgow and immediately told his father-in-law, a Glasgow bleacher, about the properties of chlorine. Together they started using chlorine for bleaching purposes and 'in 1788 as many as 1500 yds at one time were bleached under

Watt's direction'.[5] But the noxious nature of the fumes and the possible injurious effect on the cloth prevented its application in the way commonly used in dyehouses. In 1799 Pagot des Charmes wrote of chlorine that 'its action is sometimes so strong that the operator will fall down senseless. . . . Bleeding at the nose . . . and even spitting of blood are the ordinary inconveniences to be expected.'[6] Berthollet continued his experiments and discovered that the addition of alkali to the chlorine liquor deprived it of its suffocating effects. Some manufacturers in Javel absorbed chlorine in an alkali, caustic potash, and called the result *Eau de Javel.* This was marketed from about 1793, but the high cost of the alkali and of transporting the bulky product proved too great for anything but private manufacture.

In the last half of the century bleachers had experimented with lime for use in the bleaching process. (Lime was known to have been used in 300 B.C. for bleaching purposes.)[7] These experiments were conducted in secret because earlier in the century the use of lime had been banned because of the possible injurious effects. Slaked lime (calcium hydroxide) was made by heating limestone in a kiln and so had the great advantage of being cheap to produce. Charles Tennant was convinced that a successful combination of lime and chlorine was possible and after several years' experimentation he produced 'chlorine liquor' for which he was granted patent number 2209 on 23 January 1798. In his patent he described the use of lime instead of alkali for absorbing the chlorine. (When lime was shown to be both effective and unharmful, even though it was still illegal, its use was permitted.) The lime was mixed with water, forming a suspension) and the chlorine gas was passed through the suspension to form chlorine liquor. The apparatus was the same as that used for combining chlorine and alkali (Eau de Javel) but an important point was that the suspension of lime and water was perpetually stirred to obtain the maximum absorption of the gas. Extensive use of Charles' method by bleachers showed it to be very effective. Materials were unharmed and costs were lowered.

Charles at the time was still working his bleachfields at Darnley and some years earlier he had gone into partnership with four friends. The starting date of the partnership is uncertain but was probably around 1794: '... for several years previous (to the patent) ... Mr Macintosh was a partner in business with Mr Tennant. The other partners of the firm being Mr James Knox, Dr William Couper and Mr Alexander Dunlop.'[8] Charles Macintosh and William Couper were partners in a business enterprise in 1786 and Charles Macintosh and James Knox started the first alum works in Scotland at Hurlet in 1796.

Charles was wise in his choice of partners. Charles Macintosh, F.R.S., of Dunchattan, was a pupil of Joseph Black, and son of the founder of the first cudbear works in 1777 and the Turkey Red dye works the following year. He was an excellent chemist and his name is connected with the manufacture of cudbear, alum copperas, lead and aluminium acetates and the invention of macintosh waterproofing. Alexander Dunlop of Drums seems to have been the accountant and his brother James married Charles's eldest daughter Margaret. (Their son, the famous chemist, Charles Tennant Dunlop, 1821–1857, became a partner in Glasgow and head chemist at St Rollox.) Dr William Couper, Writer to the Signet, an eminent Glasgow surgeon, became the legal adviser to the company. His three sons married three of Charles Tennant's youngest daughters, Charlotte, Mary and Christine. The last of the partners was James Knox of Hurlet, Paisley, who managed the sales department. He was a friend and neighbour of Charles and his name appears in the title of this first company, Tennant, Knox & Co.

Apart from producing 'bleaching liquor' at Darnley, Charles demonstrated his method to other bleachers for a payment of £200 and soon many of them were using Charles's process commercially. Although bleaching liquor represented a considerable advance, it was clear that a solid rather than liquid bleach would be even more convenient and Charles Tennant and Charles Macintosh worked to this end. They discovered that by passing chlorine over moist slaked lime they were able to produce a solid calcium hypochlorite which they called 'bleaching salt' (renamed bleaching powder in about 1804). On 30 April 1799 Charles Tennant was granted patent No. 2312 for 'bleaching salt'. Although the patent was in Charles's name, Charles Macintosh's son claims convincingly that it was his father who was largely responsible for developing the powder from chlorine liquor.[9]

After the granting of the bleaching powder patent, Charles and his colleagues drew up a contract of copartnership. The shares in the partnership were divided Charles Tennant 20/64, Charles Macintosh 13/64, James Knox 13/64, Alexander Dunlop 10/64, William Couper 8/64. (The shares in the patent were as follows: Tennant 20/64 Macintosh 18/64 Knox 18/64, Couper 8/64.) The partnership was to end when the patent ended fourteen years later.[10]

The day before the bleaching powder patent was granted Charles and his partners bought 'two acres one rood or seventeen falls or thereby on the north side of the Monkland canal' from John Pattison of Glasgow. Thus, on 29 April 1799, for the sum of £615 19*s*. 7*d*. Charles and his partners became the owners of part of the land of St Rollox to build a factory to produce bleaching liquor and powder.[11]

It was a lonely site bordering on a large expanse of waste land and it was probably chosen for three reasons. First, the land to the north of Glasgow was cheap. Second, lime, the new basis of bleaching, was near at hand in the old lime-house bog. Thirdly, it lay on the north bank of Junction Canal which connected the recently deepened waterways of the Forth and Clyde and the west end of the Monkland Canal. The opening of the canals to traffic at the end of the eighteenth century virtually solved the problem of transport. Intending manufacturers could receive regular consignments of water-borne coal, and with both coasts easily accessible the district became favourable to industry.

The unusual name of St Rollox dates from the close of the thirteenth century when plagues were leaving a trail of death in their wake. It originated when a young *seigneur* of Languedoc by the name of Roque or Roche abandoned his inheritance to become a holy man. As a pilgrim he wandered through Italy healing the plague-stricken through the sign of the Cross and eventually returned to his native France, where he died in 1327. His fame seems to have travelled to Scotland for in 1506 a small chapel on the outskirts of Glasgow was dedicated to him, from which the surrounding district took its name of St Rollox. It became a sanctuary for those who suffered from the pestilence and in 1645 it became a burial ground. In 1665 the Provost and Council granted a 'tack' or form of leasehold of 'that Kirkyaird called St Rollox . . . the Kirkyaird was not to be digged or tilled, but was to lie in grass and the Town Council were to be entitled to use it as a burial ground for a rent of 30 shillings Scots yearly'. The Chapel was in ruins, and the churchyard had lost its sanctity.

At the time when Tennant, Knox & Co first established themselves in St Rollox the scene was still rural. Haystacks stood on the western side of Glassford Street. Houses were thatched and cloth lay bleaching in the kailyards of the Gorbals. In Buchanan Street dwellings stood in their own grounds and gardens, and sportsmen shot partridges in the fields beyond Gordon Street. In countless houses the purr and click of weaving shuttles could be heard from dawn till dusk. There was still a great deal of village life in the city, which during the preceding ninety years had increased its population from 12,500 to over 77,000.

The streets were littered with piles of rotting garbage, for before 1790 Glasgow did not possess a single sewer and water was so scarce it could not be used for cleaning the streets. In 1806 Glasgow's only water supply came from thirty public wells, with a few private ones scattered here and there. Droughts dangerously diminished this inadequate and impure supply. Charles Tennant with eight other men launched a fund for providing Glasgow with filtered water from the Clyde. Thomas Telford's scheme to bring water from Dalmarnock two miles away was adopted and James Watt's firm Bolton and Watt assisted in carrying out the plans.

An application to Parliament resulted in the incorporation of the Glasgow Waterworks Company in 1806.

The removal of the works from Darnley to St Rollox was quickly completed and the production of bleaching powder started with remarkable speed. In the first year fifty-two tons were produced at an average of £140 per ton. Increase in output and decrease in price can be seen in the following table:

1799–1800	52	tons at the average price of £140 a ton.
1805	147	,, ,, ,, ,, ,, ,, £112 ,, ,,
1820	333	,, ,, ,, ,, ,, ,, £ 60 ,, ,,
1825	910	,, ,, ,, ,, ,, ,, £ 27 ,, ,,
1870	9,251	,, ,, ,, ,, ,, ,, £ 8 10*s*. a ton.[12]

The partners were active in stimulating business and early in 1798 James Knox and Robert Tennant, Charles's twenty-four-year-old younger brother, ventured on the tedious coach and boat journey to Ireland, for the partners had decided to take their bleaching inventions to the centre of the linen manufacture. Then, as now, relations with Ireland were troubled and they felt it would be wiser to disclose their process to the Irish bleachers only in exchange for a cash payment. Obviously the Irish bleachers wanted proof of the efficacy of the chlorine liquor and the Trustees of the Linen and Hempen manufactures received the following favourable report on 3 April 1798.

> According to your orders, I sent forty-six pieces of linen to the bleachgreen of Messrs William and John Orr, to make an experiment with Mr. Knox's bleaching liquor; I saw the liquor made, and the linen steeped, being first boiled in an alkaline ley; they have had from four to five operations with ley and muriatic liquor alternatively, which has brought them to a more perfect whiteness than twelve boils of the best alkali would effect; the former was completed in fourteen days, and the fabric well preserved. The common method now in use would require at least twelve weeks in the most favourable bleaching season for such

linens; and I am of opinion the fabric would not be well preserved. This liquor has an advantage over that made with muriatic pot-ash; in the most ignorant bleacher's hands linen cannot be injured, when that made with muriatic pot-ash requires the person using it to have in some degree a knowledge of chemistry.(13)

On the strength of this they negotiated an agreement which provided that: 'In the Kingdom of Ireland, the right honourable and honourable trustees of the Linen and Hempen Manufacturers, had voted to the said Charles Tennant the sum of £10,000, as a consideration for his relinquishing to the manufacturers of Ireland the benefit of the said invention.' George Macintosh wrote: 'This proved to be a truly Hibernian vote; not one penny of the money ever reached the inventor's hands, who was paid with a cock and bull story, in the usual style of official honesty.'(14)

The decision to develop trade with Ireland involved the company in financial loss and much unremunerative work. A subsidiary company called The Bleaching Salt Company, with chemical works at Malahide, seven miles north of Dublin, seems to have been a lively source of trouble from the start. Nor were matters helped by the irresponsible and irascible Robert Tennant who remained in Ireland. Serious friction soon arose between him and the parent company over a claim made by the Irish Company that they could make detergent salt (a variant of bleaching powder developed by St Rollox) at 7*d* per pound 'which by the way', the parent company protested, 'is fully lower than what it costs here all charges included'. In spite of this epistolary rebuke of July 1801, Malahide proposed to reduce their sale price to one shilling per pound. 'The making of such considerable reduction in your prices', wrote the Scottish partners, 'may be attended with considerable risk of incurring the distrust of your customers, the avoiding of which will require some address.' (This, and other letters of 1800–2, except those concerning Sir Robert Peel, are taken from the Tennant Knox letter book in the Archives and Records Department of the Mond Division of I.C.I. Ltd. Surviving primary source material from St Rollox is very slight and this letter book is all that remains from the early days.)

Robert also failed to reply to letters and was dilatory about sending details of the company's progress. He was probably too busy travelling round Ireland explaining the technique of making bleaching liquor to other bleachers. He paid his bills very irregularly and was warned that his creditors 'are now threatening to attack your person, and for which I believe they are preparing. . . .' It is clear however that Robert improved greatly and on 7 November 1801 he received a letter 'to acknowledge that your state of last month's manufacture at Malahide is extremely distinct and accurate—Seeing you are capable of acquitting yourself so well both in letters and accounts we trust that in future you will not fail to afford the same satisfaction once every month. . . .' (Robert Tennant settled in Fintona and died on 11 August 1841.)

The Irish bleachers admitted to having saved over £160,000 in 1799 through using the Tennant process, and a feeling had arisen amongst the Irish that this saving should be acknowledged by some sort of remuneration to the company. It was a feeling that was prompted by a memorial from Messrs Tennant, Knox & Co. In April 1799 six Irish bleachers reported to the trustees of the Linen and Hempen Manufactures.

> We beg leave further to remark that Mr. Knox came to Ireland previous to the issuing of the patent in Great Britain, and voluntarily disclosed the process, relying that the wisdom of Parliament would, on a representation of its beneficial effects by your Hon. Board, liberally reward him and his partners for their valuable discovery and after his return to Scotland, on the recommendation of some of the undersigned, sent over Mr. Robert Tennant, who has, since April last, been occupied in instructing the bleachers in this process, at a considerable expense.

A suggestion was put forward on 1 April 1800 that:

> 1½d. a piece be given for the first 400,000 pieces of linen which shall be bleached in each year within the kingdom

> with the oxygenated muriate of lime either in liquid or in salt according to Mr. Knox's methods... the said premium to be divided as follows, 1¼d. to Messrs. Knox and Co. for their care and instruction in promoting the use of their invention, during the said four years, and ¼d. thereof to the several bleachers who shall claim the said premium.... Resolved:—that the sum of £800 be given to Mr. Knox as compensation for his time, and attention, and a further sum of £200 to Mr. Tennant, as a full reward for his time and labour.

James Knox optimistically thought a more fitting remuneration would be 1½d. per piece on the first million six hundred thousand pieces of linen.

In June 1807 after the Malahide Company had been closed down Tennant, Knox & Co. presented a final memorial to the Linen and Hempen manufacturers to reinforce their eight-year-old appeal but were only miserably rewarded by the token payment of £982 14*s*. 11*d*.

Though the Malahide Works had ceased to exist by 1807, branch offices which exist today were opened in Belfast in 1805 and in Dublin soon after. Agencies were established in both London and Manchester in 1801. The London agency was run by Joseph Perochon and was located at 110 Upper Thames Street which was then the most important street in London for merchant businesses because of its proximity to the river. William Maitland in 1756 described it: 'Thames-street is a Place of considerable Trade, and taken up by great Dealers, as well by Wholesale as Retail; and altho' the Street is broad enough, yet, by Reason of the Custom-house, and the several Keys and Wharfs, it is extremely pestered with Carts, to the great Annoyance of the Inhabitants and Passengers through it. This Street runneth a very great Length from East to West even to Puddle-dock, which is about a Mile, but lies in several Wards.'(15)

The first years of the new century were punctuated by trials and anxieties for the young company. The building and expansion at St Rollox put a considerable strain on the firm's capital at a time when the thread trade was slack. Letters of the time reflect the barometer of trade which, according to one, 'still continues very flate' with most of the previous years' stock unsold, the price of yarns higher, no market in Glasgow and unusually little in America. Another in July 1801 announces that 'We have much to do here in the course of this month having upwards of £1,600 to pay for which we are yet by no means provided.'

Money owing to the company was slow to come in. In the spring of that year the partners were pressing for payment from Mr William Tate, their Manchester agent. 'We have deferred writing to you these last weeks past in hopes, day after day, of being favoured with remittances from you for part at least of the outstanding debts yet due to us, many of these being so long past due that you must readily excuse our insisting on their being immediately settled. In the course of the ensuing month we shall have heavy demands upon us. We trust, therefore, in your remitting to assist us in meeting them, your account for sales of last month we have not received.'

In August of the same year Charles Tennant wrote to James Knox in London: 'We are much at a loss to advise you regarding the manganese as it requires ready money when so short of funds for our other purposes, and we feel shy in recommending it. Had we money to spare or could you sell a quantity of the sale for immediate bills on London, we would recommend picking up what could be had in the Liverpool market.'

Insurance emerged as another burden on the company's meagre bank balance and brought forth a remonstrance from Charles Tennant to Mr Muirhead of London to whom he wrote in the same month:

> I have yours of this date with the plans of our works, and noting the terms upon which your office are disposed to insure them, which I cannot help thinking are extravagant in the extreme. But this I must impute to their ignorance of our manufacture, therefore, until I advise with my partners I am not disposed to authorize you to confirm the transaction knowing that when our processes are properly

explained I shall get insurance done on moderate terms with others, if not with your office.

There are a number of instances of complaint from bleachers which received answers such as 'we . . . notice with concern the failure of your trial of our bleaching salt . . .' These problems were rectified and arose from the improper handling of the bleaching liquor or powder by the bleachers. The result was that 'several of the bleachers in this neighbourhood who had bought licences to make the article themselves have given up making it and are using it from us . . .' (24 Oct 1800). The new works were pleased with progress: 'We flatter ourselves, however, since we removed to our new works here, we have improved our salt considerably' (24 March 1801). 'We are regularly making 1000 lbs. salt a day' (20 April 1801). 'Our sales of salt are increasing in this quarter though not nearly equal to the produce of our 12 stills' (9 Nov. 1801).

At this time patents were frequently challenged and it must have been partly because of this that Charles sought a cash payment from the Irish bleachers for his bleaching liquor process. He disclosed the process to them even before the patent was granted. Tennant, Knox & Co. sought a similar agreement in England and in January 1801, a petition was sent to Parliament from the directors of the newly formed Glasgow Chamber of Commerce which stated:

> That the adoption of the said invention (chlorine liquor) in Great Britain would produce a great saving to the manufacturers in using a cheap substitute for the article of potash and would be productive of great benefit to this country, and therefore the petitioner prayed that the said Charles Tennant might be rewarded for his invention and patent rights in such a way as to the wisdom of the house might seem meet in order that the same might be forthwith exercised by the manufacturers and bleachers of Great Britain who might in that respect be put on terms of equal benefit with the manufacturers and bleachers of Ireland.

James Knox went to London to follow up the petition and wrote of his progress to Charles Macintosh:

110 Upper Thames Street,
London,
28th January 1801.

Dear Macintosh,

I await the arrival of the Glasgow petition before I call on Sir Robert Peel. Where a turn can be indirectly given in Lord Glasgow's letter, let them hint at the sugar of lead, red liquor, alum, and bleaching powder as well as bleaching liquor. I hope the Chamber of Commerce's resolution may be in this style. . . .

Yours, most sincerely,
James Knox.

Again another letter on 4 February:

> I have just been with Sir Robert Peel. He tells me we have 'our enemy' who has sent him, it seems, a parcel of affidavits, if I understood it right, from Glasgow. Can this be T. Stewart? He (Sir R. P.) did not seem to think himself at liberty to be quite explicit. He said, however, that all they had sent him was not sufficient to set aside our right, and that the communication was not anonymous; nor did he apprehend opposition in Parliament, though there might be speculative men who might wish to put in for a share of the reward. . . . I am again to be with Sir Robert Peel on Friday. I wish I had some compliment from the Chamber of Commerce, or town of Glasgow to hand him.

Fearing failure through the lack of 'some compliment', he wrote later in the month that Sir Robert Peel had introduced him to

> Colonel Stanley and Mr. Blackburn, the Lancashire Members, and they have undertaken to present the County petition. At the House of Commons everything is in confusion. [This must refer to the change of Ministry in February when Pitt was succeeded by Addington.] It is impossible to guess how our business is to be affected. . . . Sir R. Peel says we must lay upon our oars at present. He seems entirely to disregard the affidavits sent him.

Knox had to bide his time until April when he wrote his last letter from London:

> Dear Macintosh,
>
> I expected today to have been able to write you something conclusive. Government, I fear, are hesitating in our business. Administration is not so firm as the last in its seat, and it dreads the clamour of jobbing from opposition. I have the pleasure of learning it has no objection to us, or our business in particular, but wants a proper precedent. Mr. Pitt, it says, did not, during his whole administration, lay out such a sum as £10,000 on inventions. . . .
>
> Yours always,
>
> James Knox.[16]

Later in the year on 19 October James Knox wrote a revealing letter to John Foster in Dublin:

> Our bleaching powder has grown to a great extent without, what is most uncommon, a single competition for the invention—our title to our first patent, bleaching liquor, has been confirmed to us in Scotland by the decision of the Court of Session but we are still without a verdict in England for a prosecution we there commenced was suspended by petition to Parliament from the manufacturing interests, praying that the example set in Ireland may be followed in Britain by the purchase of our patent right, however we have the satisfaction of finding our patent becoming so much in value beyond what we estimated as to make us indifferent to anything the Government may be likely to offer.

The Government in fact never offered any reward, and the 'prosecution' mentioned in the letter was unsuccessful. It was against three Lancashire bleachers, James and Joseph Slater and James Varley, who having gained a knowledge of the invention had, without Charles's consent or licence, employed the process. The Slaters and Varley refused to pay Charles anything as they claimed the process was not new. Charles applied to the Court of Chancery for an injunction to restrain them from using the method. He did not proceed with this injunction but on 23 December 1802 he filed an action for infringement of his patent in the Court of the Kings Bench.[17] Numerous people gave evidence on both sides. A chemist, Hugh Foy, claimed to have taught Charles how to make bleaching liquor in 1796, and Robert Hall and others said they were already using it several years earlier. It was quite clear that lime had been used with considerable success long before Charles's patent and that his real contribution lay in his method of preparing the bleaching liquor. Mr Horridge and Mr Ainsworth claimed that Charles's process saved them £1000 and £2600 a year respectively. The Judge, Lord Ellenborough, declared the patent void, a finding which arose to some extent from the imperfect state of the patent laws. As the law at that time insisted that an invention had to be wholly new to qualify for a patent, Charles's patent was declared void on the ground that he had only improved a known process.

The Lancashire bleachers felt that they owed a considerable debt to Charles and in 1804 Mr Ainsworth of Richard Ainsworth Sons & Co. who had testified for Charles in court sent to the Chairman of the Glasgow Chamber of Commerce

> two very elegant silver cups, with suitable inscriptions, to be presented to Mr Charles Tennant of St. Rollox from the grateful bleachers of Lancashire in testimony of the sense they entertain of the great services his ingenuity has rendered to them in particular, and to the trade in general. Last night, Wednesday, the cups were delivered to Mr Tennant in presence of a number of gentlemen in the manufacturing interest, assembled in the Tontine for the occasion, when Mr. Finlay embraced that opportunity to assure Mr Tennant he and his friends present, and as far as his information went, the trade in general, in this part of the country, entirely coincided with the sentiments so handsomely testified by the Lancashire bleachers.[18]

The most expensive ingredient in the making of bleaching powder was oil of vitriol, sulphuric acid. Initially Tennant, Knox & Co. bought what they required from local manufacturers, such as the Prestonpans Vitriol Company, but in 1803 they erected their first six lead chambers at a cost of £50 each. By 1811 the number had increased to thirty-two arranged in sets of two or three.[19] This was a large number for the period.

The waste products from chemical manufacture became major pollutants in the nineteenth century and chemists continually tried to minimise them. At St Rollox, almost immediately after the bleaching powder manufacture began, the waste products of the stills were used in the production of alkali for soap making. In 1803 with the addition of the waste products from making vitriol the method used to produce alkali was altered and with slight variations continued in use until the introduction of the Leblanc system of alkali making.[20]

The sale of bleaching powder did not progress quite as quickly as the partners had hoped, in spite of the fact that it reduced the cost of bleaching from 7*s.* to 6*d.* for a piece of twenty-five yards length. The reason was that many manufacturers of bleaching agents wanted to continue to use their bleaching liquor stills until they were worn out; nor was there any impediment to making bleaching liquor after Charles's patent was declared void. In 1810 an official enquiry took place as to the merits of bleaching powder in comparison with those of bleaching liquor. Perhaps Charles initiated the enquiry. In any event the results from his point of view were most satisfactory. There are records of the evidence supplied by leading bleachers from all over Great Britain, and a report signed in April of that year by twenty-eight of the principal bleachers of linen and cotton in Scotland stated that the

> oxymuriate of lime, prepared in the dry state (bleaching powder) is more advantageous in bleaching than that prepared in fluid form: it is less liable to variation in strength and never contains redundant acid, a circumstance to which the liquid is often subject, and when so, hurtful to the different kinds of goods, and to linen fabrics in particular. In consequence of this opinion we, and the most of the Bleachers in this neighbourhood, have for many years, relinquished the preparation of the liquid oxy-

> muriate of lime (bleaching liquor) and bought it in the dry state from the makers, and we are further of the opinion, that if exempt from the duties on the salt and sulphur of which it is composed, so as to render the price very moderate, it would be generally preferred and would include a more liberal application of it to bleaching than the acid made in the liquid form is calculated to promote.

Many letters came from firms which had used the new powder since its invention, testifying that it was safer to use and not liable to injure the cloth, being superior in every way to any former process.

Four years later the Tennant–Knox partnership ended and it is thought that each of the partners placed sealed bids for the company. Charles, who was probably backed by his father-in-law William Wilson and his wife's uncle (who was a wealthy West Indian planter), made the highest bid and the company which then only employed about twenty men became Charles Tennant & Co. It is not known if there was a disagreement between Charles Macintosh and Charles Tennant but at this point Macintosh retired from the company and devoted himself to developing further inventions and to the other enterprises with which he was involved. George Macintosh wrote that his father was 'only scantily remunerated for the sacrifices which he had made in the establishment of the business', but he goes on to say that had it not been for the 'talent and industry brought to bear upon the business by the late Mr Charles Tennant the results, both as regards the partners of the St Rollox works and the public interests, might have been very different from the actual results.'[(21)]

The relatively slow development of chemical manufacture in the early years of the nineteenth century was largely due to high salt duties. Its rapid growth after 1825 was mainly the result of the repeal of that excise and the abolition of import duties on sulphur and saltpetre. Before 1798 the salt duty in Scotland was £3 per ton and thereafter £12 per ton.[(22)] In England it was much higher, being £30 per ton after 1805. Various attempts had been made to repeal this duty and some concessions had been made, such as the exemption to chlorine manufacturers. In 1815 Charles and other bleaching powder manufacturers recommended to a Select Committee of the House of Commons that salt used for bleaching powder be exempt from duty, its use for this purpose being only about one per cent of the country's total consumption. The Government's eventual agreement was of considerable benefit to the bleachers.[23]

A year later in 1816 Charles corresponded at length with the French manufacturers, Chaptal et D'Arcet, about the Leblanc process to make alkali.[24] Two years later the Leblanc process was started in a small way at St Rollox.[25] Charles was not in fact the first manufacturer in Britain to adopt thisp rocess as it had been used by John and William Losh near Newcastle upon Tyne two years earlier.

Nicolas Leblanc, the Frenchman whose invention was for many years to dominate St Rollox and the chemical industry in Britain, never enjoyed the fruits of his work. He obtained a patent on 25 September 1791 and, backed by the Duke of Orleans, built a plant at St Denis. When the Duke was guillotined two years later, the works were confiscated by the revolutionary government. Leblanc struggled on in great poverty. Although the works were returned to him in 1806 by the Emperor Napoleon, he had no capital with which to resume operations. He sought refuge in a poorhouse and committed suicide.[26]

After the final repeal of salt duties on 1 January 1825, which reduced the price of salt from £35 to £2 10*s*, many Leblanc plants were built in Britain. The expansion of the Tennant bleaching powder business can be seen from the table on page 63 and L. F. Haber wrote the following good account of Charles's successful handling of his company:

> During the 1830's and 1840's Tennant's factory was considered the largest chemical works in Europe. It had an area of over 100 acres, covered floor space amounting to about 250 thousand sq. ft., and a payroll of over 1,000. [The area of the St. Rollox works was nearer 12 acres, but

the company owned more land nearby, used for dumping alkali waste.] Dominating the scene was the St. Rollox 'stalk', an enormous chimney built between 1841 and 1842, which had a base diameter of 50 ft. and an overall height of 455½ ft. [Twenty feet of the chimney was underground.] But it was not only the size of the factory which was so remarkable; equally impressive was the technical ability of the founder and his successors, among them chemical engineers of the calibre of James Young (who was manager at St. Rollox between 1844 and 1852. He is now chiefly remembered as the founder of the Scottish shale-oil industry), C. T. Dunlop, and James MacTear, who kept the enterprise at a high pitch of efficiency. Similarly, the commercial practices reflected Tennant's personality, especially after he had become chief partner at the beginning of the century. For instance, the market for bleaching powder was enlarged by progressively reducing its price: in 1799/1800 it fetched £140 per ton, ten years later the price was £93, and with the removal of the salt duty fell to £81 in 1815; as production increased prices declined to £27 in 1825 and to £14 in 1850. The marketing policy was unusual, sales offices and local representatives being used almost from the very beginning instead of the more common practice of distribution through merchants. As early as 1800 one of the partners had an office in London and branches were opened successively in Belfast (1805), Dublin (1810), Dundee (1820), and Liverpool (1830). Not content with selling bleaching powder and alkali Tennant entered the drysaltery trade and among other things dealt in olive-oil and had agents in several Mediterranean ports. Through the Liverpool office he established friendly contacts with James Muspratt which led to their chartering ships for the carriage of sulphur and later to the acquisition of sulphur mines. Towards the end of his life, when his sons John and Charles James were in effective control, the scope of operations was extended. Thomson's chemical works at Ardwick Bridge, Manchester, were bought and Tennant's thereby became manufacturers of heavy chemicals in south Lancashire. Three new factories were also built about that time: one at Dalmuir made sulphuric acid, a second, opened in 1838 at Carnoustie, also made acid for the bleaching trade, but towards the end of the 1840's started preparing superphosphate and was one of the first British companies to enter the fertilizer business. The third was a starch, farina, and logwood works at Renfrew. The growth of the Tennant enterprises so completely overshadows that of the other businesses that they can be briefly dismissed.[27]

The drysaltery business mentioned above was established with an office at 49 Cochrane Street, Glasgow and was principally managed by Charles's second son, Charles James, with associate companies in London and Liverpool as its agents.

The Dundee branch was immortalised by Sir Walter Scott in *The Antiquary*[28] where he describes the daily scene at a post office in Arbroath—which he calls Fairport—during the sorting of letters just arrived by the Edinburgh post.

'Eh, preserve us, Sirs!' said the butcher's wife, 'there's ten, eleven, twal letters to Tennant & Co.—Thae folk do mair business than a' the rest o' the burgh.'

Later in the chapter he gives an account of how the gossips passed on the information they had gleaned from watching the letters arrive. 'Many, strange, and inconsistent were the rumours to which their communications and conjectures gave rise. Some said Tennant and Co. were broken and that all their bills had come back protested, others that they had got a great contract from the Government, and letters from the principal merchants at Glasgow, desiring to have shares upon a premium.'

In 1837 a New York agency was established with James Lee & Co. and continued till 1907 when Charles Tennant Sons & Co. Ltd., bought out their goodwill and formed C. Tennant & Sons and Co. of New York.

Later in 1865 C. Tennant & Co. built a large plant at Hebburn-upon-Tyne and six years later the combined bleaching powder capacity of St Rollox and Hebburn was 20,000 tons per annum.

ST. ROLLOX WORKS. BASED ON 1834 PLAN
IN CITY OF GLASGOW ARCHIVES
(Simplified. Not to scale)

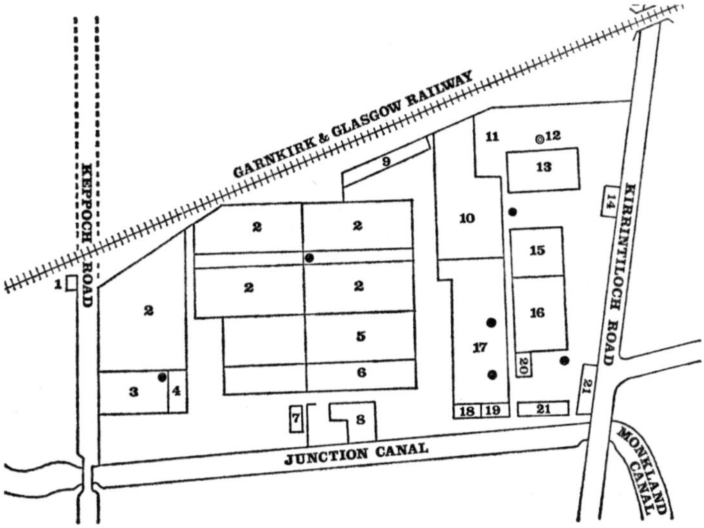

1. Booking office of Glasgow and Garnkirk Railway.
2. Vitriol chambers.
3. Steam boilers.
4. Straw and packing house.
5. Lime store.
6. Shell house and flushing furnace.
7. Lime kiln.
8. Wharf and salt store.
9. Cooperage.
10. Soda house.
11. Coal depot.
12. Site of Tennant's stalk, built 1842.
13. Soda furnaces.
14. Schoolroom.
15. Soda furnaces.
16. Soap house.
17. Furnaces.
18. Engine house.
19. Manganese store house.
20. Palm oil house.
21. Offices.

● Stalks.

CHAPTER FIVE

Charles Tennant—radical leader 1768-1838

CHARLES TENNANT had grown to manhood on the rising tide of the revolutionary ideas of the late eighteenth century. As a young apprentice weaver in Kilbarchan he had listened keenly to his elders' discussions of topical issues. Weavers, the most numerous of the artisan class in Scotland, were interested before all other classes in books and newspapers, and their workshops were hotbeds of political talk and religious controversy. They believed in religious freedom, were radical to a man and led the first political strike of any importance in Glasgow.[(1)] Many risked their personal safety by joining the secret societies, United Scotsmen and the Friends of the People, membership of which was considered treasonable. Charles, like many others who later became men of substantial wealth and influence, joined the ranks of the radical movement. They led the people of Glasgow in their clamour for political reform. It was a clamour that at first was little more than a rumble because there was scarcely any way in which public opinion could be voiced in the press. The first independent newspaper, *The Edinburgh Gazetteer*, was dubbed by authority 'a vulgar, intemperate powder organ'. The others merely reflected the established viewpoint.

Pitt's friend Dundas ruled Scotland as 'a village at a great man's gate'[(3)] and the reformers dubbed him an oppressive despot. Until his downfall in 1802 he had been virtually king of Scotland for thirty years and his powers of persecution and patronage were absolute. Political power lay in his hands and in those of a very few people, a self-perpetuating oligarchy. There were only thirty or forty privileged electors, some of whom had bought their vote by buying land at public auction. As the bidding usually went to about £500, a franchise was both expensive and a valuable asset. The Member of Parliament for Glasgow was elected solely by these men. 'The landed interest alone', said Lord Braxfield, the Lord Advocate, 'should be represented in Parliament, for they alone have an interest in the country.'

It was this same Lord Advocate who pronounced the savage sentence of fourteen years' banishment to Botany Bay on Thomas Muir, one of the most active of the radical leaders. Muir's father chalked this verse upon his door:

> Doomed from this Mansion and his native land
> To spend his days of gay and sprightly youth
> And all for sowing with a liberal hand
> The seeds of that seditious libel—truth.

This case made Fox exclaim in a Commons debate—'God help the people who have such judges.'

The trial of Muir and other Scottish radical leaders aroused public indignation in England and abroad and north of the Border spirits were aflame. Burns had drunk to the toast: 'Here is the last chapter of the Book of Kings.' The rumblings of the radical war were turning into something more like an eruption and the hunger for reform was driving men to desperation.

The intellectual life of Scotland had never been more vigorous. Revolutionary social ideas from the Continent provided a stimulus. Hume and Adam Smith were developing their ideas of political and economic rationalism. Men of vision and energy were emerging in every field of activity. Change was in the air. As John Galt wrote in his *Annals of the Parish*, 'the spirit of reflection and reasoning was more awake than at any time in my remembrance'.

Nowhere more than in Glasgow was this spirit of change

apparent. Its industry was expanding rapidly and this naturally led to an increase in its population. The 1707 Treaty of Union with England, loudly decried in Glasgow at the time, had paradoxically brought to the city the greatest benefit in material prosperity. The new leaders of its industry, hitherto without a voice in government, were now demanding their rightful status and insisting that landed property could no longer have a unique claim to political power. The cry went up: 'Shall twenty millions of bearded men tamely submit to have their just rights and inherent liberties denied them by a mere handful of thirty-five hereditary Lords? No, no!'

As a staunch liberal reformer Charles played his full share in the movements of his day. He held a position of considerable importance, not only as a man of enterprise and an employer of labour, but as a man who took a genuine interest in the affairs of the city and the welfare of its inhabitants; he became an outstanding example of the 'new man' with whom established institutions had to reckon. He fought for exclusive parliamentary representation for the city by two members. He fought for Free Trade which would provide markets and increased profits. He fought for civil liberties, religious freedom, and freedom of association, indeed for all the freedoms which have become integral to our way of life. Against a background of corruption and repression he fought with the manufacturers and intellectuals for the aims of Fox and Grey, Smith and Bentham. He organised public meetings under the constant threat of their being disbanded under the hated 'Gagging Act', or Riot Act.

At a time when liberal views could be interpreted as treason Charles upheld his friend James Mylne, university chaplain and Professor of Moral Philosophy, when the Sheriff of Lanarkshire contemplated action against him. On Sunday, 26 March 1815, the day news came of Bonaparte's escape from Elba, Mylne took the service in the College Hall and ended with the 26th Paraphrase beginning: 'Behold he comes, your leader comes!' This unconscious choice could well have been misconstrued as welcoming

Bonaparte's escape and could have had dangerous consequences for Mylne, but Charles offered to stand surety to any amount for his appearance in any trial.[4]

The Napoleonic Wars had increased the wealth of manufacturers and the poverty of the working classes. Wages had fallen, new machinery had caused unemployment and the dissenting academics and industrial middle-class had been driven underground. But it was only when the fighting was over that industrial unrest brought Britain nearer to revolution than she had been at almost any time since the Civil War. Bloodshed and disaster were only averted when the Reform Bill was passed by the minimal majority of one vote. Thus the first step was taken in the democratisation of the machinery of government.

Conditions after the Napoleonic Wars bear a close resemblance to those of this century. Charles Dalrymple Gairdner in his *Autobiography* wrote:

> I shall now refer to the state of political feeling in the country between 1815 and 1820 as compared with the years of the war. During the latter period the people were in such risk of a foreign enemy that their efforts were bent on preserving their hearths and homes from invasion, but the peace of 1815 threw an immense military population entirely idle, and in their transition to different employments and trades there was great destitution. The consequence was a large amount of bad feeling, under which the lower classes imputed all their evils to the Ministry and Parliament of the day. These complaints were shown in a demand for a radical reform. As a panacea for all their distresses, and though there certainly was much corruption in Parliament, it was very evident that no such reform could supply the grievous famine and want of food which oppressed the people. This spirit of dissatisfaction assumed a decided tone in 1819 and 1820, the whole lower classes of England and Scotland became quite disorganised. They elected a Committee of Public Safety at London, who issued proclamations of the most dangerous character, and they intimated by handbills in every town that any Magistrate who disputed their orders in a re-division of the

property of the country would be marked by them as guilty of treason to the people.[5]

During these troubled post-war years angry political meetings and processions followed each other in quick succession. Charles and his son John were well to the fore in all these demonstrations. In April 1820 a treasonable paper which had been posted up on walls all over Glasgow was torn down by the police, 'and we should suppose it to be of English composition from its dwelling much upon Magna Carta and the Bill of Rights, in which Scotland has no interest . . .' A call to strike followed which was 'implicitly obeyed' by weavers, colliers, cotton-spinners, and some of the machine-makers and founders. The city teemed with soldiers, the Glasgow Light Horse, the Sharpshooters in Vincent Square, and the Mounted Yeomen with 10,000 flints. (The Glasgow Sharpshooters were founded in 1819 by Samuel Hunter, a formidable fellow weighing twenty stone, who had gathered together 1000 trigger-happy youths armed with rifles and dressed in dark green uniforms. They would assemble in George Square to await the arrival of the London mail with a view to meeting any emergency that might arise in Glasgow from any threatened rising in the manufacturing districts of England.) The Lord Provost and civic leaders took up their quarters in the Buck's Head Hotel, Argyle Street, and 'their valuable stud of high-mettled horses, richly caparisoned, stood, ready saddled and bridled in the old circus behind'.[6] An order was issued that shops were to be shut at 6 p.m. and a curfew imposed at 7 p.m. The 'Radical Wet Wednesday' of that week has become notorious in the history of the Reform movement in Glasgow. The *Courier* reported the evening before: 'that a general attack is intended to be made by the Radicals in the city on Wednesday is now beyond doubt . . .' Pickets of Dragoons rode out on all the roads leading to and from the town to bring in any information and to announce the arrival of any body of radicals that might be marching towards the city. Despite all the excitement nothing happened, and at night the soldiers gathered again in St George's Church. A heavy downpour of rain damped the spirits of all but a few reformers, whose activities led to cruel punishments out of all proportion to the nature of their crime.

Discontent rose to a passionate climax again in November 1820. When the mail coach brought news that the House of Lords had abandoned the Bill of Pains and Penalties against Queen Caroline, the *Glasgow Herald* reported that Whigs gave vent to their feelings 'in rather unpleasant demonstrations of joy, by firing guns and pistols and carrying lighted tar barrels along the streets. Tuesday night exhibited a scene of disorder and riot highly disgraceful to the city.' Official Glasgow, in favour of the King, called out the Dragoons to restore order and disperse the crowds, which they did by charging headlong into the people.

In the cause of the Queen a meeting was called in the Black Bull ballroom on 13 December to protest against the Provost's loyal address, by then on its way to King George IV in London. Twenty-five men, including Charles Tennant and Professor Mylne, gathered together, all courting arrest on a charge of sedition. They felt sure that the address did not represent the feelings of the citizens of Glasgow, whose sympathies were with the Queen, and decided to test public opinion by organising a meeting in the Town Hall. The Gagging Act forbade such gatherings 'without the leave or licence of two or more Magistrates; or only after a lapse of a written notice of six days, served officially on the Magistrates'.(7) A delegation waited upon the Chief Magistrate who greeted them with a gruff refusal, adding 'that they had some state in the community, he was pleased to observe, but they had better not border on sedition or treason, for which some had lost their heads in Glasgow, and out of it, already'. On being refused the use of the Town Hall by the Bailie, Charles countered: 'We will get our own Trades' Hall.' 'Try it if you dare,' said the Bailie.(8) Tempers flared and 318 signatories representing the best civil and social interests, including those of Charles and John Tennant of St Rollox, were affixed to a requisition.

To the Honourable the Lord Provost, or in his absence the Acting Chief Magistrate of the City of Glasgow.

My Lord,—We request that your Lordship will call a meeting of the merchants, bankers, manufacturers, and other inhabitants, to be held upon as early a day as is convenient, for the purpose of considering the propriety of voting a Loyal and Dutiful Address to His Majesty, and representing the unconstitutional and pernicious measures adopted by Ministers, especially in the proceedings against the Queen, and the sudden prorogation of Parliament, and praying His Majesty to dismiss his Ministers, and to re-assemble Parliament without delay, that their advice may be taken as to the measures to be pursued for allaying the present discontent.[9]

This meeting was never called, so the twenty-five men announced that they would hold another for the same purpose on 22 December at John Street Church at 12 o'clock. The gloves were off. Public excitement grew. Dragoons and infantry were alerted. 'By 11.30 a.m. the John Street Church was completely filled and the crowd outside was immense. At 12 o'clock the gentlemen of the Committee arrived and took their seats below the pulpit'. Authority was represented by the auxiliary Sheriff Substitute, the Sheriff Officer, the Town Officer, and a Messenger-at-Arms with pen in hand ready to record sedition or treasonable words spoken by the Chairman, James Oswald, or by any other foolhardy malcontent. Resolutions were passed condemning the Government for their profligate policies which had resulted in much suffering and necessitated ruinous taxation, and for their impolitic restrictions upon foreign trade which 'have blasted the hopes held out to the people during the war and deprived the Nation of the blessings and benefits which ought to have been the fruits and consequences of Peace'. The crescendo of complaints ended in a tirade attacking the unconstitutional proceedings against the Queen, after which Parliament had been summarily prorogued 'in a manner unprecedented since the reign of the Stuarts', and a demand 'that on these grounds, and from the most sincere and ardent wishes for the honour and dignity of the Crown, and for the relief and happiness of the People, a loyal and dutiful Address and Petition be presented to His Majesty the King, praying that he would be pleased to dismiss his present Ministers from his presence and Councils'.[10] These resolutions were unanimously adopted. Seventeen men, including Charles Tennant, were appointed as a committee to get the petition subscribed and transmitted to London. Copies lay for signature at ten places including Messrs Charles Tennant & Co., Moodie's Court. Angry people wrote to the press against 'mischievous attempts of the factious and turbulent to influence the passions and mislead the judgment of the less informed orders . . . by abusing the public press and converting it into an engine of licentiousness and profligacy'. The reactionaries prophesied national disaster if the tide of radicalism rose much further.

The Friends of Civil and Religious Liberty celebrated Mr Fox's birthday in the Black Bull Inn on Wednesday, 24 January 1821. Dinner was on the table at 5 o'clock, with Charles acting as one of the twenty-nine stewards, who had to manage more than double the usual number of guests. Twenty-four toasts were drunk beginning with 'The King', followed by 'The Queen, and her speedy restoration to her rights and privileges'. The cry of Freedom and Reform ran through the toast list, which ended with one to 'The Independent Freeholders of Ayrshire'. Truly the tide was rising, but it had not yet reached the floor of the House of Commons, where Lord John Russell's motion for Parliamentary Reform was lost by thirty-one votes. South of the Border there was a complete lack of interest in Scottish affairs. Radical reform had still a long way to go.

It was not until he had reached the age of sixty-four that Charles finally reaped the reward of his political struggle in the passing of the 1832 Reform Bill. On Friday 25 March 1831 he and his sons John and Charles James had joined a crowd of 120,000 excited persons gathered on the Public Green to watch for the arrival of the mail bringing news of the Second Reading of the Bill. Twenty minutes before the mailcoach was due steaming horses mounted by sweating riders galloped to the Cross, and the riders waved their hats proclaiming that the Second Reading had been carried by the glorious majority of one! The crowd roared and cheered; later the mailcoach clattered in with flag flying.

Charles and a group of leading citizens signed a petition to the Lord Provost to sanction public illuminations to celebrate the great event:

> It was truly most diverting to see the mighty note of preparation going on throughout the city on that Monday, every lad and lassie cleaning their windows to let their candles shine the more conspicuously; the gasfitters eagerly fitting on their 'jettees', the painters embellishing all the sign posts in the most conspicuous thoroughfares, the wrights taking out the sashes of windows to make way for some brilliant transparency or other. . . . Every tavern in the city of any note was pre-engaged for dinner or supper parties . . . At 8 o'clock the city bells began to ring, and that was the signal for the lighting up . . . In a trice the whole city might be said to be flashing with fire . . . It was a blaze, we may truly say, perfectly unparalleled.[11]

Lord Provost Dalgleish's house at St Vincent Place had 'no fewer than 3,000 gas 'jettees' in front of his house with the words sparkling out amongst them "Let Glasgow Flourish" . . . old Mr. Charles Tennant's then new magnificent house in West George Street, had paintings hanging from its front windows, representing the King, the Cabinet and the People with the words "Hail Glorious Reform". It was a great night for Glasgow.'[12] Charles saw the fulfilment of his hopes for eventual universal suffrage. All shared in the general rejoicing.

> See Glasgow under Earl Grey
> Frae Glasgow under Castlereagh,
> Ha! Ha! the differ o't.[13]

Disillusionment soon followed and the city was torn by dissent and strife. The bill was rejected by the House of Lords and it was not until 17 July 1832 that it finally received the Royal Assent. Even then it only provided Glasgow with two new seats, for which six aspirants were battling long before the writs were even issued. All the candidates appeared in the guise of Whig reformers, but there was among them enough dissimilarity to encourage different political supporters. One or two of the candidates had only been converted when conversion became profitable. Radicalism had become almost respectable. Of the old stalwart reformers the most influential rallied round the banner of Oswald and Crawford, whose candidature was seconded by Charles Tennant. For the first time in the city's history, public hustings were erected in front of the old Justiciary Hall at the jail where the Sheriff read the Election Writ to an unprecedented crowd of 20,000 people. The poll began at nine in the morning of Tuesday, 18 December; to enable the weavers to get a good look at the candidates it did not close until Wednesday at 4 o'clock in the afternoon.

The count returned Oswald to Westminster as the first Liberal candidate to represent the citizens. The Clique, a group of Whigs, which had been driven underground during the Napoleonic Wars and of which Charles had been a member, re-emerged to support the two traditionally staunch Whig candidates. One of the first Liberal clubs, the Crow Club, came into existence and held its first meeting on 10 July 1832 in Tennant's warehouse, with the names of Charles, John and Charles James on its membership list. The exclusively Tory press ignored the Club's existence, so in February 1833 'Crow' established its own highly respectable political newspaper on the Joint Stock principle, and called it *The Glasgow Argus*. The Club had many influential members and 'The meetings of this fraternity might well be regarded as one of the most stirring, animated, delightful, and intellectual brotherhoods of all the social brotherhoods which then met in the city'.[14]

Charles Tennant and his friends who had fought for political reform against the Tory establishment were perhaps reluctant to recognise the genuine fear of the Tories at the consequences of the growth of the French revolutionary ideas in Great Britain. Nor did they always discern that the economic evils which were undoubtedly causing distress could best be solved by economic, not political, activity. However, their ideas and actions helped to create one of the most exciting and purposeful periods in Glasgow's political history.

CHAPTER SIX

Charles Tennant—railways, waterways and rewards
1768-1838

CHARLES TENNANT did not let his political activities take precedence over the main business of his life, the expansion and prosperity of the St Rollox chemical works. And this expansion was now being held up by inadequate means of transport. By 1825 St Rollox was consuming over 30,000 tons of coal a year, all of which had to be tediously and expensively transported either by the Monkland Canal or by cart from the Lanarkshire coalfields at 9*d*. or 1*s*. 6*d*. a ton per mile. The mobility of the twentieth century makes it hard to appreciate the obstacle which transport presented to the growth of Scottish industries a hundred and fifty years ago. Regular supplies of raw materials had to be assured despite summer droughts or winter frosts. Road and water carriage depended on the stamina of horses pulling carts and barges. The time was long past when it had been possible to send the whole of the St Rollox produce down to Glasgow in a wheelbarrow.

Until this time the transport of the firm had been organised by William Alexander, an old school friend of Charles Tennant. He had abandoned farming in 1798 and travelled with his family in a farm cart to join his friend in Glasgow, taking a house opposite the St Rollox works. He it was who created the fine teams of draught horses which became the pride of the firm and indeed of the town. Alexander's son

Thomas was born in the St Rollox house in 1837, started work as an office boy, rose to be a senior traveller, then became a director, and finally General Manager and Managing Director of St Rollox. He died in the firm's service at the age of 78. Thomas's son, Sir William Alexander, who himself became a partner in the firm, in giving the first Tennant Memorial Lecture in Glasgow in 1943, said: 'It is on record that Charles Tennant cut the gold buttons off his wedding coat and gave them to my grandfather to adorn his.' (Sir William's son, Kenneth Alexander, is currently Chairman of Tennants Consolidated, which owns Charles Tennant & Co. Ltd., Glasgow, and other Tennant Companies which are listed in Appendix VI.

By 1825, when rising production meant finding fresh markets beyond the West of Scotland, Charles Tennant began to apply his mind to finding new methods of transport in an effort to break this barrier to progress. He decided to make a personal study of the new system of conveying goods and people in wagons drawn by a steam engine along iron rails laid on a level road. He had heard much about them from his friend George Stephenson, the great railway engineer, and he was quick to see their potentialities as new industrial lifelines. In this year he took his entire family, including his youngest two-year-old grandson and namesake, later Sir Charles Tennant, to see the opening of the Stockton and Darlington Railway. Then he went on a visit to the North of England to see the latest developments there. He was accompanied by Mr Grainger, one of the engineers who later built the Garnkirk and Glasgow Railway, who left this description of their visit:

> The better to enable Mr. Tennant to advise and direct as to the best mode of carrying out various projected Railways in and around Glasgow, he along with myself and Mr. George Buchanan, C.E., visited the North of England, where we spent ten days most agreeably in examining the principal collieries and railways in that district. This took place in the month of August, 1825. In the course of this excursion, his desire to see everything in the district that

was interesting and the fatigue to which he subjected himself are incredible. Early or late his activity never failed, and rather outdid that of his younger companions. On arranging one evening in Newcastle to start next morning to see the various works at Sunderland, while we were hesitating about the hour, he at once resolved to take the earliest coach, at 4 a.m. which we did. But the energy and vigour of his mental powers—his keen and rapid perception of the nature of the various engineering, mechanical and mining operations which rose successively under our observation, and his just and accurate estimate of their value, and comprehensive views of their extensive appreciation in commerce and the arts, which he descried afar off—were what more especially called forth our admiration and respect. Nor did he confine himself to what was to be seen above ground; he descended one of the deepest coal-pits in Northumberland. I shall never forget the morning on which we, along with Mr. Nicholas Wood, the eminent coalviewer, rigged out in coal-pit dresses (and odd figures we certainly were) descended the principal pit of the Killingworth Colliery.

This visit was of vast importance to Mr. Tennant, the more so as the supreme object of all the railways, in the construction of which he was so deeply engaged, was the mineral traffic of the districts traversed by them.

Though Charles was not among the original promoters of the Monkland and Kirkintilloch Railway, the first public railway in Lanarkshire, by the time the line was opened in 1826 he was a prominent member of the committee of management, and appears to have been chairman of the Ballochney Railway, an eastern extension of the Monkland and Kirkintilloch (opened 1828). By using these railways in connection with the Forth and Clyde Canal he was able to break the monopoly of the Monkland Canal in coal transport from the rich mineral fields in the Airdrie–Coatbridge area. This route to St Rollox was, however, circuitous, so it was not surprising to find Charles the leading promoter of the Garnkirk and Glasgow Railway, a direct rail link with the Monkland and Kirkintilloch and Ballochney lines. Indeed its Glasgow terminus was immediately adjacent to the St Rollox

Works, and one of the first two locomotives was named 'St Rollox'. The other, 'George Stephenson' was driven by the great man himself when he opened the railway on 27 September 1831.

> The one engine, the St Rollox, conveyed the directors and a number of ladies and gentlemen to the amount of nearly 200; the other, the George Stephenson, drew a train of 32 waggons loaded with coal, freestone, lime, grain, iron, and other articles of trade upon the line, to the amount of ninety tons, exclusive of the weight of the waggons, which must have increased the aggregate load to one hundred and twenty tons; thus exhibiting, in a striking point of view, the advantages of the railway, both for the purposes of travelling, and for the transport of heavy goods. Under this prodigious load, which came to nearly twenty times its own weight, the latter engine yet advanced not only with perfect freedom, but with the speed of a stage coach; while the former, with its two hundred passengers, darted along with twice the rapidity of the mail, and seemed eventually capable of acquiring any additional speed that might have been necessary or safe. In many parts, however, the trains advanced leisurely along to give time for viewing the works of the line. The day was very favourable for the exhibition, and the scene altogether, particularly the operations of the engines, at one time advancing with their enormous trains slowly and majestically along, and at another flying past with such rapidity, amid the shouts of the assembled multitudes, was well calculated to excite the deepest interest, and to impress the beholder with a feeling of wonder and of exultation at the new and extraordinary powers which the triumphs of inventive genius had thus brought to the dominion of man.[(1)]

Thus the last main transport problem for the St Rollox Works was solved.

Charles continued his vigorous promotion of Lanarkshire mineral railways with the Wishaw and Coltness Railway, a southern extension of the Monkland network, authorised in 1829 and opened in stages between 1833 and 1844. Quite different in conception, however, was the scheme for an extension of the Garnkirk and Glasgow to Edinburgh, proposed in

October 1830, when Charles Tennant had just returned from the opening of the Liverpool and Manchester Railway, the first inter-city line in the world. An alternative line via Falkirk was ultimately constructed under an act of 1837 and opened in 1842, and Charles was a director of this company until his death. Both these schemes owed a great deal in their design to experience on the Liverpool and Manchester, so it was probably the vivid impression made on Charles by the opening of the latter that encouraged him to back them. Charles' vision of an inter-city link was ultimately realised, but his project to extend the Garnkirk line to Glasgow Harbour was unsuccessful. Mr Grainger wrote:

> The opening of the Manchester and Liverpool Railway, which took place, I think, in September 1830, was a most important event to Mr. Tennant. He was present along with his family and myself. At this time the superiority of railway communication by steam power for the conveyance of passengers and light loads had been fully established. Shortly after this Mr. Tennant took an active part in promoting a railway between Edinburgh and Glasgow by Bathgate and Airdrie, of which the Garnkirk and Glasgow and the Ballochney Railways were to form a part. It is hardly necessary to add that this project having failed to meet the support of many influential parties, it was not carried out. Mr. Tennant did not live to see, nor was he sanguine enough to anticipate, that although the Glasgow and Garnkirk line was not destined to form a portion of the railway communication between the cities of Edinburgh and Glasgow, it (as well as the Wishaw and Coltness Line) was to be part of the railway route between Glasgow and London.
>
> While Mr. Tennant left no stone unturned to carry out the railway between Edinburgh and Glasgow, by Bathgate and Airdrie, of which the Garnkirk Line was to have formed a part, he, nevertheless, when these projects were abandoned, most cordially co-operated from the beginning with those who promoted the line by Falkirk since carried out. He was all along one of the most influential of its directors down to the time of his death.

> Mr. Tennant soon saw the vast importance, not only to all interested either as coal proprietors or shareholders, but to the public in general, of having the Garnkirk Railway extended from St. Rollox to the harbour of Glasgow. With this view, various schemes were proposed, in the whole of which Mr. Tennant was prime mover. But after much exertion, the great expense coupled with the formidable opposition of Mr. Campbell of Blythswood, and other landed proprietors on the line, together with the very lukewarm support accorded by the Clyde Trustees and other public bodies, rendered all efforts unavailing; and from the rapid extension of the city of Glasgow on the West, and the consequent change in the value of properties in that district, it is now too much to expect that any such communication will ever be established on the right bank of the river to the Broomielaw, especially as such a communication with the river has now been formed on its left bank.
>
> In the promotion of these various works—with many of which I was professionally connected—and in the ordinary intercourse of friendship which I had the happiness to enjoy for nearly fourteen years—I had many—very many—opportunities of witnessing the zeal, talent, and energy of character, combined with great kindness of heart, which he possessed in an eminent degree. Whether our meeting was at four or five in the morning, as was not unfrequently the case, or at noon or night, Mr. Tennant was ever at his post.[2]

From about 1825 to his death, Charles was one of the leading West of Scotland railway promoters. He appreciated the part that railways could play in improving communications in general as well as in making the transport of minerals relatively cheap and easy. The promotion of railways in the Glasgow area was often made difficult by the fierce opposition from the canal proprietors.

However Charles did not neglect the waterways. Shortly before 1830 he started his younger sister Sarah's son, William Sloan, with some small schooners in order to carry chemical products to neighbouring markets. These schooners traded on the canals, and sailed as far south as Newcastle, Hull, and even to London.

At the time of William Sloan's death in 1848, the St Rollox Shipping Company consisted of nineteen vessels, making it the largest fleet in Glasgow. Shortly after this the firm started building steamers which sailed between Glasgow and the Bristol Channel. These gradually replaced the schooners.

By 1857, forty-five years after Henry Bell's six horse-power *Comet* had made history on the river Clyde, the company had two screw vessels plying between London and Glasgow. Another steamer traded its produce to Baltic ports and returned with goods for its own use. Many coastal vessels were regularly employed in bringing pure quality limestone and salt from Ireland and sulphur from Italy. Mineral resources could now be exploited to ensure regular supplies of fuel to the factories and foundries.

Within forty years Burns' 'Wabster Charlie' lived to see his empire grow and the child of his imagination become the largest and most important chemical works in the world, manufacturing the chemicals necessary to the heavy acid and alkali industries.

When the St Rollox works were first started they were isolated, standing alone in a desolate area. In 1831 Charles, with his office in Moodie's Court, was one of the few manufacturing chemists in Glasgow. By 1858 the number had grown to fifty-five, and the whole district was teeming with manufacturing life, potteries, glassworks, sawmills, timber-yards, flax and cotton mills, iron foundries, machine-shops, earthenware factories, and railway stations. Between 1828 and 1858 the progress of trade and manufacture was so rapid that Port Dundas and St Rollox became an integral part of Glasgow. St Rollox products and by-products contributed not only to the city's development, but to the prosperity of industries in the neighbouring counties, and to the wider pre-eminence given to this branch of the chemical industry throughout Europe. In this, Charles Tennant played the leading part.

Charles's personal prosperity became plain to all, for in 1829–30 he built the large square stone mansion, 195 West George Street, Glasgow, whose dignified façade became well known to the people of the city. A basement, two storeys and an attic were allowed by the Blythswood Estate for the building of houses. (A third storey was added after it was sold. First it became the head offices of Nobel's Explosives Co. Ltd, and it was recently demolished.) Within these instructions rose the noble five-windowed Georgian frontage. A flight of steps led to the front door. The large entrance hall and central well were lit from a skylight surrounded by a frieze depicting scenes of slaves bringing gifts to conquering Romans. A handsome chandelier hung from a long chain. A staircase with an ironwork banister and a mahogany rail led up to the first floor. The ballroom, with its ornamented ceiling, faced on to West George Street and extended through the whole breadth of the house.

Acknowledgement of his services and success came to Charles on Wednesday, 4 July 1838, when the Lord Advocate, John Murray, wrote:

> My dear Sir,
>
> I can assure you that it is very generally thought that a person who has rendered the services which you have done to the Commerce and Manufacturers of the country ought, on the present occasion, to receive some mark of Her Majesty's favour.
>
> I conversed with Lord John Russell on the subject some time ago. I had the pleasure of receiving a note from His Lordship this evening, in which he says that if it would be pleasing to you to receive the honour of Knighthood he feels sure he would be able to obtain Her Majesty's sanction to confer that distinction upon you.
>
> I hope to hear from you soon on this subject, and I remain,
>
> My dear Sir,
> Yours truly,
> John A. Murray.

Following his elder brother David's example, Charles replied two days later.

My dear Sir,
I beg to acknowledge the receipt of your letter of the 4th curt., and to thank you for the very flattering notice it contains of the slight services I have rendered to the Manufactures and Commerce of our Country.
Assure Lord John Russell of my grateful feelings for the honour he intended me, which, however, I beg leave most respectfully to decline for reasons too numerous and peculiar to be mentioned in this note, and
I have the honour to be
My dear Sir,
Ever gratefully yours,
Charles Tennant.

On 1 October 1838, this pioneer of seventy died at his house in West George Street. He left a grown-up family and a widow, who lived her last five years in the fine new mansion, waited upon by six maidservants and one man-servant.

The following letter was written by a friend to Charles's son John, dated 3 October 1838:

It is now fourteen years since I first knew your father and having been so much in his company and lived and travelled so often with him, I acquired a feeling towards him more as if he were father rather than acquaintance. Indeed, I enjoyed more pleasure in your father's society than I ever did with my intimate friends of my own age. His kindness of disposition and scientific acquirements removed the difference between youth and age and when we travelled together I felt I was always accompanying another youthful companion. The bereavement was the more unexpected, for your father, from his excellent constitution and regular habits, was a person likely to live to a good old age.

On 13 October the *Glasgow Argus* published this obituary notice, written by Mr Henry Ainsworth of Manchester.

A few days since died Charles Tennant, Esq. of St. Rollox, one of the ablest of the Scottish Reformers. The loss of Mr. Tennant will be deeply and widely felt. He was an earnest and indefatigable promoter of economical and educational improvement, an uncompromising friend of civil and religious liberty. His own inborn energy of character and clear intellect placed him among the foremost of that class which, by wedding science to manufacturers, has at once extended their field of action, and elevated them to the rank of a liberal profession, with all the deep sustained power of a comprehensive mind, to which we can scarcely apply a feebler name than genius. Mr. Tennant was in his disposition singularly mild and retiring. A constitutional nervousness—remarkable in one of large and healthy frame—was allied with that sensitiveness to the beautiful which is usually its concomitant. We have more than once listened with delight when he, whom most men thought engrossed in scientific and commercial speculation, began to expatiate on his youthful reminiscences of Burns. In every respect—as a domestic man and citizen—a more pure and upright soul we have not yet known than his, whom society, and still more his family have lost.

The loss of the accomplished energy of Alexander Dunlop has been too soon followed by that of the quiet shrewd power of Tennant, and where are they of the next generation who are to fill their places?

Inventive genius demands one kind of ability and business enterprise requires talents of a different order. Charles's contribution to the science of chemistry was significant, but it is for his achievements as an entrepreneur of amazing ability that he has first claim on the recognition of posterity. By putting into practice his ideas and those of his colleagues at St Rollox he built the largest chemical company in the world.

CHAPTER SEVEN

John Tennant of St Rollox (1796-1878)

CHARLES TENNANT's eldest son John was born in 1796 in the parish of Eastwood, Glasgow. He was one of a family of seven girls and two boys. He was educated at Glasgow High School and entered the university at the age of twelve. Two years later he was joined there by his brother Charles James. Neither boy took his Arts degree. At this time chemistry was taught in the University by Thomas Thomson, the first Regius Professor. He was a utilitarian and a radical, a life-long friend of James Mill. John, one of his youngest pupils, would have received first-class tuition in chemistry and this must have laid the foundation of his successful running of St Rollox, where he pursued the then unusual policy of employing trained chemists. Later he became a firm friend of his former tutor and finally one of his legatees.

He entered his father's business when he was nineteen and he and his brother both became partners in the Glasgow and London houses in 1820. John's business ability coupled with his good grounding as a practical chemist soon earned him the post of Managing Director of the Company. When he was twenty-two he met Robina Arrol, an employee at the St Rollox works, and fell in love with her. The family legend tells that she was lovely and intelligent. History does not relate why they were not able to marry. Had she been married before? Whatever the reason, John treated Robina as his legal wife and although they were only married 'by habit and repute' their union gave the family arms the bordure compony. Her name is absent from all records (except from her daughter Marion's death certificate, 1902. In the registration of his death John was described as a retired chemical manufacturer, single, died 17 April 1878, at 195 West George Street, aged 81 years), nor is she referred to in John's obituary notices, which only mention his children; nor is she buried in the family vault in the Glasgow necropolis.

It is said that she was persecuted by her 'mother-in-law' who hated the alliance, and that most of the family refused to recognise her. Charles James would not countenance his 'sister-in-law'; nor do John's sisters seem to have played any part in his and Robina's life. No mention is made of them or of their descendants in any of his letters or diaries; but he may have remained on speaking terms with his eldest sister Margaret, whose son Charles Tennant Dunlop became the firm's celebrated head chemist and subsequently became a partner in St Rollox and the London business. (He introduced important improvements in the filtration of chemical solutions, and also for the recovery of manganese during the manufacture of bleaching powder.)

John in his turn disapproved of his fashionable, good-looking dandy of a brother who was known as 'The Vipe'. A skilled yachtsman and a famous rider, Charles James was one of the young bloods of the West of Scotland. At the age of twenty-two he married a great beauty called Jane Pollock and carried her off to Ballikinrain, an estate which he had bought in Stirlingshire, where they lived until she died in 1870.

The rift between the brothers never truly healed. As an old diary says: 'Each was too proud to speak first, and there was never any explanation.' Despite this estrangement, they remained in the business as co-partners for twelve years after the death of their father. Finally they quarrelled outright and in 1850 Charles James left the business.

John was a complex character, a mixture of blunt gruffness and great kindness, of hard-headedness and generosity. He was forceful in his speech, yet retiring and unassuming.

He was a most hospitable man and a *bon vivant*; a man of honour who hated all shoddiness or meanness. At the start of their life together he and Robina lived in a modest way in a house by the St Rollox works, close to the Monkland Canal. A young boy who was employed in the house at this time and who later became the butler recounted that John married Robina by consent under Scottish Law, proclaiming this fact by placing a brass plate on their front door engraved with 'Mr and Mrs John Tennant'. Their first child, Marion, was born in 1819; John and Charles followed at two-year intervals. They kept open house to their many friends, amongst whom John was known as 'Jakey'. At one of his dinners in 1825 the seeds were sown for the formation of the Western Club of which he was a foundation member.

In 1838 the death of his father brought John to the head of the firm, but he did not move in to 195 West George Street until after his mother's death in 1843. Then he made it his home for the remaining forty years of his life. Work was synonymous with breathing for him. He formed the habit, so the story goes, of inviting his head salesmen to dine early in January each year to decide the price of bleaching powder.(1) 'Well,' he queried, 'what's to be the price this year?' On their naming a figure which would be the envy of a modern manufacturer, he answered, 'Very well,' and the contracts were fixed accordingly.

He managed to find time to follow his favourite sport with the Renfrewshire Hunt. As a young man he was an indefatigable sportsman, an enthusiast for the game of golf and one of the hardest riders. When he was long past seventy his compact, close-knit figure, sitting his well-bred horse in an unmistakeably workmanlike manner, was well known to all who took their walks abroad around Glasgow. He travelled much on business. As late as 1850, when he was fifty-four, on journeys to Dundee he always rode on horseback by way of Perth, eschewing the postchaise because it would have carried him past a beautiful view without his being able to enjoy it. He owned a yacht called the *Ruby Queen* in which he sailed to the Faroe Islands in 1856. Three or four years later his travels took him to Italy and Sicily to visit some sulphur mines of which he was part owner. No comment on the mines has survived, but a rebellious cry made its way into a letter: 'Let me see no more Italian gardens!'

In November 1850 John's elder son and namesake died tragically at the age of twenty-nine. He left a young widow who had two children and was expecting a third. Writing to his sister after the funeral, Charles expressed surprise that their uncle Charles James had been present.

> My Uncle's coming was quite unlooked for, the announcement of John's death reached him at Ballikinrain, without a moment's delay he set out and reached Mr. Clow's at two o'clock on Sunday—I cannot tell you how much we were all touched of this very great mark of his affection and regard—my father felt it not a little . . . it was the talk of everyone and has confirmed the opinion I have already entertained of our Uncle's attachment and esteem.

In the same letter he reveals another facet of his father's nature: 'My father testified towards her [his widowed daughter-in-law] the utmost tenderness and affection; he is in possession of rare qualities of heart and mind.'

Charles had been devoted to his brother and in writing again to his sister Marion he said: 'We two had no interest, no hope, no thought indeed apart from each other . . .' He ended the letter with some advice:

> Write to me as often and as long letters as you feel inclined but to my father be brief—you know this is his desire—he is a man of few words, and long pious reflections, and expression of excited sentiment and feeling do not harmonise with a mind so active and practical and so much employed. You know I say this in thoroughly good part as you desire so much to please your father I know you will not neglect my kindly admonition.

Two years after this Marion married the Rev. Robert Wallace, minister of Dalrymple in Ayrshire, a widower with a family of five children. It is said that she told her step-

5. The opening of the Garnkirk and Glasgow Railway, 27 September 1831, with the engine 'St Rollox', at the St Rollox works.

6. 195 West George Street was built by Charles Tennant in 1830, and remained the Glasgow headquarters of the Tennant family for the next seventy years. It was demolished in 1970.

7. Robina Arrol who was married to John Tennant 'by habit and repute' and was the mother of his three children.

9. *(opposite)* St Rollox in 1844, showing the 'Stalk', large Gossage towers on the left and a sailing barge in the canal probably carrying salt and limestone, also coal barges. The glass cone on the right was probably part of the St Rollox flint glass works.

8. John Tennant of St Rollox (1796–1878) who built Tennant's Stalk in 1842. He was the son of Charles, founder of St Rollox and father of Sir Charles Tennant.

10. *(below)* Four generations of the Tennant family:

(front row)

(Sir) Charles Tennant, (1823–1906); his sister Marion, (Mrs Wallace); Charles James Tennant (1801–1870)

John Tennant of St Rollox (1796–1878)

(standing)

Mr Clow (partner in Tennant Clow & Co. Liverpool). Bust: 'Auld Glen', John Tennant (1726–1810). Picture: Charles Tennant (1768–1838)

11. Sir Charles and his brother John Tennant's family in 1864: *(back row)* James, Charles, John, (children of John), Pauline *(second row)* Edward, Margot, Lucy, Frank, Laura *(front)* Charlotte.

12. Emma Winsloe (1821–1895) married Sir Charles in 1849 and had six sons and six daughters.

13. Sir Charles Tennant (1823–1906), by Sir Daniel Macnee, 1870. He was one of the greatest of Victorian entrepreneurs. He was a Liberal member of parliament for six years and was created a baronet by his friend W. E. Gladstone.

children that, although she was fond of them, she was not 'passionately attached', and she proceeded to turn them out of the house. She had only one child of her own, which did not survive.

In politics, true to the family tradition, John was a Whig and a supporter of the Reform Bill of 1832. With his father and his eight-year-old son Charles he took part in the protest march through the streets of Glasgow in favour of the passing of the Bill. He campaigned for the repeal of the Corn Laws and the removal of all 'oppressive fiscal duties'. He could have contested a parliamentary seat in Glasgow had it not been for his retiring nature. He disliked public speaking, for all his sense of public duty, and it was only in the General Election of June 1841, which brought a four-cornered fight in the constituency of Glasgow, that he overcame his reticence enough to second the nomination of his friend James Oswald, an ardent liberal reformer.

John's imposing house in West George Street became a meeting place for many distinguished visitors, more especially Whigs and men of radical opinions. He entertained them lavishly. The dining-room was square, solid and spacious. The ceiling was supported by pillars. A noble mahogany sideboard showed off the victuals, strong chairs supported the guests, blazing gas jets gave them light and a large coal fire warmed them. The remarkable Mrs Houston was a cook of genius, and Cunningham, an equally remarkable butler, presided over the wine from a connoisseur's cellar. He was a butler of the old school, who was nicknamed 'The Cat' and many of whose remarks appeared in *Punch*.

John's friends lived to bless the bounteous charity he lavished on individuals and on many good causes. The Company's cashier spent a large part of his time cashing mandates brought to the office by needy customers whom John had befriended. His anonymous giving far exceeded his public benefactions, and many who flourished in later life owed their start or their success to his encouragement and practical help.

One of the many stories told about John concerned his

close friend James Merry, a steel magnate who, on hearing that John had given £10,000 to build a church, said to him that it was the biggest fire insurance premium he ever heard of. This raised an argument on religion and Merry bet John £100 he could not say the Lord's Prayer. John accepted and began: 'The Lord is my shepherd, I'll not want'—when Merry stopped him saying: 'You've won. I didn't think you knew it.'

John was for many years one of Glasgow's most prominent citizens. He was also 'a gentleman of uncommon energy and ability, and was esteemed one of the most honourable and upright of the merchants and citizens of Glasgow; and every movement for the social, commercial or educational advancement of his native city found a ready claim to his support.'[12] He did much to promote the spread of knowledge and technical education by encouraging in various ways the Mechanics' Institute in Bath Street and Anderson's University in George Street, both of which became merged into the Royal College of Science and Technology, Glasgow, since 1964, the University of Strathclyde.

It was becoming customary to look upon Glasgow as an undesirable place in which money could be made, but one which was to be left as soon as possible for fear of being dubbed 'provincial'. Businessmen were moving out to the suburbs or to country estates and they sent their children to English public schools. Not so John, who was first and foremost a Glasgow man. He never left the city and his children were educated in their native land.

He was a man of many interests. In addition to owning the St Rollox works, he was a partner in the chemical works at Jarrow and Newcastle. He was a member of the underwriters of Glasgow and Lloyd's. In 1857 he became the owner of large cocoa and sugar estates in Trinidad. His interest in railway development extended beyond the Garnkirk and Glasgow railway to lines which would link the coal and iron centres of Scotland. He was Chairman of the Ballochney Railway (opened in 1827) and was connected with the Monkland and Kirkintilloch line, the Wishaw and Coltness line, and the Edinburgh and Glasgow line via Bathgate. He was also a keen promoter of the Volunteers when these first started. He financed and equipped the Fourth Regiment of the Lanarkshire Volunteers (first called the First Northern; subsequently becoming a battalion of the Cameronians), which was recruited mainly from men at the St Rollox works, and he became its Honorary Colonel at the age of sixty-four. Another of his interests was the Jumble Club, a whist club founded in 1799 which numbered amongst its members many leading men of Glasgow. He was extremely fond of the game, though he was never by any standards a good player; nor was he a good loser.

As far back as 1827 John had been the prime mover in building and maintaining the St Rollox school at the north end of Castle Street near the works. He was far ahead of his time in his concern to educate his employees' children, for it was long before the law decreed that factory schools should be built. Mr Masterman, or 'Corky' as his pupils nicknamed him, the second headmaster to be appointed, had lost his left arm as a factory worker in his youth. He was a good teacher, who had the welfare of his pupils at heart. Many parents who would have removed their young children from school to earn their living working long hours in the mill were persuaded by him to leave them learning a little longer. When the first St Rollox school became inadequate to meet the needs, John drew up a scheme for building a better one in Garngad Road to hold about 800 children. He hurried and harried the builders until it was opened in 1850 as the first school in the district. He was never given to strut 'in his ain kailyard', so was not a well-known figure to the pupils. Once only he caused a sensation by escorting over the premises a company of Serbians, who were dressed in full national costume, with towering hats and lavish moustaches.

As the years passed John became a somewhat forbidding figure, quick-minded and quicker-tempered. When he was eighty-one he visited the magnificent chemical works at Hebburn-on-Tyne which had been opened in 1865 to meet the demands for chemicals from London. He was shown round by a man named T. W. Stuart who worked for three generations of Tennants. Stuart recorded that although it was a bitterly cold winter's day John Tennant insisted on being shown over every corner of the Works for, as he said, 'the last time'. This led to the greatest 'spring cleaning' ever administered; even the vitriol chambers' floors were scrubbed. Everything seemed perfect. When he climbed to the chambers he found the plumbers had knocked a hole in the wood flooring, whereupon he gave his guide a never-to-be-forgotten lecture on the principle of 'A stitch in time'.

In 1908 there were still old employees who remembered his visits to the London House, and the rising trepidation his footsteps occasioned as he was heard puffing on the stairs. In 1932 his twelfth and youngest grandchild, Harold John, wrote of him: 'I can just remember him and my principal memories are of his grand manner and his kindness to me. At Christmas he often came to Glen, bringing a small bag of new sovereigns which he distributed among all of us. I used to play billiards with him when I was so small that I had to carry a footstool round the table to reach my ball. He must have been a poor performer, as when I could only have been ten or eleven years old I beat him occasionally. His language on these occasions was very forcible.'(3)

John's life was dominated by St Rollox. Its financial success and its organisation were a source of constant concern and pride to him. When he took command in 1838 he inherited what was the most extensive group of chemical companies in the world. Its interests were spread widely over Britain and Europe, so that when a recession struck Scotland production could be redirected to other markets. Thanks to men such as his father the bleaching industry had grown out of the flourishing textile industry, and John and his fellow capitalists were now investigating possibilities in such new fields as metallurgical extraction which later in the century was to bring further fame and prosperity to the Tennant family and to Glasgow.

As the works expanded so the noxious fumes increased. Although chimneys or 'stalks' were reaching high into the air where the prevailing winds could carry the poisonous fumes away over the empty bog country, yet people still continued to complain of the tainted air. It was these chimneys that gave John's eighteen-year-old son Charles, who was serving his apprenticeship in Liverpool, the idea of building a mammoth 'stalk' to release the fumes even higher in the atmosphere to reduce their effect further. It is said of him that during a dreary sermon in church one Sunday, he sat with his hand on his brow, seemingly sunk in deep concentration on higher things. Those next to him heard him repeating under his breath, 'I've got it . . . I've got it . . . I've got it.' 'It' was the idea of building the tallest chimney in existence. His vision became a reality.

The chimney shaft was projected by Professor W. J. Macquorn Rankine and designed by Professor L. D. B. Gordon and L. Hill. The engineer was Andrew Thomson.[(4)] Dugald Campbell McIntyre, once foreman bricklayer at St Rollox and by then a builder on his own, was approached to given an estimate for the work. At first he regarded the proposition as a joke and beyond the realms of possibility. He was assured that it was not so and his estimate was accepted. On 29 June 1841 the concrete foundations of the outer wall were laid twenty feet below the surface on a bed of solid sandstone rock, and exactly a year later the coping stones were laid 49 feet higher than the Cross above St Paul's Cathedral, thrice the height of Nelson's Column. The twin chimneys of this structural marvel were concentric; the outer one was 40 feet in diameter at the surface of the ground, tapering to 14 feet 6 inches at the 430 feet summit, and both took five months to complete. To alleviate the human suffering caused by smoke from the works, underground channels were tunnelled through the solid rock from various furnaces to the giant 'stalk', with one great main tunnel receiving the branches before it joined the chimney. *The Mirror* of 4 December 1841 predicted that: 'The Stalk when completed, will be about the height of the Great Pyramid of Egypt'. (Their article is reproduced as Appendix III.)

Excitement mounted when Mr McIntyre offered to take

guests to the top before the stalk came into use. Gentlemen ascended in buckets, and ladies in iron-hooped baskets made for the purpose. Both were hoisted through the inner chimney by a steam pulley and took 2½ minutes to reach the top. The *Glasgow Herald* reported that 'some of the fair sex have displayed a degree of courage superior to many of the Lords of the Creation'. The murky journey gave the guests no unpleasant feeling as they held on by a rope, then climbed out on to a secure platform surrounded by a parapet sufficiently high to banish all fear of falling over. No one had ever seen such a panorama. The lengthened course of the Clyde divided hill and dale; the shores of Dunoon, the Isle of Arran, the beauty of Ben Lomond, pride of the Western Highlands; faintly the outlines of Edinburgh and the Firth of Forth flanked by the Kingdom of Fife shadowed the skyline. Down below the grey smoke of the great city hung over a patternless mass of masonry. To mark the opening day a Union Jack was unfurled from a fifty-foot flagpole, and Mr McIntyre, his work accomplished, celebrated with his friends on whisky and beef. For the next eighty years, both nationally and internationally, 'Tennant's Stalk' became a city landmark, and entered into the speech of the people as a symbol of the incredible. In a local ballad it became synonymous with the impossible: 'Until Tennant's Stalk down Buchanan Street walk.' When asked why trees did not grow in the streets and squares of Glasgow, a Glaswegian would point to the chimney as the reason; when he walked abroad over neighbouring hills he would look to see if the dark elegance of the Stalk was still visible. It held pride of place in his memories of Glasgow. George Dodd in 1847 wrote,

> They (the works) are, necessarily, black and dirty; and some of them are as infernal in appearance as we can well imagine any earthly place to be. The heaps of sulphur, lime, coal, and refuse; the intense heat of the scores of furnaces in which the processes are going on; the smoke and thick vapours which dim the air of most of the buildings; the swarthy and heated appearance of the men;

the acrid fumes of sulphur, and the various acids which worry the eyes, and tickle the nose, and choke the throat; the danger which every bit of broad-cloth incurs of being bleached by something or burned by something else—all form a series of *notabilia* not soon to be forgotten. The buildings occupy an immense square, from which shoot up numerous chimneys. Many of these chimneys are equal to the largest in other towns, but they are here mere satellites to the monster of the place—THE Chimney.(6)

As the works expanded immense and increasing quantities of solid odorous wastes defiled the nearby land and polluted the streams. By the 1860s the filth was said to cover about eighty acres. According to the Alkali Report of 1883, 'There were nearly 100 acres of crude calcium sulphide constituting a vast grey desert, a mass of three million tons, in some places eighty feet thick.' Bog waters and springs took some of the waste into the Pinkston Burn, thence into the Kelvin and finally into the Clyde. In the course of the Kelvin the sulphide of calcium liquors from St Rollox met the waste of other concerns, especially acid from the distilleries, producing hydrogen sulphide, which gave forth so unbearable a smell that people suggested the works should be removed elsewhere.

Drainage was the logical answer. A shaft was driven 40 or 50 feet down into the sandstone rocks below the bog, and galleries were driven in various directions. Pumping was continued night and day for years. The problem remained recalcitrant, and in 1864 the Company laid a nine-inch pipe all the way to the Clyde, and a large reservoir was made.

This gave rise to a new problem. Shipowners protested that the copper sheathing on the hulls of their ships was corroding as a result of the alkali waste passing straight into the Clyde. In 1871 James MacTear, the then Manager at St Rollox and a fine chemist, therefore turned his fertile mind to solving the problem of pollution, and a process which bears his name was the result. Success exceeded hopes. Not only was the drainage problem solved, but the sulphur thus recovered became a profitable by-product.

The foremen of the works under John Tennant found one other use for the huge pile of waste. At the expense of the firm, they kept trotting horses and held races on a course laid out at the top of the waste. This irregular activity was firmly stopped when Charles Tennant took over from his father.

Apart from the recovery of sulphur and the racing, the waste was a constant liability and a cause of public complaint. Although they were not entirely successful in solving the problems of waste and pollution on the ground, John and Charles Tennant can claim that the noxious fumes were dispersed higher in the air at St Rollox than at any other industrial factory.

John was also concerned about the welfare of his employees. He never disassociated himself, as many leaders of industry did, from the appalling social problems which arose as a result of the industrial revolution. In this new society, with its *laissez-faire* philosophy, the old ideas of paternalism were dying out. That an employer should bind his employee to him by personal links or adopt any social responsibilities on his behalf was incompatible with contemporary rationalism. Although Tennant's works could not claim exemption from the abuses of human labour which were customary in those days, it was generally considered at the time that the management of the St Rollox works had always been progressive towards their employees. They attempted to provide the most sanitary conditions possible at the time, and were generous in voluntarily giving compensation for temporary injury, permanent disablement and death, very long before legislation compelled manufacturers to recognise and discharge obligations in this respect. They also retained the services of a doctor for their employees.

However, such mitigating circumstances must still be viewed against the background of some of the worst working and living conditions imaginable. It was no disgrace at this time to use child labour or to employ women in work such as mining, which destroyed their health and turned them into crumpled old hags at the age of thirty. But judgement of

Victorian employers must be made with understanding of the prevailing belief in a rugged individualism at a time when men of enterprise could rise from humble circumstances and amass fortunes. People generally held that it was spiritually stultifying to give assistance in the form of Poor Law relief, which would hinder the development of independence of character. Hunger was no reason to receive relief.

The home of the average Glasgow worker was in 'a giant tenement, the colour of mud, built to last forever, cut up into boxes with a top on the staircase', dark, damp, low-ceilinged rooms spilling over with people, homes providing among the worst social conditions in Great Britain, with privies and drains unknown, 'and the dung heaps received all the filth which the swarms of wretched inhabitants could give, and the rents of the houses were paid to a considerable extent by the produce of those dung heaps'.(7) The natural corollary to these conditions was recourse to liquor which led to crime on an appalling scale.

The composition of Charles Tennant & Company changed a good deal during John Tennant's period of office.

In the thirties the company had lost two of its original partners, Alexander Dunlop and William Couper, whose places were filled by William Stevenson and George Brown. This led to a long association between the Stevenson and Tennant families in the chemical trade. George Brown strengthened his ties with the family by marrying the irascible Robert Tennant's daughter Jane, a niece of the founder of the firm, and he worked for many years at St Rollox from where he became a partner in the London business.

In 1846 two partners were added to the Glasgow business: Alexander Morison, who only stayed for five years, and the brilliant chemist, Charles Tennant Dunlop, whose death at the age of thirty-six was a serious loss to the firm. Other partners joined the company, including William Galbraith who was commercial manager from 1855–79. He was followed by James MacTear, who experimented with making diamonds as a side product. He believed that diamonds might be formed from small particles of carbon inserted at a high temperature in an iron cannonball which was then contracted by cooling. The diamonds were to be recovered by dissolving away the iron with waste effluent hydrochloric acid. The experiments did produce a substance which, to quote his own words, 'was so like diamond dust in appearance as to deceive even experts'.(8) In 1856 John invited William Dalrymple Tennant, great-grandson of the earlier David Tennant who had been Latin master at the Burgh School in Ayr, to join the business. Four years later he became a partner, and for the last twenty years of his life from 1873 to 1893 he managed the London business. Thus was laid the foundation of an association between two branches of the family which has continued until the present day. William Augustus Tennant of Ugley in Essex 1861–1941; his son Ernest Dalrymple Tennant, 1887–1963; his son, Julian Tennant, born in 1924 and currently Chairman of C. Tennant & Sons & Co. London. All were partners in the London office. This long association has proved invaluable to the life and prosperity of the Tennant companies. Some indication of the prosperity of the company at the time of John's death is given by James MacTear when he records that in 1878 St Rollox produced 37,400 tons of chemicals, mainly bleaching powder and sulphuric acid. In order to produce this, 29,000 tons of salt, 50,000 tons of limestone, 18,000 tons of pyrites, 7,000 tons of manganese (manganese dioxide) and 127,000 tons of coal were consumed.(9)

On 17 April 1878 John died in his sleep after a short illness at his West George Street home. He left a fortune of about a million pounds sterling. At the funeral his coffin was drawn in an ornate hearse along Lochburn Road by black horses. Their progress was slowed to a halt by the low bridge under the Forth and Clyde Canal. The cortège of mourners, in their tall hats with mourning weepers waving in the wind, waited while the plumes adorning the top of the hearse were unscrewed. Only then was it able to proceed under the dark bridge, lit night and day by the old fishtail gas burners, and so make its way to the necropolis. Here John Tennant's remains were laid to rest amid the heartfelt sorrow of a large gathering of friends and relatives.[10]

Part III

CHAPTER EIGHT

Sir Charles Tennant, Bart., J.P., D.L., of the Glen in the County of Peebles and of St Rollox in the City of Glasgow 1823-1906

CHARLES TENNANT, the second son and third and youngest child of John and Robina, was born in 1823 in his father's house close to the St Rollox works. He lived his life to the full until his death at 83; he married twice and had sixteen children, the eldest of whom was born in 1850 and the youngest in 1904—a remarkable span of fifty-four years. He was to become one of Glasgow's leading merchant princes and indeed one of the greatest men of commerce in the country. He was an industrial pioneer and an international financier whose important dealings on the London Stock Exchange influenced prices on Wall Street. When, on his father's death, he became head of the family firm he was one of the largest employers of labour in the British Isles. He enlarged the Tennant empire to include interests in mining, steel and marine engineering. His energy was boundless and he had no use for marking time. He liked to travel by railway sleeper so that the entire day could be devoted to work. For seven years he was a Liberal Member of Parliament. He was a keen sportsman; he was a connoisseur and collector of pictures, mezzotints, books, china and objects of vertu. As his daughter Margot Asquith wrote in her autobiography, 'He had courage for life and the enterprise to spend his fortune on it.'[1]

At the age of five Charles was sent to school at the Ayr Academy where he proved to be a promising pupil. An annual examination card records: 'Mr Charles Tennant, student in the 5th Junior English Class, obtained by Proficiency and Exemplary Conduct this Public Token of Approbation.'

At the age of nine, as we have seen, he was initiated into politics when he walked with his father in a procession of 150,000 demonstrators to demand the passing of the great Reform Bill of 1832. The procession was preceded by a large live ox with a board affixed to its chest announcing: 'I am reformed, the patriotic spirit roused; all dangers scorn and take corruption's monster by the horns.' Banners proclaimed: 'He that hath not a sword, let him sell his garment and buy one,' and 'Better to die in a good cause than to live in slavery,' and 'By the bones of our fathers we shall be free.' It was an exciting experience for a small boy and the memory of it must have remained with him all his life.

Later he was sent to join his brother, who was two years older than he, at a well known boys' school at Tillicoultry. This school was run by the Reverend Archibald Browning, an unusual and stimulating teacher who had only the most rudimentary education himself. Virtually self-taught, he had formed his own method of teaching in which he devoted a whole hour to one particular subject. A few minutes at the beginning were spent in listening to and memorising the lesson; the remaining time was occupied by teaching as he saw it. His method was not only to impart knowledge but to stimulate his pupils to think and act for themselves. It was a grounding which undoubtedly exercised a profound influence on Charles' character and development. The boys learned no Greek, but in Latin lessons passages were meticulously studied and explained and then the boys were examined on them. The headmaster demanded perfection and exercises often had to be written out three times before they were passed by him. Charles learned to write in beautiful copperplate handwriting in which no error, blemish or carelessness was tolerated. Throughout his life he would carefully scratch out with a penknife any accidental blemish or spot of ink in the letters he wrote. Discipline at Mr Browning's school was strict and he administered beatings to the accompaniment of a leonine roar that no erring pupil ever forgot.

Charles' memory, fostered so sedulously at school, became phenomenal in later life. He attributed it to his early love of learning poetry and prose by heart, reciting it to himself as he went to and from school. It was so reliable throughout his life that he never carried a notebook or a diary for his engagements. At the age of eighty-one he was able to stand up before the assembled company at a Tweedale Shooting Club Dinner and recite the 224 lines of Burns' 'Tam o' Shanter' without a single mistake.(2) Burns was one of his favourite poets but he also had a wide knowledge of Shakespeare, Tennyson, Dryden, Milton and Wordsworth. In his younger days he read most of the Waverley novels as well as the works of Dickens and Thackeray, but as he grew older his tastes turned more to history and biography.

When he was sixteen Charles became apprenticed to his godfather, William Nevett, a well-known Liverpool merchant and friend of John Tennant. He remained in his employment for about five years. At first he was a mere office boy who took the letters to the post; but it was not in his nature to remain long doing menial tasks. Soon he became the youngest and best judge of the indigo and madder dyes which he was sent to inspect on their arrival at the docks. It would appear that he mastered early the ramifications and intricacies of commerce and its manifold opportunities in a free-trade world, for Mr Nevett wanted to take him into partnership. John Tennant would have none of this, having made up his mind that his promising son was destined for the family business. It was during this period of his life in Liverpool that Charles set himself to learn French. After office hours he studied with John Brunner who came from Zurich. It was something of a coincidence that he should be the father of the future Sir John Brunner of Brunner, Mond and Co., which became the rival firm to Charles Tennant & Co. in the eighteen-eighties.

In 1843 John took his son away from Mr Nevett, and at the age of twenty made him and his elder brother, John, partners in Tennant Clow & Co., Liverpool and Manchester, which in 1913 merged to become Tennants Lancashire Ltd. The following year Charles went to London to work in C. Tennant & Co., 110 Upper Thames Street. His father gave him an allowance of £400 a year and £2000 to start life. One of his first acts on reaching London was to persuade Mr Gurney of Gurney's Bank to advance him a considerable loan to invest in Midland Railway Shares. Mr Gurney acceded to this confident request; the only security required was that the shares should be lodged at the Bank. This first venture, timed to coincide with the beginning of the boom, resulted in profits which enabled the loan to be repaid in two weeks, leaving the happy young man with a substantial surplus, which laid the foundation of his fortune.

On 24 June 1847 Charles wrote from his brother's house in London to his sister Marion in Edinburgh, telling her he was—'still a house-bird, an occupant of the sofa' as he was suffering from a 'swelling' which had been cut, 'but has not decreased much in size. Patience and quiet are the only restoratives, the former is a virtue I hope to become perfect in before long, of the latter I have at least as much as I choose to accept, my own thoughts being my only enemies. The Church before me ought to remind me of all that is beautiful and holy, but share lists will obtrude themselves and stir the avarice of all bad passions. . . . I spend my time, of course, principally in reading, poetry is my favourite, and Byron, as you know, is "my soul's delight", his works and life are the only books I ever asked my father to give me. . . . Business, however, is such an enemy to the Beautiful and Sublime in thought . . .'

On 8 July a letter to 'My dear sister' tells of his sorry state of health, and his journey with Mr Clow from Liverpool to Malvern to take the water cure as administered on the hydropathic system by Dr Wilson, a doctor of high repute. He wrote: 'I have a high regard for cold water, and shall give its qualities a fair trial before leaving here.' By 23 August he writes: 'I am heartily tired of this hospital life and want active employment whether in business or pleasure I care not which,' and that he is 'well enough to return to business in the course of a week or ten days, remaining a week in Liverpool for business, and hoping to get a day or two's fishing'.

In appearance Charles was short, and at the age of seventeen he was blackballed from the Everton Club on account of his stature, surely a quaint reason for exclusion. He was slight in build, neat and meticulous in dress, light of foot, quick and graceful of movement. His impressive forehead was framed by dark curly hair, rather bushy over the ears. His large grey eyes were deep set, their glance penetrating. His face was long, with a finely-chiselled aquiline nose, and classically shaped, kindly mouth. His hands were delicately shaped. Early in life he followed Victorian fashion and wore carefully trimmed side-whiskers and a beard, with clean-shaven upper lip. He was always immaculately dressed in tail coat and top hat and usually arrived at his office smoking a cigar. It was customary for merchants and bankers to attire themselves in dress clothes and ride on horseback to their places of business, for there were many livery stables in London. Charles preferred to travel in a hansom cab, although in later life he always drove in his private brougham.

Charles's next business *coup*, after his success with the loan from Mr Gurney, resulted from a large block of shares in an Australian land company which he bought in 1847. In those days of sailing vessels communication was a matter of many months and it was not until the following year that the Australian mail brought him the news of an enormous rise in the value of his shares. The realisable profit was said to be over £80,000. George Pinnock, an office clerk present at the time, reported that the consequence was an extremely lively day at the office.(3)

In 1849 Charles made a return visit to Malvern where he

met for the second time a Mrs Winsloe and her daughter Emma. Two months later the young couple became engaged. In a letter to his daughter Marion, John Tennant wrote: 'as far as a day's intercourse can enable me to judge of looks, both mother and daughter, I think Charles has a good chance of happiness in the marriage state.' The marriage took place on 2 August of that same year at Leamington Spa. It was to last for forty-nine years, during which time Emma bore Charles six boys and six girls; six were fair and six were dark, six had curly hair and six had straight.

Emma Winsloe, who was two years older than Charles, was born on 6 September 1821. Her grandfather Richard Winsloe was Rector of Ruishton, near Taunton, and his first wife was Catherine Walter, daughter of the founder of *The Times* newspaper. Their son, Richard, was sent to Oxford to study for the Church. Instead of pursuing divinity, he pursued Charlotte Monkton who was finishing her education at a nearby convent school. She was brought up at Taunton by her grandfather, Admiral Monkton, who had led the *Marlborough* to victory under Admiral Howe on the Glorious First of June, 1794. The couple eloped, Charlotte making her undetected escape through a convent window. Later they were caught at Evesham, brought back to Taunton and safely married there the following day. The young man was made to return to the university to finish his studies, but marriage does not seem to have increased his sense of responsibility. After the birth of their two children Richard and Emma, and after having spent all her money, Richard deserted his young wife. She was left to live on an allowance of £200 a year from her father-in-law. First she took her two young children to Honiton, then to Cullompton, then they settled in Le Havre. Later they spent two winters in Paris, where Emma learnt to speak perfect French. After she married Charles preferred that she bought her clothes in Paris.

Emma and Charles were of totally different temperaments. 'She was as timid as he was bold, as controlled as he was spontaneous, and as refined, courteous and unassuming as he was vibrant, sheer and adventurous.'(4) She was utterly selfless, never cared about her appearance and only on rare occasions looked in a mirror. She thought that there was no reason why anyone should be interested in her and as a result she had no really close friends. Placid and even-tempered, she wanted to be dependent on no one and for no one to be dependent on her. She loved to be in the country surrounded by flowers as much as she hated being in London surrounded by 'good society'. She never enjoyed her prosperity and her preachings on economy were a constant source of amusement to Charles who made and spent fortunes.

Their first London house was at 14 Craven Hill, Bayswater. Mrs Winsloe came to live with them there, for Charles was deeply attached to her. The *ménage* was described by one of their daughters:

> In 1849 we find them in a pleasant house, close to the Park, arranging their possessions. Emma superintended the planting of a vine in the greenhouse. The Tennants, unlike the Winsloes, were always political, and Papa was fond of hearing debates in the House. Lord John Russell was then Prime Minister, Lord Palmerston Foreign and Lord Grey Colonial Ministers, and Cobden and Bright were at their zenith. Papa and Mama also had stalls at the French Play, when Mademoiselle Rachel electrified the world. The young Queen, in cruelly trying toilettes was often present with the Prince; once even doing herself the injury of garlanding her head with red fuchsias. For Papa and Mama no actors, singers or dancers ever came up to the giants of those days, Jenny Lind, Grisi, Taglioni, etc. Mama used to wear those pretty tartan dresses, blue and white, and leghorn bonnets in the Marie Stuart fashion.

Emma Tennant was adored by her numerous children, but the dynamic vitality and the exceptional qualities which made many of them famous must have been inherited from their father, because the Winsloes were noted for 'the low vitality inherent in their family'. Their fifth son, Jack, wrote of her: 'she was a most gentle, lovable and beautiful woman, and although she had nothing in her of governing capacity, she had sure sense and shrewdness, and her advice, which was given with such delicacy as to appear almost timorous, was generally full of reason and wisdom.'(5)

By the time their third child John Aubrey was born Charles and Emma were on the look-out for a property in Scotland. Their lawyer Tom Sprot wrote to say that a perfect sporting estate in Peeblesshire had come on to the market and they lost no time in taking the train north to Galashiels. When they arrived at the Glen, Innerleithen, they were immediately enchanted by all they saw. On 2 February 1853 Charles completed the purchase of the estate of just under four thousand acres, which he bought from Colonel George Allan for the sum of £33,140. On Charles telling his father what he had done, John Tennant asked how much money he had. '£90,000,' replied Charles. 'The devil you have,' was his only comment.

The name of Glen is known in records as far back as 1296. Almost as soon as Charles became its owner he proceeded to demolish most of the existing house. An army of masons and workmen were billeted in the surrounding cottages of shepherds and labourers, where they slept in rows on the kitchen floors. Work began on the new house which was designed by David Bryce and was to be in the Scottish baronial style. The main grey stone building, with its twenty-nine bedrooms and six reception-rooms, was completed in 1858; the larger tower was added twenty years later. Two landscape gardeners were in constant attendance to supervise the laying of spacious terraces around the house, the planting of the avenue and the lavish arrangement of gardens and greenhouses. Soil for the kitchen garden had to be carted up from the valley.

The setting was magnificent. Cradled among hills, miles from roads or railway, the Glen looked out on moor upon moor, where heather swept down to the garden walls. Margot described it much later as 'a place buried in the restful hills where the echoes of the burn are never heard except by the peewit and the curlews and the moor mists wreathe round the sun'.(6) Charles took great pride and delight in his creation and was able to keep a watchful eye on the progress of the building by renting first Prestonfield House near Edinburgh and then Kailzie, six miles away. The family finally moved to Glen in 1858. Later, as his children grew up, it was to become the scene of much brilliant entertaining. Charles had learned from his father the art of hospitality; he was a generous and genial host with a gift for telling a good story really well.

Charles was a man of many sporting interests and not least of them was shooting. Every winter there were shooting parties at Glen. In a letter to Lord Rosebery Charles wrote: 'I forgot in my last to tell you that my boys begged me to bring you down here with me for our shoot today. We missed your gun much—the shooting was not up to the mark. Sir Graham Montgomery and I killed the most—we got 359 head in all. 234 pheasants, 2 woodcock, 4 black game, 77 hares, 42 rabbits. We ought to have had 100 more pheasants & I daresay they will pick up 50 tomorrow!'(7)

One of Charles' sons-in-law, Lord Ribblesdale, wrote to Lord Rosebery about Charles as a shot: 'We spent Christmas at Glen—the parent bird in great form and fair spirits. I missed the cover shooting which was pretty good this year. Next year we will both go, it is really rather fun. The Parental one dropping on one knee and fetching a high one out of the skies, a sight not to be forgotten, and the murmer of admiration which his retainers and family give vent to, almost touching.'(8)

Charles was also a keen rider and an accomplished fisherman. As a young man he had often been to Ireland for his holidays and rejoiced in fishing for trout in the lakes. Many years later, when he heard that his son Frank had caught his first salmon, he wrote: 'I well understand Frank's feelings—his first salmon! A great event in anyone's life—I shall never forget it in my own case as I was fishing for trout in the lower lake of Killarney 56 years ago!'

At the age of twenty-eight he had already become an enthusiastic golfer. When he first played at St Andrews there was no clubhouse and players met in the parlour of an old inn to arrange their matches. The captain of the club, Major Playfair, when playing, wore a type of dress coat with pockets at the sides and a top hat. Charles enjoyed the game throughout his life. On his seventy-fifth birthday he went round the course of the Glasgow golf club in eighty-three. A contemporary said, 'he did not put off much time playing the game and as a rule in a match was first up to his ball, with the smartness which was characteristic of him throughout life.'

Charles formed a fine library at Glen. In accordance with the fashion of the day, he had many of its five thousand volumes beautifully rebound in morocco leather by Bedford and Rivière. It was a very readable collection, devoted mainly to eighteenth- and nineteenth-century English, Scottish and French literature. Naturally there were many of Burns' writings, including the Kilmarnock edition. The poet wrote a charming inscription in *Letters concerning the religion essential to a man*, which he gave to James Tennant of Glenconner. (See page 32). Among the books on politics there were three autographed works by Mr Gladstone.

But perhaps his main interest outside his business affairs was his collection of paintings and other works of art. He had always had a taste for rare and beautiful things and began by collecting mezzotints. His earliest purchases cost only a pound or two, but the popularity and price of mezzotints were increasing rapidly. In 1890 he created a stir in the saleroom by outbidding George Vanderbilt's agent and paying a record price of £372 15*s* for a mezzotint of Reynolds's 'The Three Graces Decorating a Statue of Hymen'.

In about 1880 he began to take an interest in the paintings from which the mezzotints had been copied, and through his chosen dealer William Agnew he bought English eighteenth-century portraits, nineteenth-century landscapes and contemporary Victorian paintings steadily for the rest of his life. At his death his collection was one of the finest in private hands. He greatly prized paintings by his contemporaries and the high esteem in which works by Victorian Royal Academicians were held often made these works more ex-

14. 40 Grosvenor Square, the London house of Sir Charles Tennant from 1881 until his death in 1906. Sir Charles' well-known Phaeton carriage with his coachman Andrew Brown and horses 'Dornus' and 'Merlín' stands outside.

15. The Glen, Innerliethen, Peebleshire, in about 1900. It was bought by Sir Charles Tennant in 1852 and rebuilt in the Scottish baronial style by the architect David Bryce. Lord Rosebery wrote to Mr Gladstone in 1890 'I regard the Glen as the most perfect of all modern country houses, architecturally speaking.' It is now the home of The Honourable Colin Tennant.

16. Four of Sir Charles Tennant's daughters, *(above left)* Lucy Graham-Smith, *(above right)* Laura Lyttelton, *(below left)* Charlotte Ribblesdale, *(below* right*)* Margot Asquith.

pensive than paintings by earlier artists such as Reynolds and Gainsborough. His Victorian collection eventually included works by G. F. Watts, W. Q. Orchardson, David Cox, David Wilkie, William Etty, William Powell Frith, John Phillip, William Mulready, Clarkson Stanfield and many other famous painters of the time.

Charles was clearly fond of portraits and he owned ten Reynolds, five Gainsboroughs, six Romneys and three Hogarths. He also bought five landscapes by Turner, three by Constable, two by Bonington and ten by Morland. Charles regularly visited Christie's and Agnew's on his way to the city. In Agnew's inner sanctum he was shown hundreds of paintings and from these he selected those which appealed to him. Gainsborough's delicate and beautiful portrait of 'The Ladies Erne and Dillon' was bought in 1882. Four years later he bought Hogarth's portrait of the actress Peg Woffington and Sir Joshua Reynolds' 'The Fortune Tellers', which portrayed two of the 3rd Duke of Marlborough's children. Of the latter William Agnew wrote to him: 'There can be no doubt whatever that in point of *colour* it is Sir Joshua's masterpiece.'

Romney's 'The Countess of Derby' joined the collection in 1887 and in 1890 Reynolds's magnificent 'Diana, Viscountess Crosbie' was bought direct from her County Kerry descendants. The artist was so delighted with his first glimpse of Diana coming towards him across the lawn that he painted her in that setting. Her freshness and beauty live through her portrait and she still looks today as if she is poised ready to walk from his canvas.

Portraits of children greatly appealed to Charles and two of the most attractive were Raeburn's 'Leslie Boy' bought in 1894, and Reynolds' 'Collina' (Lady Gertrude Fitzpatrick) purchased in 1896. He bought 'The Frankland Sisters', one of Hoppner's most beautiful portraits, in 1899. Charles filled 40 Grosvenor Square with people and in *one* room he could sit with Lady Gertrude Fitzpatrick (Collina), Lord Henry and Lady Charlotte Spencer (The Fortune Tellers), Viscountess Crosbie, Marianne and Amelia Frankland (The

Frankland Sisters), Miss Ridge (by Reynolds), and Mrs Jordan (by Romney). Seeing Charles surrounded by these portraits inspired his daughter-in-law, Pamela, to write 'The Children and the Pictures' in which she brings the subjects to life. Romney's 'Mrs. Inchbold' beautifully describes Charles to his granddaughter, Clare:[9]

> Do you think if your Grandpapa had never loved us in the way he did that we should be here walking and breathing—we, but semblances of human form dwelling in pigment and paste? It's only love that can make alive and he did it. Sometimes, after all the lights were out and the folks in bed, the door would open and he'd enter. I can see him in his dressing-gown and slippers, the light shining on the mahogany door; his clean white hair, and shrewd face. His hands so swift in movement, so beautifully kept, his beard trimmed so neatly. Did you ever see him untidy, I wonder, or harassed, or wasting time? Never—it all went so easily, he had the long-houred day of a busy man. Time to read aloud to others, time to look over his old French books, time to saunter out and play golf earnestly, and time, above all, to spend, upon us. How he loved us. We shall never have that again.

The nineteenth-century landscapes, such as Bonington's 'The Fish Market, Boulogne' were as fine in quality as the portraits. Of this, bought for Charles in 1895, William Agnew wrote: 'I cannot refrain writing to express my delight that this great masterpiece of Bonington's shall hang with your glorious pictures. So long as I live, the knowledge that it is yours will be a joy to me, for I am proud of my handiwork and brain-work at No. 40.' The large Constable, 'The Opening of Waterloo Bridge', one of the artist's acknowledged masterpieces, joined Sir Charles's collection in 1891. He also bought five Turners which illustrate the artist's different stages of development. Ruskin wrote of the beautiful and visionary 'Approach to Venice': 'I think when I first saw it it was the most perfectly *beautiful* piece of colour of all that I have seen produced by human hands, by any means, or at any period.'[10]

This painting hung in the library at 40 Grosvenor Square with two other Turners, 'Van Tromp's Shallop at the Entrance to the Scheldt' and 'Newark Abbey on the Wey'.

Among pictures of the Norwich school of painters, Charles owned 'Yarmouth Beach' by John Crome. At a time when George Stubbs's work was not so much appreciated he bought the superb 'Greenland Falcon', the only known work by Stubbs of a bird.

Charles did not buy pictures as investments and he fervently hoped that the collection would remain intact. Unfortunately death duties made it necessary to sell the cream of the portraits during the 1920s, by which time their value had increased enormously. (See Appendix V.)[11]

Charles loved to show his treasures to his family and friends and he was unfailingly generous in lending them to exhibitions. Between 1900 and 1904 he gave seven works to the Glasgow Museum and Art Gallery in Kelvingrove Park, the most important of which was Sir John Millais's 'The Forerunner'. Four of the gifts were marble busts: of his father, his grandfather, James Oswald his father's Liberal politician friend, and Garibaldi. In 1893 he became a Trustee of the National Portrait Gallery and was also a Trustee of the National Gallery from 1894 until he died in 1906.

He also had a fine collection of Meissen and Chinese porcelain, in particular *Famille-rose* and *Famille-verte* pieces made during the reign of K'ang Hsi. Objects of vertu brightened his furniture, and he employed a special housemaid with a small pair of bellows to dust all the more fragile and valuable pieces.

Max Roldit writing about his collection in the first issue of *Connoisseur* in September 1901 mentions the existence of French and English miniatures, Battersea enamels and antique furniture. An evocative description of the pleasure Charles derived from his collections was written by his son, H. J. Tennant:

'The pains he took with the arrangement of his possessions was notable . . . it was the embodiment of his . . . desire for perfection . . . He enjoyed his possessions in a delightful and almost childlike way . . . Sometimes late at night we would find all the electric lights blazing in the big drawing rooms of Grosvenor Square and there was my dear old father gazing at his Sir Joshuas or Hoppners in rapt delight. "Doesn't Lady Crosbie look splendid this evening?" he would say and he would rejoice in our fervid agreement.'(12)

CHAPTER NINE

Sir Charles Tennant, industrialist

WHEREAS JOHN TENNANT's ambitions had been limited to the confines of St Rollox and to the efficient running of the enterprises started by his father, those of his son Charles were considerably more far-reaching. He was one of the first industrialists to combine chemical, mining and metallurgical enterprises. He became one of the most skilled experts in the handling of company formation and he revelled in taking large speculative risks. With his restless energy and powerful personality he quickly dominated any negotiations in which he was taking part. By moving the centre of his activities from Scotland to London, where he became one of the great market operators of his day, he helped to close the gap between the industrial north and the financial world of the City. His lightning mind was always quick to spot the business potentialities of one situation after another, and even in times of national adversity he showed an uncanny facility for turning the situation to the advantage of his many business interests.

In 1843 when Charles was still only twenty, his father made him a partner in the Glasgow and London branches of the firm. Seven years later he went into his first partnership outside the family business when he joined Edward Humphreys in forming the marine engineering business of Humphreys, Tennant & Co. This company had a long era of success. Their first contract was carried out in 1854, after which they continued to prosper until economic factors, over which they had no control, led to the closure of the works in 1907. A family diary of 1860 tells:

> Among those who visited my parents was Mr. Humphreys the famous marine engineer (he was Chief Engineer at Woolwich Dockyard) with whom Papa went into partnership. Papa told the story of his association with him. It was a remarkably pleasant and profitable one upon which he dwelt with natural pride for, though the success of the great marine engine works at Deptford was primarily due to the scientific skill of Mr. Humphreys, Papa's genius in lighting upon, and then adhering to the man in whom he trusted first showed itself.

Edward Humphreys died in 1870, and Charles gave up his interest in the firm. (Among the important British warships engined were: 1875 *Dreadnought*, 1877 *Alexandra*, 1879 *Polyphemus*, 1881 *Conqueror*, 1882 *Collingwood*, 1886 *Rodney*, 1888 *Sans Pareil*, 1889 *Blenheim* and *Trafalgar*, 1906 *Shannon*, 1907 *Invincible*.)

As a result of the financial crisis of 1857, Charles and his father acquired sugar and cocoa estates in Trinidad, which produced between eight and nine thousand tons of sugar per year. But the sugar crop failed in 1877 and this brought about a depression throughout the islands. Charles lent money to Bernstein & Co, the Trinidad merchants, who mortgaged many estates to him as security. When the crash came these estates were offered to him and they included the Pitch Lake for which at that time there was no known use. However, Charles preferred to return many of the estates to their owners and only kept the cocoa estate of Ortinola, Maracas Valley and some sugar plantations in the south. His refusal to take the Pitch Lake was deeply regretted by his descendants when tar macadam was developed for the road surfaces which today carry millions of motor vehicles all over the world.

1866 was a year of great importance in Charles Tennant's life, marking as it did the beginning of his interest in the Tharsis Company.(1) As far back as 1838 his father, in partnership with James Muspratt, had bought a brimstone mine in Sicily,[2] realising that sulphur was essential to alkali makers using the Leblanc process. But the King of Naples, urged to action by the jealousy of the Italian sulphur magnates, imposed a large duty of £4 per ton on all sulphur exported to Britain and later extended it to the rest of the world. It therefore became necessary to investigate other possible sources of sulphur.

> Pyrites had become the subject of eager experiment: by 1866 not only was an efficient method of sulphur extraction available, but a subsequent process for the recovery of copper from the residue had been developed by the Glasgow chemist, William Henderson. A leading spirit among the British Alkali makers, Charles Tennant, master of the great St. Rollox works in Glasgow, saw clearly the potential of the new situation. The Alkali makers should form a syndicate, raise capital, acquire Henderson's patent rights, and develop a major Spanish pyrites mine.[3]

For many years a close liaison had existed between British alkali makers, with John Tennant and James Muspratt at their head, so it was an easy matter to bring them together. The meeting took place in Liverpool and plans were made. Charles was to act as the negotiator for the group and the French-owned Spanish mine of Tharsis became the object of his quest. In March 1866 Charles wrote to his father: 'I hope we are to become possessed of the most valuable mine and mineral properties which have yet been developed. I will only say that I have never had anything to do with anything I liked so much. It is the most important negotiation I ever took part in.' John Tennant was unenthusiastic about the negotiations and it was some time before Charles was able to get the necessary support from him.

The Tharsis mine in the Huelva province of south-west Spain was worked as far back as three thousand years ago. Later the Romans worked it; more recently Spaniards and Frenchmen, and finally Scots and Englishmen. The French company, under the guidance of M. Mercier, had made great progress. 'Exploratory work had been carried far enough to indicate a safe reserve of cupreous pyrites. A good deal of experience had been gained in mining practice and in ore treatment.'[4] However, without the use of more capital Mercier was unable to test the mine's profitability. Charles Tennant and Mercier met to negotiate. The French owners did not want to sell outright and the British syndicate did not want to make an outright purchase. Finally it was agreed that Charles and his colleagues should take over the working of the mine and pay a royalty on each ton of pyrites extracted.

The Tharsis Sulphur & Copper Company Ltd was incorporated in Edinburgh as a public company on 27 October 1866 with Charles Tennant as Chairman. Its head office was in Glasgow. The new management immediately injected the necessary capital and for the next forty years Tharsis was the most profitable copper mine in the world. The French and English companies merged in 1880.

In April 1867 Charles wrote from Tharsis: 'All day I have been on a stretch in this extraordinary mine. I can quite understand the opinion of the gentleman who said there were two things worth seeing in Spain—the Cathedral at Seville and the "ciel ouvert" at Tharsis. They are both the finest things of their kind existing. The ride of 32 miles up from the Huelva is fatiguing to one not accustomed to long promenades.'

The great prosperity of the Tharsis company was due to their skill in developing ways to exploit each component of pyrites. Crude pyrites was exported to the alkali makers in Britain who extracted the sulphur; the cinders, which remained the property of Tharsis, were then sent to the Tharsis metal extraction companies where the copper was recovered. 'Altogether, by 1872 the company possessed seven metal extraction works, dispersed over the principal chemical producing areas of Britain. Though there were vigorously conducted metal extraction companies that remained independent, the Tharsis metal works represented by far the most considerable group in Britain, if not the world. In addition to its mines and metal works the company held perhaps the most important range of non-ferrous metallurgical patents in existence.'[5] After the extraction of copper there remained the iron oxide residue or purple ore nicknamed 'Blue Billy' which represented about seventy per cent of the weight of the pyrites. After much experiment it was made usable in blast furnaces to produce pig-iron. Soon methods were devised so that even minute quantities of other precious metals were recoverable.

The success of Tharsis inspired the formation in 1873 of an internationally backed London based company to redevelop the Rio Tinto mines along the lines of Tharsis. Charles was offered the chairmanship of the neighbouring Rio Tinto Company but his co-directors thought interests might have clashed and would not agree to his accepting. The resultant competition between Tharsis and Rio Tinto halved the price of sulphur.

The prospect of the direct production of steel from 'Blue Billy' attracted chemists and entrepreneurs alike and many experiments took place under the aegis of the Tharsis Company. In 1872 it was decided to form a new company, the Steel Company of Scotland, with Charles as its Chairman. Unfortunately, after the works were built, it became clear that the experiments had failed and that 'Blue Billy' could not be made into steel. Either the company would have to be wound up or another method of producing mild steel had to be adopted. Sir William Siemens had been working on the 'Blue Billy' problem with the Tharsis company and they therefore chose to pioneer in the United Kingdom the Siemens-Martin acid process. This produced a reliable mild steel which gradually came to supersede iron in the making of ship plates. Soon vessels built of mild steel earned preferential rates of insurance at Lloyd's over those built of the best iron plates. Consequently mild steel was supplied to most of the navies and railways of the world. Although in the first few years the company had cost Charles a considerable amount of money, by 1900 it was producing one million tons of steel a year and entered on a long period of prosperity. It is of interest that Charles and his co-directors, rather than the

Scottish iron makers, were responsible for introducing the steel age to Scotland.

In 1873 the idea was conceived of building a railway bridge a mile and a half long over the Firth of Forth. The first plan was not executed owing to the collapse of the Tay Bridge in 1879. In 1883 a new cantilever bridge was designed and started. It was a major and imaginative engineering project which involved the use of 54,000 tons of mild steel, and it attracted world wide interest. The bridge was completed in 1890 at a cost of £2,500,000. Charles sat on the management committee of the Forth Bridge Company, representing both the Steel Company of Scotland and the North British Railway Company of which he was deputy chairman. (He also held a large block of shares in American railways. So large was his holding in the Chicago Great Western Railway that a small town in Shelby county, Iowa, was called Tennant after him.)

A famous Chinese diplomat, Li Hung Chang, who was visiting Britain at the time when the bridge was almost completed, asked if he could see the largest cantilever bridge ever built in this country. He was shown every courtesy and Charles walked some way over the bridge with him. As they gazed down on the waves threshing against the great girders, Charles was somewhat startled when the diplomat shot three questions at him: 'How old are you? How many children have you got? and how much money?' The reply came back in a flash: 'I am a hundred years old. I have twelve children, and I have enough money for one dinner a day and I can't eat two.'

On 4 March the official opening was performed by the Prince of Wales (later King Edward VII). A westerly gale of hurricane proportions roared unmercifully, but with a fine disregard of the elements the crowds thronged to the bridge on both sides of the water. Thousands of people arrived by special train, horsebrake and steamer at South Queensferry. The distinguished company included every manager of note from the four participating British Railway Companies, and from Germany, Austro-Hungary, and France. In the last delegation could be seen fifty dress coats decorated with the Légion d'Honneur. A French engineer referred to the British railway system in his speech: 'We look upon the British Railways, managed by Companies, as models. Your nation does not accept the State interference system. You are satisfied to go on, on the old lines of freedom, and to secure the steady results obtained by self help.'

The Royal party arrived headed by the Prince of Wales, the Dukes of Edinburgh and Fife, their host, the Earl of Rosebery, followed by the other guests including Charles Tennant. At Dalmeny the party boarded the train which took ten minutes to reach North Queensferry Station, and passed drenched bluejackets who lined the track at intervals. The air was punctured by a warship's guns firing the Royal Salute. The Fifeshire Volunteers presented arms as the party alighted. After presentations they boarded a steam launch and a steamer to view the bridge from below. Tossed by the churning sea, drenched by clouds of spray, they returned to the shelter of the train as soon as decorum allowed.

The final ceremony took place at the centre of the northernmost cantilever where the Prince drove home the last of the eight million rivets, its head was gilt, its plate of blue enamel: so the Bridge was declared open. The *Daily News* of 5 March reported that during this ceremony: 'Such a hurricane had not been known in Scotland for many years, but the Bridge remained uninjured.'

At last the battered party reached the haven of the Model Room where they were joined by the *élite* of the land, law officers for Scotland, Members of Parliament and the two engineers. Although one of the Queen's chaplains was in attendance, as well as the Bishop of Lichfield, no grace was said, and no one remarked on the omission as this saturated, frozen company enjoyed the unblessed Whitstable oysters, foie gras, chicken cutlets, roast turkey, tongue, lobster mayonnaise, ham, lamb and mint sauce, all to be washed down with wines, mostly of the 1880 vintage. The menu cover had a North British Railway engine pulling a luxury carriage with 'Progress' written in bold letters along the destination board: 'Through carriage Aberdeen to New York, via Tay Bridge, Forth Bridge, Channel Tunnel and Alaska'. At that time the sky was the limit in men's minds. In the centre were the galaxy of guests surrounding the Prince of Wales, with fur collared coats, top hats, and ample beards. In 1960, seventy years later, Katharine, Baroness Elliot of Harwood, Charles' fifteenth child, was invited to attend the opening of the Forth Road Bridge which runs alongside the bridge of 1890.

Charles and his fellow Tharsis directors had earlier turned their minds to extraction processes because of the fact that pyrites contained minute amounts of silver and gold. Frederich Claudet, working for Tharsis, invented and patented a cheap and simple silver extraction process in 1870, from which the company subsequently made approximately £21,000 per annum.

From extraction of gold and silver it was a natural step to the mining of these metals. It so happened that Charles was told about the ancient, disused gold mines of Mysore by John Hunter Blair, a friend who had been in the Madras Civil Service. Fired by his success over the Tharsis mines, Charles decided to risk some of his capital in this new and exciting venture. In 1880 he formed the Mysore Gold Mining Company Ltd and the Gold Fields of Mysore Ltd, which included the soon-to-be-celebrated Champion Reef. Unfortunately the company had to face many difficulties during its first six years. The sinking of six shafts had involved them in heavy expenditure without any immediately foreseeable gain and the majority of the shareholders were becoming discouraged. At the Annual General Meeting of 1884 Charles said from the chair: 'Gold mining, as you are aware, is a lottery. We all know this, but having £13,000 now left we are inclined to go on and give the concern another chance.[6] Later, at a directors' meeting, the majority expressed again a desire to wind up the company. Charles declared that he had not come all the way from Glasgow with that intention and reiterated that he thought they should sink further shafts before deciding to abandon the property. He was supported by the lone voice of Mr Taylor, the manager of the engineering firm in charge of operations. With the exception of Captain McTaggart all the other directors left the room—and the company. Thus the fate of these fabulous gold mines rested upon three men who were prepared to risk laying out the unexpended balance of £13,000, all that stood between the great property and liquidation. Charles, with his usual generosity, bought back unwanted shares at the price the shareholders had originally paid for them, thus amassing an enormous quantity himself. He and his two staunch supporters carried on alone. Twenty years later the Mysore Company was employing 40,000 people at the great Kolar gold field, which had been no more than a desert when they first came.

In the early years no large gold deposits were found and the method of gold extraction used was still highly inefficient. But Charles persisted in his belief that Mysore would eventually pay off. He employed metallurgists to research into new methods. In his eagerness to find a solution to the extraction problem he was persuaded into backing Henry Renner Cassel's electrolytic process. On 15 December 1884 he and four other Tharsis directors formed the Cassel Gold Extracting Company. Unfortunately the system proved to be unreliable, but before this became generally known Cassel, who had sold his shares during the Company's boom, disappeared. Presumably he retired in comfort to New York where he came from. The wags of Glasgow made reference to 'Cassels in the air', but Charles was undaunted.

He proceeded to put the gold extraction problem in the able hands of John Stewart MacArthur, who had worked as a chemist in the Tharsis company since 1873. MacArthur and his colleagues, the two Forrest brothers, evolved a brilliant process, using cyanide and zinc shavings, which is still in use today. The Cassel company purchased their discovery which they had patented in October 1887. Charles's perseverance was indeed rewarded. Now 95 per cent of the gold, instead of the previous 55 per cent, could be extracted from ore. Development costs had been high and the Cassel company decided to license the use of the process to other companies on a royalty basis of roughly 7.5 per cent of the value of the gold recovered. As the process came to be universally adopted mining companies baulked at paying such a high royalty. As a challenge the patent was deliberately breached in South Africa and the mine owners won their case in court. The immediate result for the Cassel company was the loss of £3,000,000 of royalties owing to them. It was not such a crippling blow as it sounds, for by this time they had become large-scale producers of the cyanide which was needed in the extraction process. In 1906 the name was changed to the Cassel Cyanide Company.

The new method transformed the financial position of the Mysore mines. From 1889 the profits soared. Between 1896 and 1905 the dividend paid by the Mysore Mining Company was always over 100 per cent and in 1898 it reached a peak of 150 per cent. The Gold Fields of Mysore Company, which included the Champion Reef mine, also paid a dividend of over 100 per cent from 1897 to 1905 and in 1903 it reached the fantastic figure of 165 per cent. At the 22nd Annual General Meeting in March 1902 the best telegram ever received from the mine was read to the company: 'Remarkable developments in Tennant's Shaft—huge increase of reserves—200 shares sold 18 years ago at 9*d* each which have realised £4,905.' (Mr Taylor, manager, had framed in his office, a transfer passed in January 1884 for 200 shares worth ninepence each. This humble investment of £7 10*s* at that date, produced a return of no less than £4905 eighteen years later.)

When Charles, the seventy-nine-year-old chairman, rose to address the meeting cheers broke out. During the course of his speech he said: 'We have obtained from this Mysore Mine £5,307,090 worth of gold, and distributed among the shareholders £2,830,652! I think if that does not encourage a man not to give up, or, at least, to do so most unwillingly, pushing on the operations of a mine on the Kolar field, then I should like to know what would.'(7)

The *Mining World and Engineering Record* of 22 March 1902

reported: 'The Mysore Mine appears to be wanting in no element that can conduce to continued success. At home and abroad it is splendidly managed, and it is an object lesson to some other mines that we are thinking of, perhaps as rich, but whose wealth does not come to anything like the same proportion to the shareholders. . . . It has no surprises for its shareholders unless they be of an agreeable character.' Some however questioned the wisdom of distributing such enormous dividends but Charles maintained that those who had the courage to risk such speculative investments should be amply rewarded. His own reward was in the region of two million pounds and it was this which put the crown upon his fortunes.

Charles' mining activities had already led to an interest in the developing explosives industry. He was an important shareholder in Nobel's Explosives Ltd from its inception in 1876. In 1885 he was made a director in order to help organise an international trust uniting makers of dynamite and so preventing cut-throat competition. In the following year the 'Nobel Dynamite Trust Company' was formed and was the first important instance of a true holding company. When it was reorganised in 1900 Charles became Chairman.

In 1878, when Charles became head of the St Rollox group of companies on the death of his father, its days were already numbered. This was due to a decision taken at the works six years earlier. In 1872 a young Swiss, Ludwig Mond by name, travelled to St Rollox with the purpose of demonstrating and selling a new ammonia-soda process for the manufacture of alkali. This system, invented by Ernest Solvay in Belgium, had the obvious advantage of not requiring sulphur for its working. But it was still unproven commercially and a vast capital outlay would be needed if St Rollox were to change over from the Leblanc process, which was still supremely successful and highly profitable. It was felt that they were too committed to accept the possibility of a potentially more economical process. James MacTear, the distinguished manager of St Rollox at that time, would almost certainly have argued against the new process. He would probably have realised that the solid-salt-using St Rollox site could not compete with the brine-using sites in Solvay soda production. This conjecture is supported by the run-down of soda production at St Rollox. Disappointed, Mond turned to John Tomlinson Brunner. A partnership was entered into in February 1873 and in 1874, under licence from Solvay, Brunner-Mond began to use the ammonia soda process at Winnington near Northwich in Cheshire. 'By 1882 they were producing 52,000 tons annually. This challenge came to the Leblanc men almost like a thunderbolt out of the sky. By the mid-eighteen-seventies the Solvay system was regarded by objective judges as technically the better of the two. Yet this did not settle the issue. The Leblanc producers, with their very large commitment in plant and skill, and the potential of their by-products, fought back.'[(8)] The history of the British chemical industry in the last quarter of the nineteenth century is dominated by this struggle.

Inevitably Charles was in the middle of the battle and was looked upon as the leader in the long fight against Brunner-Mond. His attempt to maintain an obsolescent method might seem strange in someone who was brilliant at both spotting and utilising new ideas. But the Solvay system was not without its problems, and his financial commitment to the Leblanc process coupled with the fact that there was an assured supply of sulphur to the alkali industry from the Tharsis company, weighed heavily in making his decision.

Charles was both the master and the captive of the Leblanc process. Each year he saw his predicament becoming more acute and when he met Brunner by chance in Bournemouth in 1881 he was alternately threatening and deferential. Brunner wrote to Mond on 7 November describing the meeting: 'He was very, very doleful about the prospects in view of our competition. . . . Was it true, he wanted to know, that we could make Alkali at a penny. I replied that it was true. In that case, he rejoined, I might depend on it as a certainty that they would all go into the Ammonia process,

17. Portraits of three of Sir Charles Tennant's sons and Mr Gladstone, painted by his daughter Lucy Graham-Smith, *(above left)* Francis John (Frank) Tennant, *(above right)* Harold John (Jack) Tennant, *(below right)* Edward Tennant (later 1st Baron Glenconner) *(below left)* Mr Gladstone at Hawarden.

18. Mr Gladstone visiting Glen, November 1890. Left to right; Lucy Graham-Smith, Sir Charles Tennant, Mr Gladstone, Mrs Gladstone, Margot Tennant, Jack Tennant, Frank Tennant.

19. Glenconner, North Berwick, named after Glenconner, Ochiltree. The house, which Sir Charles bought and altered in 1902 for Marguerite, is now lived in by their granddaughter Henrietta Reader-Harris and her family. The photograph dates from 1905.

and fight us on our own ground. They would *not* be ruined. I asked how the entire loss of their existing plant was to be distinguished from ruin. . . . Finding that threatening was the wrong dodge, he changed again very suddenly, and gave me an immense amount of soft soap.'[9]

The only hope for Charles and the other Leblanc users was to draw together and face their common enemy. Instead of producing soda which was now more efficiently done by the Solvay system they decided to concentrate on bleaching powder, which was a profitable by-product of the Leblanc process and one that the Solvay method could not compete with. In 1884 Charles withdrew the Tharsis company from the pyrites price-fixing ring and then reduced the price of sulphur for the sole purpose of helping the Leblanc users. Matters were further helped when James MacTear's sulphur recovery process was greatly improved upon.[10] The next step was a formal amalgamation of all the major Leblanc producers. This entailed such widespread negotiations that it was impossible to maintain secrecy. In the summer of 1890 *The Times* vehemently attacked the scheme and advised the public not to invest in this attempt to salvage a dying industry. Charles and the other promoters replied by emphasising the opportunities for increased efficiency, lower distribution costs and the need for bleaching powder. Unfortunately *The Times*' attack coincided with the severe financial crisis in the autumn of 1890 and it was impossible to raise enough capital on the open market. As an alternative a private company was formed in November and in February 1891 The United Alkali Company Ltd was incorporated and an issue of stock was made providing the company with capital of about £8.2 million, which was for that time a very large sum. Sir Charles Tennant was appointed President of the world's largest chemical concern which consisted of forty-eight factories (all but three were chemical) and there were Leblanc departments of five other firms.[11]

By the time the St Rollox companies (with the exception of the soap works) were absorbed by United Alkali in 1890 they were already in a state of decline. In the previous thirteen years alkali production at St Rollox had fallen from 14,000 tons to 9,000 tons per year, the labour force had halved to approximately 600 and sulphuric acid became its most important product. Other figures tell the same story—in 1874 the world production of alkali was 525,000 tons, of which 495,000 were produced by the Leblanc process; and in 1902 world production was 1,800,000 tons, of which only 150,000 tons was produced by the Leblanc process. By 1893 the Brunner-Mond profits had overtaken those of United Alkali. The company had another major setback when Castners' newly developed electrolytic method of chlorine production greatly weakened the company's competitive position in terms of bleaching powder, their principal alternative product. Charles and the Leblanc producers were at the end of a technical and industrial cul-de-sac and they had lost the battle.

By the mid-nineties the Tharsis Company was also having to face problems. Like most mining enterprises the company and its shares experienced ups and downs which were caused in no small part by the instability of the price of copper. Charles and other copper miners made various attempts at stabilisation. A syndicate was formed in 1886 by Hyacinthe Secretan, director of the largest European manufacturing company, with the purpose of controlling the market. The Tharsis dividend picked up from 7½ per cent to 20 per cent which was what it had averaged in the previous decade. However three years later the difficulties of controlling copper producers throughout the world proved insuperable. The scheme ended in disastrous collapse, and Denfert-Rochereau, who was responsible for backing the syndicate, committed suicide.

The supply of good quality cupreous pyrites was running low during the nineties and Charles and his fellow directors were on the look-out for new mines to buy and work. In 1900 four prospecting engineers were employed full time to search the globe for suitable mines for the Tharsis Company to purchase. They presented one possibility after another but Charles and his board turned down each in turn. Several of these rejected mines, such as the Ray Copper mines in Arizona, later became fabulous successes. It is difficult to understand why Charles and his fellow directors, who appeared to be in such a strong position with large capital reserves and great experience, should not have taken part in the great mining boom of the early nineteen-hundreds.

The various enterprises that Charles initiated seemed to follow one another in logical sequence but they were too different for him to be able to unite them. Only in 1926, twenty years after his death, were some of them united when Imperial Chemical Industries was formed from Brunner-Mond, United Alkali, Nobel and the British Dyestuff Corporation. This giant contained three of Charles's enterprises, the Cassel Company, Nobel's Explosives and St Rollox.

The London office of Charles Tennant & Co was started in 1801 as a selling agency for St Rollox bleaching powder. It soon began to carry stocks of other goods and developed a merchant business of its own, exporting a variety of commodities to the colonies. Until the 1850s chemicals and the export of coal to the West Indies formed its main business. In 1857 the firm became interested in produce as owners of sugar and cocoa estates in Trinidad. In 1870 the firm opened ferrous and non-ferrous metal departments, based on the sales agencies obtained from the Tharsis Sulphur & Copper Company and shortly afterwards from the Steel Company of Scotland. Seven years later Charles Tennant & Co. helped to found the London Metal Exchange.

William Tennant and Edward Tennant, Charles's distant cousin and eldest son respectively, joined the London firm after the office was moved from its original location of 110 Upper Thames Street, to 9 Mincing Lane. It remained there until it was bombed on 10 May 1941. All the company records were destroyed. William left a description of life when he joined the London Office on the second floor of 9 Mincing Lane. He became Chairman of the firm from 1920–28 succeeding Edward Tennant, 1st Lord Glenconner, and he was yet another member of the family to refuse a knighthood.

There was no lift, telephones or typewriters. The practice was to telegraph offers of business to our various clients, after the incoming letters had been read in the morning, for reply by 5 p.m. It was impossible to begin handwriting letters until replies came in. Then it often happened that a letter would be spoilt in the copying, which was done in a book of tissue sheets damped and then pressed down in a machine like a printing press. If the tissue sheets were too wet the copying ink ran and the letter had to be written all over again. As it was essential to catch the mails mainly to Scotland, a hansom cab was kept waiting outside the door to carry the letters to the mail train, leaving Euston at 8 p.m. . . .

The office was lit by open gas burners and by the end of the day, in winter, one could cut the atmosphere with a knife—to add to our discomfort, the clerks' lavatory was in a sort of a cupboard in the middle of the office. . . .

When visiting works in the country, the etiquette was that any representative of the London office had to wear city clothes and I can see myself now, marching over the Welsh hills from one works to another in a top hat and tail coat. . . .

When I was made a partner in 1884, and for many years after, the management of the staff was under a strict old Plymouth Brother, J. H. Smyth, who was responsible for keeping the books and getting out an annual balance sheet. No auditors were employed and we were entirely in his hands for getting out the results of each year's working. No figures were supplied to us to show where we stood from month to month, so I never knew, until the balance was struck, usually in May, whether my drawings had exceeded my earnings or not, and I used to go through a period of intense anxiety each year, especially as Mr. Smyth was never optimistic in his forecasts. In the end I insisted on having a better system. Some of our old Balance Sheets, which had to be signed by each partner, may one day become quite interesting for today, with modern methods, the cashier is able to say exactly where the firm stands at a few minutes notice.

> The first telephone was installed in the 1890s. There was intense opposition to overcome from the older partners, but as telephones were coming into general use we had to have one; but it was only permitted on the condition that the noise of the bell should not be heard in the partners' rooms and was therefore, installed in the cupboard which used to be the clerks' water closet. As the drains had never been properly closed the smell was quite unbearable and my senior partners refused to have anything to do with the telephone and any messages that came had to be written down and taken to them so that an immediate reply was often impossible.[12]

William's later involvement in the London business meant that the control remained with the Tennants, whereas in Glasgow after Charles retired from the business in 1891 control started to pass to the Alexander family. Although all three of Charles's sons were large shareholders and on the boards and often chairmen of many of the companies in the Glasgow group, they never took an active part in the day-to-day routine and had no detailed knowledge of the business. Their time and interests were fully engaged in other pursuits. The result was that after Charles died all active control of the Glasgow business passed out of the family. Today Charles's grandson, Lord Glenconner, is head of Tharsis, and his great-grandson Colin Tennant runs Tennant Estates (1928) Ltd which has large interests in the West Indies. The present Chairman of C. Tennant Sons & Co Ltd in London is William A. Tennant's grandson, Julian Tennant.

CHAPTER TEN

Sir Charles Tennant, politician

IN 1879, when Charles Tennant was fifty-six years old, he was asked by the Liberal party to stand at a by-election for Partick, one of the three Glasgow parliamentary seats. He agreed and was unanimously adopted at a meeting in the City Hall on 15 July. The *Glasgow Herald* reported: 'The entire Liberal party in the city accepted his candidature, a unity supposedly non-existent since the last General Election in 1874.' In his address Charles covered a wide field, speaking on foreign affairs, the depressed state of agriculture and the need for land reform. He spoke with feeling about the misery and famine in Ireland and vigorously supported Gladstone's policy of Home Rule. There was a prophetic voice from the floor: 'Is Mr Tennant prepared to advocate the settlement of all international disputes by arbitration (Hear! Hear! and laughter) and the establishment of a High Court of Nations for this purpose?' (Laughter). To which he answered: 'I am essentially a man of peace, and I am very anxious indeed to find in the proposal of our friend a practical solution of international difficulties.' He was the only candidate and at the end of the meeting he was elected by a show of hands. On the following day the Sheriff Clerk declared him to be the elected Member of Parliament and at noon he received the congratulations of his friends and of the crowd gathered in the street outside.

Shortly afterwards, in November 1879, Gladstone embarked upon his famous Midlothian campaign in preparation for the general election in the following year.

> Gladstone's long term object was to raise the moral standards and ideals of the people by improving their material conditions. He had no trust in the efficacy of State action to achieve that end. His method was to remove all restrictions upon trade, and to extend its area. All taxation in his view, operated in restraint of trade, and therefore, in order to reduce prices and to secure full employment, it was necessary to keep taxation and public expenditure to a minimum. For that reason he was tireless in pursuit of opportunities to reduce the numbers of Civil Servants alike in the highest and the lowest grades. Individuals might suffer hardships, but he was certain that the permanent interest of the mass of the people would thereby be served.[(1)]

This political philosophy suited Charles perfectly.

As the 1880 general election approached Charles was pressed to give up his safe Glasgow seat and stand for the Tory-held combined counties of Peebles and Selkirk. The sitting member, Sir Graham Montgomery, had represented the constituency for twenty-eight years. He only made two brief speeches, on the hustings in Peebles and Selkirk, during an election. There is a story that on one of these rare occasions he had been addressing a meeting for five minutes, when a voice from the audience shouted: 'Noo, Sir Graham, noo for the perroration!' He never made a political speech between elections, but he opened bazaars and flower shows, and attended agricultural meetings. He was a most kindly, popular and courteous gentleman.

Charles was persuaded to stand for Peebles and Selkirk by Mr Walter Thorburn, Chairman of the local Liberal Association, who later, by an ugly twist of fate, seceded from the Liberal Party, stood as a Liberal-Unionist and turned Charles out in the 1886 Election. The Liberal Committee saw that Charles could cement the union of the party still further by his local connections, and his influence could sway the floating voter. A contemporary newspaper reported:

> He is a gentleman having a heavy interest in the County of Peebles. During a long series of years now he has manifested a lively interest in every movement having for its object the moral and social advancement of those less favoured by fortune than himself. As a large employer of labour in Glasgow he could sympathise with and give advice to those engaged in industrial pursuits. As a politician his views are in entire accord with the majority of those in the country and he is regarded as a gentleman by everyone, no matter whether under blue or buff (Tory—Liberal) colours. Mr. Tennant is already in a constituency far more important from a numerical point of view than Peeblesshire, and difficulty was experienced at the outset in persuading Glasgow to allow him to leave. His re-election to Glasgow was considered a foregone conclusion, and he was throwing aside a certainty, for what, at the outset, looked like a great uncertainty. Success of the Liberal cause he put higher than personal considerations.

On 25 March 1880 Queen Victoria dissolved Parliament; Polling Day was on 7 April. Between these two dates Charles conducted a characteristically vigorous campaign. Selkirkshire was Montgomery's stronghold, with his strength lying in the faggot votes at his command. 'Faggot voting is a device, dating back to the days of the early Stuarts, for extending the right to vote on the basis of a property qualification. Where the rooms of a tenement building were leased to a number of individuals, the right to exercise the franchise which the property conferred upon its owner or lessee could be split amongst the inhabitants of the building, thus creating a multiplicity of votes where there should have been only one. Even the Reform Act of 1832 failed to abolish this practice, which continued well into the nineteenth century.'(2) Peeblesshire was Tennant's political stronghold. The unfairness of the faggot vote system was a burning issue at the time and Charles mounted an attack on the Tory agent for buying up small bits of property with the intention of selling them for the enfranchisement of the voters.

'Having made the purchase, he looked abroad for owners, and in London, Edinburgh and Glasgow and other centres of industry was able to obtain names of gentlemen whose overflowing patriotism would not permit them to rest content with the vote on the property in which they had more immediate interest, but were willing to purchase a nominal interest in property which would give them the legal right to disenfranchise their distant countrymen. It is quite evident that if some measures are not speedily adopted to remedy the present state of affairs with respect to voting, some strenuous efforts will be made by the electors themselves to purge the rolls, and the result may not be at all very comfortable for the faggot voters.' Charles opened his speech at Innerleithen by saying: 'I believe some of you are real voters of Innerleithen' (Laughter and cheers). He had a warm reception at all his meetings throughout the campaign. 'On the various questions he discussed Mr. Tennant has intimate knowledge, and, as he speaks with all the fervour of a gentleman convinced of the honesty and straightforwardness of the cause he pleads, rarely fails to carry conviction.'

31 March was a great day. Gladstone, on his way to a big meeting at Stow, spoke at Peebles and at Innerleithen on behalf of Charles Tennant. He too laid stress on the need to fight the iniquitous faggot vote, saying: 'I am here in the very citadel of sham representation and you have undertaken to make a great effort to break down this unconstitutional and mischievous system . . . One would think the days of intimidation had passed away with the birth of the ballot: but it is not so. In large towns the voter has come to know by experience that the way he votes cannot be discovered, but in Peebles and Selkirk, where the ballot has not been in operation before, they have a lingering idea that their lairds will find out how they have voted and financial ruin may be round the corner, a feeling worked on by the Tories to an extent scarcely credible—direct intimidation . . . We have a

Government, Gentlemen, that increases our taxes yet does not pay our debts.'

The *Glasgow Herald* reported at the end of three weeks' campaigning that:

> Mr. Tennant's eight day round of the United Counties was brought to a triumphal conclusion on Tuesday night at Innerleithen. Earlier in the day Mr. Gladstone passed through the town when the good folks turned out in their thousands: but if I may be allowed to use a comparative phrase: in the evening they turned out in their tens of thousands to welcome Mr. Tennant on his return from the great demonstration at Stow. The streets were lined with youths to the number of 800 or so, who carried blazing torches, whilst the pavements were crowded with ladies and others not taking any active part in the procession. At the entry of the town, Mr. Tennant's carriage was met by the local band who, on their way to the Volunteer Hall, discoursed lively music, striking up amongst others, 'See the Conquering Hero comes' and 'Charlie is my darling'. The carriage passed down the centre of the streets; the torch bearers walking on each side. Ladies waved their handkerchiefs, and young men and old shouted themselves hoarse. The spectacle was highly picturesque and, I should think, remains in Mr. Tennant's memory. It was perhaps the most striking manifestation that could be given of the popularity of the laird of The Glen in the district. Such a demonstration too, was a fitting conclusion to a political tour which has been unprecedented in the history of the representation of Peebles and Selkirk-shires, because of the admiration and sympathy it evoked.

Polling took place on 10 April. Mill girls left their work to join the fun at the station when the 11.30 train came in bringing thirty or forty faggot voters in two coaches from Edinburgh, which included Lord Elcho, an Edinburgh baillie and various Writers to the Signet. As they walked with a police guard following, the young greeted them with effigies of the Tory agent, Captain Black of Kailzie, and a board bearing 'Peebles-shire Faggots' in bold letters. When they stepped out of their first-class compartments they were 'dressed in the whitest of linen and the triggest of clothes'; ten minutes later when they reached Chambers' Institute to register their votes, they were unrecognisable, having walked through a hail of mud, stones, and peasemeal.

Opposite the Drill Hall posters declared 'Vote for Tennant and Political Independence'—'Vote for Tennant and down with the Faggots', 'Wha waddna vote for Charlie?' Shortly after 6 p.m. people streamed in from all parts of the neighbourhood; there must have been a thousand assembled in the street. A few minutes after 7 p.m. Sheriff Orphoot appeared at a window in the Chambers Institute and announced the result: 'Mr Charles Tennant—516 Votes. Sir Graham Montgomery—484 Votes.' So Charles became the first Liberal to represent the constituency with a majority of 32. When he appeared at the windows he was greeted with long, loud cheers. Simultaneously the Post Office door was opened and the news came 'They've got in!' Cheers broke out everywhere, hats were thrown in the air, bells pealed and the Waverley Mill whistle spread the news far and wide. The throng increased to 2000 rejoicing people, nothing like this had ever been seen before. The crowd set out to meet the new member, in a body headed by St Ronan's Brass Band. The young set fire to a stretch of whins along the railway embankment, and the glow added lustre to the night. When Charles's carriage appeared, with a rousing cheer the crowd rushed to meet it, instantly unharnessed the horses, and drew the carriage in triumph towards the centre of the town, the band again striking up 'See the Conquering Hero comes', and on to the Volunteer Hall where the new Member addressed the people. Rockets were fired and the cavalcade continued to the railway station to see off the extra police who were returning to their homes. 'A great Liberal victory had been gained; the united counties were at length to be represented in the true sense of the word; assimilation of the franchise was in fair prospect, and best of all a most noble triumph had been achieved by Mr. Tennant over the horde of faggots that infest Peeblesshire.' Lord Napier wrote a letter describing the final return home to the Glen that night.

'Lights had been placed in all the windows of the Glen castle. It was fine and clear and the stars looked down on our joy. Posie was on the steps with a flag [Pauline, wife of Thomas Gordon Duff of Drummuir, Charles and Emma's 5th child]. The people of the place were all in the courtyard with a kindly shout. He alighted. He was embraced. The door was closed, the play was over and we went to supper. . . . After 44 years under the domination of the Faggot, I have lived to see the Faggot broken.'

This General Election of 1880 resulted in an overwhelming Liberal majority under Gladstone's leadership. Queen Victoria wrote in her diary—'To me The People's William is a most disagreeable person half crazy', and on 4 April a note reached her Secretary, Sir Henry Ponsonby, from Baden-Baden, where she was staying, stating that: 'She will sooner ABDICATE than send for or have anything to do with that HALF MAD FIREBRAND who would soon ruin everything and be a DICTATOR.'(3) She vowed that she would never submit to his democratic rule. On 23 April Lord Granville and Lord Hartington had an audience with her at Windsor, and implored her not to delay in sending for Gladstone to ask him to form a government. Finally she yielded and summoned her *bête noire*. Gladstone proceeded to form a government in which he himself held the offices of Prime Minister and Chancellor of the Exchequer.

In 1885 Charles's name appeared in the Honours List. A Baronetcy had been conferred upon him by the Queen. Twice before Tennants had declined honours; this third offer was accepted some sixty years after the first had been made. In 1911 a fourth offer came to Charles' eldest surviving son, Edward, who reverted to the family's Ayrshire origin and took the title of Baron Glenconner of Glen, in the county of Peebles.

During the seven years that Charles was a Member of Parliament he made only one speech and asked only two questions in the House. This is surprising in a man with so active a mind and who had fought five elections. The fact is that he found the procedural frustrations of the House of

Commons and its daily routine unsympathetic to his temperament, which was not endowed with the necessary patience or contentment with a politician's tribulations and compromises. His daughter testified this when she wrote of him: 'Born a little quicker, more punctual and more alive than other people, he suffered fools not at all. He could not modify himself in any way. . . .' He 'was a man whose vitality, irritability, energy and impressionability amounted to genius'.[5] Clearly a man not made for the back benches.

Although it was still some years before 1894 when Charles became the father-in-law of H. H. Asquith, politicians of both parties were constant visitors to Glen. Always a staunch supporter of Mr Gladstone, he must have impressed one of his guests, Emma, Lady Ribblesdale, mother of his son-in-law, Tommy. She writes to her son in October 1884:

> From Edinburgh I went to Glen. Mr. Tennant towards the end of Dinner gave his views on the deadlock between the Houses of Parliament. He said Mr. Gladstone had only to raise his finger to draw all the people and sweep away the House of Lords; no ability there, compared with the Members of the House of Commons. 'Peers to be elected, and all to be drawn or selected from the House of Commons.' He saw no good in the House of Lords and might as well be abolished! Yet the Barons of England obliged the signing of Magna Carta![5]

No doubt conversations at dinner are of transitory interest, but the letter shows how radical were the views of those who supported Home Rule, and it is interesting to reflect that in 1968, 84 years later, a proposal to make a part of the House of Lords an elected Chamber was defeated by the House of Commons, although the Bill had a large majority in the House of Lords. By this time, Charles's fifteenth child Katharine was a member of the House of Lords and voted for the Bill.

In June 1885 Gladstone resigned after a defeat in the House of Commons and Lord Salisbury became prime minister. A general election was called for December. At his adoption meeting Charles spoke of a proposal to reform the procedures of the House of Commons itself. His last years' experience had shown the difficulty caused by the obstructions of the existing system in carrying on the ordinary business of the country, not to speak of great and important measures. He also made a prophetic forecast that the Irish question would come into the forefront again, Mr Parnell having shown he was determined to free his country, Ireland, and get independent government at any cost. Gladstone at this time was perilously unaware of the rapid deterioration of the Irish situation.

Charles then mentioned the Land question which was occupying many minds. He thought the country had made up its mind that the laws of entail should be done away with. The landed proprietor must be put in real possession of his land, and be able to dispose of it. If the landlord had power to sell, he thought the result would be that many of the landlords would be able to spend a considerable amount on permanent improvements, buildings, drainage etc., and do a great deal to increase the fertility of the land. Many would be inclined to do what seemed most desirable, to reduce the size of very large holdings, and have smaller farms to enable small capitalists to invest their savings in this way.

Mr Herbert Gladstone spoke in support of the candidate and Charles's son-in-law Alfred Lyttelton followed him, saying: 'Having received from Sir Charles Tennant by far the choicest gift which any human being can receive (cheers and laughter) he felt it would be, at any rate, unchivalrous not to say a word in support of his candidature.'

As the election drew nearer excitement grew. This time Walkerburn posters asked 'Wha wad'na fecht [fight] for Charlie?' On 2 December the polling booths were open from eight in the morning until eight at night. A carter paraded the streets with his horse gaily decorated in the yellow Liberal ribbons, and a dog trotted by with his tail trussed up in the same style. The evening became wet and stormy; the poll closed quietly, and the extra police imported from

Edinburgh were only onlookers. A small band of shepherds were said to have driven eighteen miles to take part in the election for the first time. The remoteness of some of the polling stations, especially in Selkirkshire, delayed the count for a day. Charles's carriage, driven by his daughter Margot in a yellow hat, came from Glen to Peebles at 12 noon where a great crowd, including workpeople from Damdale Mill, had gathered for the declaration of the poll. Charles was re-elected, having increased his majority from 32 to 708. When he appeared at the County Buildings' door he was at once cheered to the echo and carried shoulder-high to the Town Hall. Then his carriage was pulled by supporters amid banners proclaiming 'Tennant for ever'. Mr Thorburn was treated in the same way.

The November 1885 General Election ended in a dead heat. The Liberals held 335 seats, the Conservatives 249 and Parnell led his Irish Nationalists to win 86. Provided that Salisbury and Parnell held their two parties together, their voting power equalled that of the Liberals. Thus Lord Salisbury remained Prime Minister. Gladstone, the Grand Old Man, shut himself away in his country home of Hawarden, where his relaxation was cutting down trees, and he vexed his followers by withdrawing all signs of leadership. He was biding his time, hoping that Lord Salisbury would settle the Irish question by sinking party differences and sending for him and Parnell. No summons came and on 15 December his pent-up anxiety drove him to approach the Prime Minister through his nephew Arthur Balfour, with the warning that unless Home Rule was granted at once violence would break out both in Ireland and in England. So strongly did he feel about it that he was prepared to support the Prime Minister in the introduction of Home Rule even though it would certainly split his own party. He already knew that three leading members of it, Hartington, Chamberlain and John Bright, would not countenance the move. Salisbury put the proposition to his Cabinet and it was turned down. On 1 January the Queen's Speech from the Throne announced that the legislative union between the two countries would be maintained, but that there might be a necessity for a new Irish Coercion Act.

The storm broke twenty-six days later when the Government gave notice of its intention to introduce this Act. The Grand Old Man appeared in full fighting array, determined to turn out the Government. And indeed at one o'clock the next morning the Government was defeated by seventy-four votes. On 3 February 1886 Gladstone became prime minister for the third time.

The struggle for Home Rule continued to dominate Parliament. On 27 March Joseph Chamberlain resigned over the issue. On 8 April Gladstone presented his Home Rule Bill to a packed House. Never had there been such a scene in the Commons. As he rose from the front bench he received a standing ovation from his supporters. He spoke for three hours and twenty minutes. 'I cannot allow it to be said that a Protestant minority in Ulster is to rule the question at large for Ireland. . . . But I think that the Protestant minority should have its wishes considered to the utmost practicable extent in any form which they may assume.'

The second reading of the Home Rule Bill began on 10 May, and on 7 June 1886 Gladstone rose to close the debate with the foreboding that failure awaited him. At 1 a.m. on the following morning the Bill was defeated by 30 votes, 93 Liberals voting against their leader. The Queen dissolved Parliament at once, probably with a sigh of relief, and the General Election began. Gladstone's most cruel and pungent public critic was the thirty-seven-year-old Lord Randolph Churchill, whose invective struck home. On 11 June he said at a meeting in South Paddington: 'This design for the separation of Ireland from Britain . . . this monstrous mixture of imbecility, extravagance, and political hysterics, is furnished by its author with the most splendid attributes, and clothed in the loftiest language . . . but . . . the united and concentrated genius of Bedlam and Colney Hatch would strive in vain to produce a more striking tissue of absurdities . . . For the sake of this . . . all business other than that which may be connected with political agitation is to be impeded and suspended . . . all useful and desired reforms are to be indefinitely postponed . . . the British Constitution is to be torn up, and the Liberal Party shivered into fragments. And why? For this reason and no other: to gratify the ambition of an old man in a hurry . . .' The attack increased to a crescendo: 'At this moment, so critical, we have not got to deal with a Government, or a Party, or a Policy. We have to deal with a man; with a man who makes the most unparalleled claim for dictatorial power which can be conceived by free men. Mr. Gladstone, in his speech in Edinburgh on Friday, recommended himself to the country in the name of Almighty God. Others cannot and will not emulate such audacious profanity.'

It was against this background that Charles came up for re-election as a Gladstonian Liberal on Saturday, 3 July 1886. His was a straight fight with his former local Party chairman, Walter Thorburn, who opposed him as a Liberal-Unionist. Charles opened his campaign in the Chambers Institute in Peebles, packed to capacity, where he was greeted by an outburst of applause. He was accompanied by his son, Edward, and many others. Throughout the campaign his theme was the same. He started his speech by saying that he was not a blind follower of Gladstone, but he had to decide whether the cardinal principle of government of Ireland was to be conciliation or coercion. Coercion had been tried for eighty-six years and failed. The condition of Ireland was a disgrace to the Empire. To govern each man, woman and child in that country cost the government exactly twice as much as in Britain. Why should they not try another course now? The people of Ireland wanted to be allowed to manage their own affairs, and he maintained that was a perfectly reasonable demand. Did they think that a poor country like Ireland with no army or navy could possibly, if it wished, separate itself from Britain? They lost America by denying her autonomy (Hear, hear). It was the policy of coercion which lost them that great country (Cheers). He did not believe there would be any persecution of the minority. The great province of Ulster contained a majority of Protestant population, but they sent a majority of Nationalists to the House of Commons (Cheers). He did not think the complaints of the Ulster people were well founded. The disturbances were principally among the Orangemen, who were but a small body, but a very noisy one. Mr Parnell in his speech on the evening of the Division, had pledged his party on behalf of the Irish people not to abuse the powers which the Bill conferred, and he thoroughly believed that Mr Parnell's statement was seriously and honourably made (Cheers). He thought, therefore, they should dismiss from their minds the fear of the supremacy of Parliament, or the integrity of the Empire, being damaged. On the contrary he believed that the moment that question was settled the people in Ireland would return to their duties and industries, and develop a wholesome desire to improve their position (Cheers). He had himself a considerable stake in Ireland. He had had a house of business in Belfast for upwards of half a century, he had business relations with Cork and with Dublin, and he was not in the slightest degree apprehensive of any injury befalling him, or his property being confiscated (Cheers). On the Land Purchase Bill, he had himself, with other Scottish Members, indicated to Mr Gladstone that he did not see his way to approve of the Bill, and he believed that it would never again be brought in in the shape in which it had been, but if it were he would not support it (Cheers). So he was not a blind adherent of all Mr Gladstone's policies.

When the result of the poll was declared Charles Tennant was shown to be defeated by fifty votes. His supporters were surprised and shocked. Addressing a large crowd outside the Town Hall, Charles said that they had had to fight against an unholy alliance of Tories, faggots and Unionists, men who were deserters from the Liberal cause, who had wrecked the Liberal cause in the country. Mr Thorburn spoke also, from his committee rooms, but was obliged to stop because of the continued yelling of the crowd. When the defeated candidate left, his carriage was drawn by thirty or forty stalwart men, leaving the horses to follow behind. The extra police drafted into the town had a rough time; windows were broken in the Conservative Club rooms, and the evening's proceedings were very noisy. In the final national results the split in the Liberal party ensured their defeat and on 20 July 1886 Gladstone submitted his resignation to the Queen.

The one happy outcome from Charles' point of view was his acquisition of Sir John Millais's fine portrait of Mr Gladstone. This came about as a result of the Grand Old Man's having written a letter of condolence to the defeated Liberal candidate in Chester, in which he said that the Duke of Westminster had struck 'a *fresh* blow at the aristocracy'. The angered Duke retaliated by ejecting the portrait from his great collection and Charles, equally annoyed at this slight to his great friend, immediately bought it. In 1898 he gave it to the National Gallery and today it hangs in the National Portrait Gallery.

In 1892 the country was again embarked on a General Election. After his defeat Charles had pledged himself to stand again for the joint counties, but nearer the election he was pressed by Glasgow Liberals to stand again for the Partick Division which had a Liberal Unionist majority of 801. 'Young Radical' wrote a letter on 19 April 1890 to the *Peeblesshire Advertiser and County Newspaper* saying: 'It is almost certain he will stand for Partick again at the General Election. Anyone who knows these Counties thoroughly knows that Sir Charles is the only man who can win them back to the Liberal cause . . .' At the same time he received a letter from Gladstone. 'You are, in the eyes of the Liberals, not only the fit man—that goes without saying—but the indispensable man, so I do earnestly hope that you will grant their prayer, provided that they show you that you have a good chance of winning. Your return among us in the House of Commons will be an occasion of jubilee. Whatever you say or do, I rely on you to stand by Glasgow in her need.' The reference to a 'good chance of winning' reads strangely because the Division was a stronghold of Tories and Unionists. The Leader's call was imperative, and Charles became the Gladstonian candidate in the Partick Division; his opponent was Mr J. Parker-Smith, the Liberal Unionist candidate.

Charles pursued an active campaign, and his speeches were in advance of contemporary thought. Referring to the ladies who worked so hard but who had no vote: 'It may come some day,' he said, 'the difficulty is that the public has not yet made up its mind,' but he felt that opinion was veering that way. He was in favour of election expenses being paid out of the rates, not by the candidate, so that working-men would be able to stand, and of salaried Members of Parliament. He attacked the Tories for opposing the Reform Bill, the abolition of slavery, the abolition of the Corn Laws and Free Trade . . . 'Almost all that had rendered this century remarkable in the annals of political and social progress. They opposed these measures because they said they would be injurious to the State.' The conviction of the people had passed these measures in spite of Tory opposition, and they had been productive of the greatest good, and every step in the direction of liberty had also been one in the direction of loyalty and contentment. At the eve of the poll meeting on 10 February, a heckler probably employed in the St Rollox Works shouted out that he was 'hurling a barrow as big as a donkey cart for 12*s* a week!' When questioned as to the truth of this statement Charles said: 'My best answer to this question is that we have been in St Rollox since 1800 and we have never had a strike or a difficulty with our men during all that time.' (Cheers.)

Gladstone won the 1892 General Election with a majority of 45 and, at the age of 82, formed his fourth and last administration. But Charles himself was defeated by 219 votes. Gladstone wrote to him:

My dear C. Tennant,

I do not think as a party we have any reason to murmur or complain about the result of your gallant effort. Even for you personally I can hardly regret that you have had such an opportunity of distinguishing yourself by such

> high public service as leading the attack on such a stronghold as Partick of Toryism and wealth. It is a great service and will no doubt be remembered by our friends.

Charles never again contested a parliamentary seat.

CHAPTER ELEVEN

Sir Charles Tennant, an avant-garde *family*

'Is Papa really Papa, or only a kind of visitor?' Charles and Emma's twelfth child Jack once asked his mother. It was an understandable question. Charles, like many Victorian fathers, played only a small role in the upbringing of his children as his business commitments kept him away from home a great deal. They always looked forward enormously to his visits, although neither they nor their mother ever knew exactly when or how long they would be. He thought all his children were beautiful and brilliant and was always paying them compliments, whereas Emma never complimented them and thought none of them beautiful. With a slow smile she would say: 'Pay no attention to your father, darling . . . he is so impressionable.'(1) She had little faith in the fortunes and futures of her daughters and was clearly perplexed by their later successes. Charles, on the other hand, was ambitious for them and often told them it was foolish to marry poor men. When it came to the point, however, he allowed them to marry the men of their own choosing, none of whom was very rich, and his generous dowries made much difference to their marriages.

Charles' and Emma's first child Janet was born in 1850 after which they added regularly to their family. But their happiness at the birth of each child was counterbalanced by tragedy. Charles, born in 1851, died of brain fever at the age of four; John Aubrey, two years younger than his brother, died of appendicitis at the age of eight; and a third son, also called Charles, was killed in a train accident on the Peebles railway when he was seven. A family diary records: 'I can scarcely tell of this succession of shocks, sudden deaths and sorrows, or write about this fearful night when they never rested at all, but suffered an agony of grief. Papa could not be comforted . . .' The diarist adds realistically 'but in their full life there was not time for brooding'.

Pauline Emma, known as Posie, was born in 1855; then came Charlotte Monkton, or Charty, in 1858. There followed in rapid succession Edward Priaulx, Katharine Lucy, Francis John and Octavia Laura. Emma Alice, or Margot, was born in 1864, and in the following year Emma's twelfth and last child arrived, Harold John who was always known as Jack. But there was yet another tragedy when Janet, the eldest child, died of tuberculosis at the age of sixteen. Charles and Emma had now lost four children and Margot claimed that it was this great sadness which prevented her mother from showing many signs of emotion and from communicating on anything but a superficial level. The fear that tuberculosis, which haunted the family, might attack others of her children was the reason for her frequent visits to health resorts with the delicate Posie, who was now her eldest surviving child.

The eight remaining children grew up in the beautiful Border country, isolated from the outside world. The education they received was limited and Margot recalls that even the mildest of questions put to their governesses were considered impertinent. 'It was only because my father had a fine library and we were fond of reading that I learned anything at all before I was sixteen.'[(2)] Charles and Emma did not particularly encourage their daughters to read or study, and it was largely because of their natural curiosity and their own intellectual gifts that they were able to develop their many talents and increase their knowledge. They were all very different in mind and character and stimulated each other with endless discussions. Though devoted to each other, they were hot-tempered, so that discussions often became fiery disputes. Emma Tennant could not bear these complicated wranglings and tended to put a damper on all her children's intellectual activities.

Whereas he thought it unnecessary for his daughters to be educated away from home, Charles was determined that his three sons should have the best education that money could buy. In 1872 his eldest son Edward became the first Tennant to be educated in England, at Eton. Later both he and his youngest brother Jack went to Trinity College, Cambridge. The three boys were unlike their sisters in that they disliked argument and society. They adored the country and excelled at country pursuits such as fishing and shooting. It is not surprising that their lives were to be more conventional. At times their sisters clearly got on their nerves. One day, after he had been heavily snubbed, Jack yelled out, 'You are more like lions than sisters.'(3)

Both boys and girls were, however, united in their deep-rooted and passionate love of Glen. Laura wrote about it in her diaries and letters. 'I am really quite happy simply because I could never be unhappy in the most beautiful place in the broad earth. Such proud purple, such glowing green and such shadows under the trees such pink lights on the hay fields! Oh it is very very beautiful and all dearly beloved. I know every light on the heather, I know every gleam on the Tweed and you must know it someday George, and we will walk into the moor mists and faraway into the sky.'(4)

Margot writing in 1933 said, 'There was not a stone dyke, peat bog, or patch of burnt and flowering heather with which I was not familiar, and I made friends with wandering tramps, and every shepherd, farmer and fisherman on the Border.

'Looking back today—over many and long years—I can truly say that the influence that has permeated my whole existence has been my love of Nature, and an inner anchorage to the wide horizon and beautiful moorlands of the Border country—nothing that can happen to me in the future will ever rob me of the morning glory of my Glen background.'(5)

Later, just before she got married, Margot looked back nostalgically to the Glen of her childhood:

> It seems as if my time were up. I must prepare myself for leaving Glen the Glen wh. is my very own—for all things belong to those who can best appreciate them.
>
> Paying the bill only ensures ownership in a court of law, there are the chambers of the mind in wh. we can secure what we want, undisputed by anyone and in these chambers of head & heart my Glen is secure. My life here has been so even so regulated so exquisite—to rebuild all by matrimony is so sad I think & wants such courage & so much fancy. I sleep in the red night nursery with the old guard green painted bars & a brass rail round the top, a slate mantle piece wh. used to have our little boots & shoes but has been hidden for a long time under a claret coloured plush covering. The night nursery has 2 turrets & a large window facing the bed wh. is small & low with no hangings only a brass railing & knobs . . . I hear the turret door wh. is just below my room give a muffled swing as the housemaids begin moving in the morning but I sleep heaviest from 5 till 9 & these sounds mingle with my sleep. I hear the Doocot [Laura's and Margot's sitting-room] blinds pulled up & the water of papa's big bath turned on—his dressing room is just below mine & the water pipes pass near my writing table—I hear the quiet steady tread of Maggie the housemaid with the hot water in her hand & my glass of milk both of wh. she puts on the nursery table (—the unused ante room to my bed room) while she pulls up the nursery blind & opens the double window near my bedroom door to do it. I know the frou frou of her dress & the faint slide she gives before opening my door to pull back my white linen curtains.(6)

Her brother Edward also felt deeply about his home. One day in India when he was asked what he was thinking about replied, 'Oh, always the same . . . Glen.'(7)

A visitor to Glen during the early years of Charles's and Emma's marriage could hardly have imagined that later it would become a favourite meeting-place of many of the greatest men of the late Victorian age. Charles had not yet started forming his magnificent collection and, apart from an interesting library, there were no paintings or works of art of distinction. Visitors were mainly business partners and friends from Glasgow. Charles's father was a frequent guest, as was his small, unattractive sister Marion, whom the children remember sitting silently in the window of the dining-room, sipping non-vintage port and eating cake.

Posie, the eldest daughter, was nineteen when she was brought to London in 1874 for the season. It was here that she met and fell in love with a fellow-countryman, Tom Gordon-Duff of Drummuir, Banffshire. They became engaged in October and thirteen-year-old Frank's amusing letter from Cheam preparatory school shows the close relationship that existed between the brothers and sisters:

> My dear Posie
>
> I was taken back fearfully and I could not believe it at first at all but I suppose it is, is it not? I am sorry, but I am glad for your sake & I congratulate you upon being so lucky & I wish you many many days with Mr. Gordon Duff and that you will never disagree when you are married and hope you will have every comfort and everything you wish for. The only thing I wish is that you had not been engaged so soon and not to the same Person. I don't like him very much but now that you are engaged to him perhaps I will learn to love him as you say.
>
> I must now shut up, so goodbye darling Posie and I hope that you will have a very good time of it.
>
> Love and kisses to everyone
>
> I am
>
> Your true & most loving brother
>
> Frank J. Tennant
>
> P.S. When is it to be, I suppose in about 3 and a half or four years. F.T.
>
> October 28th 1874

Tom and Posie waited four months, not four years, and on a beautiful day in February 1875 they were married at Glen amid much rejoicing. Posie's cousin John described her thus: 'Posie united the warm affections of her father and the peculiar equableness of her mother and she combined with both the most beautiful and simple faith in her saviour that I ever met'.[8]

Their honeymoon lasted months and included visits to the Tennant estates in Trinidad and travels on the Eastern seaboard of America and Canada. Posie's life was overshadowed by ill health and she was forced to spend much of it abroad. They spent eight years in South Africa, where they were hospitably looked after by a cousin, Sir David Tennant, who became Speaker of the Cape parliament. Charty, Eddie, Laura and Jack all visited their sister there and many letters survive between Posie and her mother which give vivid accounts of life in South Africa in those days. She and her husband returned to Europe in 1885 to try the mountain air of Switzerland; but in those days nothing could cure tuberculosis and she died at Davos in 1888. Charty, writing to George Curzon in January 1889, said: 'Posie was more to me in some ways than anyone in the world; now I have nobody to scold me, nobody to advise me, as she could, and I feel as if I could not keep good. She sanctified everybody who came near her, and hallowed everything she touched, and the dullest domestic duties became lovely with her.'

In 1911 Charty herself died of tuberculosis.

Charty was the tallest and best looking of all the daughters. Her brother Jack described her thus: 'She had distinction both of mind and presence. Her tall, graceful figure, her golden hair surmounting a pure and clean profile, her fine eyes and beautiful carriage, made up a whole that arrested attention and compelled admiration. When you add a wonderful charm to that armoury of beauty, it is natural that she should be surrounded by a multitude of friends.'[9] Margot said she had 'less vanity than anyone that ever lived and her social courage was a perpetual joy'.[10]

When she was eighteen at a ball in London she met a twenty-one-year-old army officer called Thomas Lister. After they had waltzed together, a friend, perhaps hoping for an introduction, asked Tommy if she was his sister, to which he answered 'No, thank God!'[11]

Tommy Lister's first visit to Glen caused a considerable stir amongst Charty's brothers and sisters because of his memorable good looks, fine manners and sense of humour. Tommy's father died suddenly in August 1876 and by Christmas Charty and Tommy, now the 4th Baron Ribblesdale, were engaged. They were married the following April in St George's, Hanover Square. Margot said: 'It was difficult to find a better-looking couple than Charty and Ribblesdale. I often observed people following them in picture galleries; and their photographs appeared in many of the London shop windows.'[12]

Charles and his new son-in-law, despite their very different backgrounds, were genuinely devoted to each other. They shared many tastes in art, sport and politics, but their closest bond was a love of beautiful objects. They frequently went to Christies, where Jack Tennant noted that 'it was a joy to see them together'.[13] Charles also made Ribblesdale a director of several of his companies. He told Margot that 'Tommy is one of the few people in the world that has shown me gratitude'.[14] Indeed he had reason to be grateful, as Charles also paid off a £20,000 mortgage on his family home of Gisburne as a wedding present and gave Charty a handsome London house, number 57 Green Street.

After he had left the army Ribblesdale became interested in politics, allying himself with the Liberal cause. He was an appropriate candidate for the appointments of Lord-in-Waiting to the Queen, and Master of the Buckhounds. A fine portrait of him, painted by Sargent, hangs in the Tate Gallery. As Barbara Tuchman wrote: 'he looks out upon the world in an attitude of such natural arrogance, elegance and self-confidence as no man of a later day would ever achieve.'[15]

Charty and Posie were of an age to be companions and so were Margot and Laura, but Lucy was not close to any of them. Thus, although she was her mother's favourite daughter, her childhood was a lonely one. She was kind and gentle, and she shared her mother's 'stubborn modesty and delicacy of mind'.[16] She was the most artistically talented of the sisters and she spent much of her life in the country painting beautiful watercolours. In 1879, despite her parents' misgivings, Lucy married Thomas Graham-Smith, a country squire whose main interest was hunting and horses. They lived at Easton Grey, a charming Georgian house near Malmesbury in Wiltshire. Later Lucy became crippled with arthritis and suffered terrible pain. She endured these hardships and the difficulties of her marriage with a gaiety which commanded the love and respect of all who knew her.

Charles's business life was becoming more diversified and profitable and in 1879, when he became a Member of Parliament, he decided that he needed a London house. He wanted it to be large enough to house the fine paintings and works of art which he was beginning to collect; and he wanted it to be in a fashionable area so that he could bring out into London society his two youngest and most fascinating daughters, Laura and Margot. In 1881 he bought from Lord Gerard number 35 Grosvenor Square, which exactly fitted his requirements. In 1888 it was renumbered and became 40 Grosvenor Square.

London society in the eighties consisted of a small circle of rich and leisured people who led monotonous lives of elegance and artificiality. They rode or walked in the park, gossiped over the tea-table, dined and danced until the early hours of the morning; and although the *milieu* of the entertainment might alter, the company was generally much the same. They adhered closely to certain unwritten conventions. Lady Frances Balfour described 'good society' as being 'composed of people who knew how to behave, were well bred and felt their obligations to live according to the position in which they were placed . . . certain things were not done, certain people not received'. With some regret she continues, 'Where it broke down was among the coming generation who grew impatient of the many bonds and restrictions which admittedly bound them. The first movement of change undoubtedly came with a family highly gifted of totally unconventional manners, with no code of behaviour, except their own good hearts, the young women of the Tennant family.'(17)

Margot and Laura entered London society without any preconceived ideas of how to behave in it, for their father knew little of its ways and their mother was completely uninterested in it. At first they were not readily accepted into the established circle, where their unconventional behaviour and provincial background were frowned upon. Margot was disappointed not to receive more invitations. She recalled the first dance that she and Laura went to together. They stood against the wall in their new ball gowns, wondering if they would ever meet anyone of interest.

'We did not mind being spectators since we were together—we had a great deal to discuss & observe in the gay illuminated crowd of beautiful strangers. I did not dance once I remember—*Laura* was engaged twice by civil and industrious dancers. I reminded *Laura* of these moments later on when she was the centre of almost universal interest.'(18)

Laura, presented at Court in May 1881, was amazed by the glittering spectacle. She wrote in her diary how insignificant it made her feel. Margot came out the following year. Charles gave a dance for her at 35 Grosvenor Square at which she fulfilled her desire of starting the ball by dancing the quadrille with Mr Gladstone.(19)

During the season her elder brother Eddy usually acted as Margot's escort; but as he did not enjoy dances they each had a key to the house and returned home separately. She also persuaded him to take her to Ascot. With considerable difficulty they obtained tickets for the Royal Enclosure, which led to a meeting with the Prince of Wales. He must have been very struck by Margot as he first asked her to look at the horses in the paddock with him and then to lunch. The following day she claimed he sent her a gold sharkskin cigarette case with a diamond and sapphire clasp. 'After my introduction to the Prince of Wales I was invited to London houses where I had never been, and danced and talked with him at every ball and party.'(20) She made innumerable new friends and Laura recorded in her diary of 8 May 1883: 'Who could help being conquered by her—she carries victory in her eyes.'

What is remarkable about Laura and Margot is not so much that they took London society by storm, but that they did so entirely on their own terms. It was society which had to alter. Their vitality, spontaneity and disregard for conventions attracted the most interesting young men in London, and mothers' disapproval certainly could not prevent them from pursuing and proposing to these two entrancing girls. As Lady Frances Balfour explained: 'It was unnatural if every man did not propose to them after a few hours' acquaintance, and they got distinctly confused concerning the identity of those who certainly had not proposed, but thoroughly enjoyed the delights of their society.'[21]

Their admirers soon included men such as George Curzon, Arthur Balfour and his brother Gerald, 'Doll' Liddell,[22] Hugo Charteris, Rennell Rodd and Alfred Lyttelton.

Laura and Margot's lively parties at The Glen and Grosvenor Square were highly entertaining. Charles encouraged his daughters to turn Glen and Grosvenor Square into meeting-places for some of the most remarkable people of the age. Emma took little part in these activities and often did not know who was sitting at her own table.

Margot described entertaining with Laura in Grosvenor Square:

> In the first years of our Gros. Sq. home, entertaining was a perpetual delight, excitement & irritation. Our standard of success was so high that nothing short of Sir W. Harcourt dancing or Ld. Acton becoming spontaneous satisfied us. Papa's servant used to bring me hurried lines on the 'Menu' to talk across the table or start one particular topic of general possibility. If we were in reach of each other's eye the sympathy was telegraphic & the conversation general. And so we spent four years in & out of society in the most perfect accord & 21 years of uncontradicted intimacy. Discussing Life, Lovers, letters and literature—reading together, praying together, laughing and crying together.[23]

'Doll' Liddell was the wistful and bearded secretary to the combined department of the Lord Chancellor's office and

Crown office, who was pleasantly surprised by life at Glen.

> The life and habits of the younger generation at the Glen were in those days entirely novel to me, and though somewhat startling to an early Victorian caused a "joy of eventful living" that I never thought could exist except in a book.
>
> There was no attempt at anything like chaperonage, all the old-fashioned restrictions as to the manner and place of companionship between young men and maidens being entirely ignored but with such an entire freedom from self-consciousness that after a time it seemed just as natural as it does to suspect the ordinary rules in regard to the attitude of the sexes during a valse. Indeed, the life at Glen from its gaiety and abandon might have been compared to a perpetual valse, not without a good deal of interesting and sparkling talk in the intervals of the dance.[24]

'Doll' here makes reference to the fact that Margot and Laura entertained young men in their bedrooms, discussing books, plays and politics animatedly until the early hours of the morning. An unheard-of habit for young people in those days.

Mary Gladstone, daughter of the Prime Minister, wrote a letter to her cousin Lavinia Lyttelton about her first visit to Glen:

> Since then I have had the strange, rather mad experience of the Tennant circle. I couldn't describe it—it is the maddest, merriest whirl from morn. till night—wonderful quickness, brightness, wit, cleverness—the 4 sisters all so pretty and fascinating in their different ways. Lady Ribblesdale tall, distinguished, and a sort of sunny serenity about her, aged 25. Mrs. Graham Smith, married straight from the schoolroom, small, pretty, clever . . . She draws with great spirit and dash, plays the violin capitally, sings and is full of ardour and interest over everything in the world, books, politics, art, great men. Then comes Laura, the sharpest little creature, like a needle, delicate and yet able to do everything beautifully, like riding, lawn tennis, playing, etc., full of life and fun and up to anything in the world, and yet some 'Weltschmerzen' in her eyes and full

of aspiration in her graver moments . . . She is fair and quite different in looks to the others, but very piquante. Lastly comes Margot, aged 18, perhaps the most really pretty and clever of the lot, her hair curling darkly all over her head, eyes large and deep, skin very pearly without much colour, and the most bewitching mouth. She sings, draws, plays violin and pianoforte, all with originality and charm . . .[25]

Godfrey Webb was a frequent visitor to Glen and always spent Christmas there. He was a bachelor whose wit and good nature made him welcome in country houses everywhere. Although nearer Charles's age than his children's, he was devoted to Laura and Margot, and produced several poems about them. In 1884 he wrote in the visitors' book at Glen:

In olden times before they fled
Before the steps of men,
Dryads and nymphs and fairies too
Were tenants of the Glen.
The times are changed, the dryads gone,
But even yet, as then,
Two nymphs more dangerous than those
Are Tennants of The Glen.

A picture of the life at Glen when the family were alone is drawn by Margot in her diary entry for 20 October 1893:

We return to find Lucy hard at her water colours for her bazaar & the boys just come in from shooting wet & waiting for tea, papa writing hard at the library table very impatient & nervous but sweet tempered as ever. I come up here & write or arrange papers or look over old letters or stick things into my album till dressing gong. Eddy generally comes up & smokes a cigarette in my arm chair staring into the fire & he & I throw out talk to each other about the future. We love each other so dearly & have such complete understanding of all that most concerns us. I like the tick of the clock & the noise of the wind howling down the valley & my pen scratching on in silence 'Any letters Miss'—'Here'—& then I go & have my bath—

Lucy comes too sometimes—it is so very big & we laugh as I read her my letters in the bath till Gee knocks at the door to tell us we shall be late or Eddy yells through the door to know when we shall turn out. I stare at the old dyed mulberry drugget in the bath room while I dry myself & hand Lucy the towel. I am generally first down & find Eddy reading *The Times* on the billiard table; if we are alone papa takes the *Evening News* in to dinner 'Two awful railway accidents in America 4 killed & 8 seriously injured. Eddy—What a boon for the Evening papers. Lady disappeared at Maidenhead—Richards on the spot! or a cuckoo in November—! I know the sort of things in the papers'. Then papa will read us out loud some begging letter of his from an old soldier or a former worker in St. Rollox & he will tell us how he was taken in once & as we well know the story we wink at each other & mama says he is a great goose, or he will tell us about Mama's first present to him of ivory backed brushes wh. touched him so much & how he got the bill a month afterwards. This never fails to amuse him & Mama & we don't get tired of hearing it. This led to other little anecdotes of byegone adventures wh. lose nothing by being repeated or by mama's cute & unsentimental corrections. If we get on politics we are not so lucky as Eddy & I are Whigs, Jack a Radical & papa Gladstonian. After dinner Lucy hands me a letter of Grahams wh. she cannot read: it begins with a long quotation from his old Col's letter about troopers saddles & continues by telling her how he & his saddler & partner 'have gone to the root of the evil—(sore backs among troopers) & there is a percentage of 40 per cent after autumn manoeuvres etc.—' it is not to be xpected that she'd read it! Mama plays the piano with energy & conscience while I smoke a cigarette & refuse coffee wh. keeps me awake. When the boys come in from their claret (wh. now by the way is champagne) if Eddy is in good form as there are enough of us we play pencil games—Styles—or poems or great men beginning with 1 letter in 3 min. or letters on given subjects. I invented a very good new game. Everyone telling the story of a novel as shortly & graphically as possible reading it out & letting the others guess. Lucy took Rob Roy—I did David

> Grieve Jack Tess & Eddy the Old Testament wh. was quite xcellent & took us all a long time to guess. At 11 Eddy gets restless & I with the kind of regularity of my animal nature begin to yawn & we all go into the billiard room & after a little fooling or giving early morning carriage orders we file upstairs. Charty looking lovely, with a candle in her hand—in the semi obscurity of a pretty staircase. As we sit talking in each others rooms & crossing the passages a faint smell of cigars—the click of billiard balls & delighted applause reach our ears & after rubbing my head against my little dog's hairy pretty little face I go to bed.

In September 1883 Laura was invited on a two-week cruise in Sir Donald Currie's new 400 foot, 4,000 ton steamer *Pembroke Castle*. The party included Mr and Mrs Gladstone and their daughter Mary, and their cousins Arthur and Herbert Lyttelton, the Poet Laureate Lord Tennyson and his son, Sir William Harcourt and his son and Sir Algernon West.

The steamer sailed from Barrow on 8 September, cruised up the west coast of Scotland, and stopped at Kirkwall where the Freedom of the Burgh was conferred on Gladstone and Tennyson. The cruise continued across to Christiansund in Norway, then to Copenhagen, where on 18 September, a royal party fifty strong were given lunch, after which the steamer returned to Gravesend on 22 September.

Mary Gladstone, who had arranged to have Laura invited on the trip, wrote a beautiful description of her:

> She had the naughtiness, the grace and quickness and mischievousness of a kitten. Her sense of fun, of antithesis, sometimes led her into daring expressions, dangerously near forbidden ground. Nothing was safe in heaven or earth or under the earth from the sallies of her wit. One trembles to think what she would have been had it not been for the restraining influence of her spiritual side. She never seemed capable of being bored, distributed herself pretty equally all round, and talked to bores (we were not without them) with the same eagerness and animation as to poets and premiers, could strike sparks out of dead wood, and make the heaviest natures shine and sparkle . . . I

> never knew anybody with such unique powers of attraction to shine in this way. It was generosity carried to a pitch I had never seen before. She was ready and willing to sacrifice herself to anybody. She would give away the most precious things she possessed, if she thought they would please others.
>
> Extraordinarily brilliant in conversation, though apt to be run away with, the life and soul of the company one minute, the next she would be an altered being, with that curious, indescribable weird, far off look in her eyes, so sad, so wistful, her face small and pale and pitiful as a suffering child's, you could cry simply by looking at her, and at those times I used to feel she did not belong to us, the little body was here, frail and white, but the soul, it seemed to escape.[26]

Laura enjoyed herself to the full, and noted in her diary on 10 September:

> I am immensely happy and having the greatest fun in the world. Tennyson and I get on like a Palace on Fire and he calls me 'little witch'. He is kind and gruff and big . . . most people quail before him. The G.O.M. I look upon as too sacred to . . . Oh! Tennyson was so funny today—he asked me to kiss him! which I promptly did and would any day! I love him. We talked of Swinburne and Rossetti—of fame—and cabbages and kings. He said to me this morning 'I find it much harder to realise matter than spirit' . . . I understand so well what he means, and would much sooner doubt my body than my soul . . . It is so wonderful living with two Kings on board—Bless them.

At one point it was decided that the ship would go to Norway and then to Denmark and Laura decided she must leave; she wrote in her diary: 'I told Tennyson I must leave him. "Nonsense, little witch, you must not go, you are the life of the party—Gladstone and I will sign a round robin to prevent you going." It is the first time and probably the last I shall be asked to do something to please a Poet Laureate . . .' she concludes.

Laura described the Royal lunch party thus:

Copenhagen Tuesday Sept: 18th 4 P.M.
Two hours ago I was in a crowd of human beings, or is it too familiar to speak of Kings and Queens and Chancellors and a sprinkling of Imperial Majesties as human beings? It was a curious experience—I was sitting by the King of Denmark's brother, one door off the Queen of Greece. At my back the Emperor of all the Russias next Mrs. Gladstone, the Queen of Denmark, the King, the Empress of Russia, the Princess of Wales (his two daughters), Prince Eddy and the three princesses and a dozen children. Altogether forty to fifty Royalties. Interesting to see the Czar and Czarina and wondering how long they will sit on their thrones, and which will be blown up first—a ghastly thought and a ghastly state of things. The Czar said he would rather be King of Denmark than Emperor of Russia. Our Princess looked lovely as ever. Tennyson read to them in the tiny smoking room, between the Empress and the Princess of Wales and patted them just as he does us. Among all the crowned heads Gladstone is King of Kings.

Charles wrote to his friend, Mr Gladstone, after the trip and received the following reply, dated 28 October: 'On the 4th you kindly wrote to thank for your daughter's reception and entertainment on board the *Pembroke Castle*. But in nautical language she really paid her passage for she gave more than she got, charmed everybody and perceptibly helped to raise the temperature of the party.'

Laura's pleasure was increased by the fact that the letter arrived on her twenty-first birthday. She characteristically noted in her diary after the cruise: 'It's all nonsense to say I have social qualities and genius and all that sort of thing . . .' In fact her success in society did not entirely meet with her own approval, as can be seen from another diary entry for 30th July 1882: 'I've wasted quite five months of this year. I don't know if it is right to look at my London season philosophically as a time to be made up for afterwards or practically as a time that should never exist.'

Underneath her gaiety there was a deep-rooted seriousness and a firmly-held religious conviction. At an early age she realised the transitory nature of life, and in March 1879 she had composed an inscription for her tomb: 'Laura Mary, A child of the Sky.' Two months later she was confirmed, one of the most important events of her life. Laura yearned for a freedom of mind and body. On 19 November 1879 she wrote: 'am I very rebellious & unkind & unwise—no I only long for something broader than I have, away with the horizon & those lines and rules that appear every minute—can I break loose and be like no other girl can I be free & pure & broad & loving.' She continues that she has 'a sort of serene longing—a longing for Death—the key to this riddle of life—the interpreter of all there is to interpret & god knows how much there is . . . In 5 years I will be out of this sad girlhood—perhaps out of this sad world. God help me.'

Nearly every page of Laura's and Margot's early diaries contains a long religious soliloquy. The other sisters held strong religious convictions too. Writing many years later, Margot found it difficult to explain this because neither parent ever mentioned the subject of religion to them. Even the minister at Glen only succeeded in making Laura and Margot giggle.

By the end of 1884 the complexity of Laura's love life was putting a great strain on her. Her three favourite suitors, Gerald Balfour, 'Doll' Liddell and Alfred Lyttelton) saw the New Year in at Glen with the entire Tennant family except for Posie who was still in South Africa. Laura recorded in her diary the intricate happenings which ended with Alfred proposing to her and being accepted just before the gong sounded for dinner on 3 January 1885. This was Margot's description of the scene:

> Laura came into my room and asked me what she should put on (she had a dressing-room just off our bedroom densely populated by books and hung with Burne-Jones's and illuminated by pansies). I said 'Your white muslin. Mr. Lyttelton is strumming in the Doocot. Go and entertain him.' She told me afterwards that she tied her blue ribbon in her hair, and thrust her diamonds into her fichu with lightning rapidity; and with her eyes very big, and

> her whole being very small and shy, she went into our sitting-room—the Doocot—and shut the door, leaning against it.—Alfred was playing—he turned round and gazed at the little white figure so near him, so delicious in her dainty muslin next to his great rough travelling clothes—he was going to London that night. He began to break the conspicuous silence by saying something about not many leaving Glen without telling her they loved her, but it all broke down; in a minute his great figure was bending over her, and she was in his arms.[27]

There was something extraordinarily romantic about this union. Both combined irresistible charm, youth and unusual powers of enjoyment, and both held an ideal in their hearts. Margot said that Alfred, whose prowess at games was unparalleled, 'could have taken out a patent in himself as an Englishman'.[28] After his death Henry Asquith said in the House of Commons that Alfred 'of all men of his generation came nearest to the mould and ideal of manhood which every English father would like to see his son aspire to and, if possible, attain'.[29]

Laura wrote to her close friend Mary Gladstone:

> Oh! Mary, isn't it all wonderful and mystic! I feel it is like a sacrament and can never be understood but only dwelt in. The sense of perfect rest and perfect truth and the knowledge of his strength are the feelings that float the uppermost in my well of delight. He is so big and I am so little and why should he have ever cared for anyone so wee. That's what's so generous to start with and then it was such a break to think he didn't expect me to jump and to fly down his throat! And he was so darling about it and his arms are great walls round our God-given world, so that even the ambassadors of lower worlds cannot enter in.[30]

The reactions of Laura's parents were characteristic. Charles wrote to Lord Rosebery;

> You know Alfred and I think you will agree with us that he is likely to make her a good husband. We all like him much. We wish he were a little less dependent on his professional work, which is, no doubt, a precarious source of

> income—he is doing fairly well, however, and everyone tells me he is one of the rising men at the Bar. Laura is a determined worker and thinks she will be able to help him. She might have married a rich man—she could not have married a better stamp of man and I think they have every prospect of happiness.(31)

A letter from Posie to her mother-in-law explains Emma's reaction: 'I am amused by what you say about my mother not saying anything to you about Laura's engagement. It is so exactly like her. The first letter she wrote to me about it was most funny, three sheets were filled up with trifles about the garden, the visitors etc. before she attended to the subject, on the 4th sheet she said, "I was not very surprised when Laura told me she had promised to marry Mr. Lyttelton," etc. for a few lines, and then she began about something else; funny little mother.'

On 21 May 1885, Alfred and Laura were married at St George's, Hanover Square, and Mr Gladstone proposed the toast of the bride and groom. The closeness of Margot and Laura can be gauged from a letter written to George Curzon on the night of the wedding. 'I can't help it, it may be selfish but it's true I *mind* Laura going, she's part of myself & I shall shriek at the empty bed now & work off what I've wanted to say by biting my pillow and burying my head, no one, no one takes that place, say what you like, 21 years just we two in the most perfect closest intimacy you can imagine . . . and now it's all over—I mind her letters, her kisses, her hair round my neck nothing of that sort makes up, it's just like sealing wax to fix the gap.'

Alfred's and Laura's life together was supremely happy. Soon came the promise and excitement of a child. Shortly after the marriage Mary Gladstone introduced Laura to a young American called Mr Chapman. After this meeting Mary was startled by a letter she received from him: 'They call Mrs. Lyttelton a charming woman and they none of them see that she is dying. I wake up in the night and thank God for having given me one half hour of this woman, who calls out all that lies buried, that is best and noblest in us.'(32)

Laura herself had often written of death. Early in April 1888 shortly before her baby was due Margot visited her before going to stay at Easton Grey and Laura told her, 'I am sure I shall die with my baby . . . If I die, Margot, I want you to read my will to the relations & people that will be in my bedroom. It is in that drawer. Promise me you will not forget.'(33)

On 16 April her son, after a long struggle, was born, but the effort had been too much for her frail little body. She fought for life for several days, but on Easter Saturday she murmured 'I think God has forgotten me' and died. Margot remembered what she had promised Laura and fetched her will, which included this moving passage about Alfred and their married life:

> I want first of all to tell Alfred that all I have in the world, and all I am and ever shall be, belongs to him, and to him more than any one, so that if I leave away from him anything that speaks to him of a joy unknown to me—or that he holds dear for any reason wise or unwise, it is his, and my dear Friends will forgive him and me.
>
> So few women have been as happy as I have been every hour since I married—so few have had such a wonderful sky of love for their common atmosphere, that perhaps it will seem strange, when I write it down, that the sadness of Death and Parting is greatly lessened to me by the fact of my consciousness of the eternal indivisible oneness of Alfred and me—I feel as long as he is down here—I must be here,—silently, secretly sitting beside him, as I do every evening now—however much my soul is on the other side —and that if Alfred too were to die, we should be as we were on Earth—love as we did this year—only fuller, quicker, deeper than ever—with a purer Passion and a wiser worship. Only in the meantime whilst my body is hid from him, and my eyes cannot see him, let my trivial toys be his till the morning comes, when nothing will matter, because all is Spirit.(34)

The tragedy of her death was felt by an extraordinarily wide circle of people. Mr Gladstone's letter meant more to the family than any others they received. It was to Alfred:

'How eminently true it is of her, that in living a short time, she fulfilled a long time. If life is measured by intensity, hers was a very long life; and yet with her rich development of mental gifts, purity and singleness of heart, made her one of the little children of whom, and of whose—is the Kingdom of Heaven.

'Bold indeed would it be to say that such a being died prematurely.

'All through your life, however it may be prolonged, what a precious possession to you she will be . . .'

Mary Gladstone received a letter from Edward Burne-Jones: 'We shall all feel it, all of us, to the end of our days: it will be a never healing wound. What a brief delight it was. I am as unhappy as an outsider can well be—and so are we all. It is never out of our minds and the year feels darkened hopelessly.

'But when I go back to London—in a fortnight or so—I will call in Grosvenor Square and arrange about the book, and about any other scheme that may have been thought of to show our undying love for her sister.'(35) Laura wrote a children's story which was much admired by John Ruskin, and Burne-Jones had undertaken to design a cover for it. It was never published. Burne-Jones also designed a beautiful memorial plaque to Laura which is in Mells parish church, Somerset.

The desolation of her brothers and sisters is summed up in a letter Jack wrote to Lord Rosebery on 6 May from university:

> Everything looks so superficially the same—only rendered more beautiful by the glorious weather. It is only I who am wretched. It is all such mockery. I have very few associations here with her which only makes it worse. I feel as if I should never care for anyone who either didn't love her or whom she didn't love & one has to go about just as if nothing had happened and life was as sweet now as ever.
>
> I have not yet, to my regret, learnt to look full in the face the argument which says—a very happy and wonder-

> fully perfect life passed away amid sunshine and peace. I can only think of what she was to Alfred and me and all of us & what she would have been to her boy. It is such an impossible argument to say she is more wanted where she is than with us. It seems as though there was no justice in the world to take [away] one who breathed more good into the foul nostrils of this world, and looked more sympathy out of her dark blue far-reaching eyes in 23 summers than anyone else in a hundred.(36)

The imperishable nature of her personality is described by Dr Holland, who wrote after Alfred's death:

> . . . we recall now, over his grave, the tragic wonder of that first marriage—the amazing fascination of the tiny little lady whose very being was a shining flame, who enthralled and bewitched the world; who moved about encircled by a crowd of rejected lovers who remained her adoring friends: who gave herself wholly to him who won her soul: who left those overwhelming records of her young wedded life: and who died within the year to leave an incomparable memory as of a vision that had come and gone in a moment's glory. There was never anything quite like her. And the pathos of her love hung about him to the end.(37)

Kenneth Rose in his book on Lord Curzon wrote the most recent account of Laura in 1969, and confirms this account. 'The legend of Laura Tennant resists scepticism. It cannot be diminished or explained away by the pity of her early death or by the extravagant delight which her coterie took in each other's company.'(38)

Charty and Ribblesdale went to live with Alfred in Brook Street and Charty looked after Laura's child as if it were her own. Alfred began to enjoy the company of his son and wrote 'he is beginning to throw a gleam upon my life'. But this was sadly short-lived for in May 1888 Alfred Christopher died of meningitis. He was buried beside his mother at Glen on the anniversary of his parents' wedding. Charty supported Alfred through all this period, and writing many years later to a friend, Alfred said of Charty that she 'was for years my greatest stay and comfort and remade my broken life'.[39]

Margot's relationship with Laura was the most intimate and perfect of her life; and although she has been criticised for being self-centred, and full of self-praise, her acknowledgement that her sister was the more remarkable of the two is surely genuine. When discussing the differences between them, Margot wrote:

> I have never succeeded in making anyone the least different from what they are, and in my efforts to do so have lost most of my female friends. This was the true difference between us. I have never influenced anybody but my own two children, Elizabeth and Anthony; but Laura had such an amazing effect upon men and women that for years after she died they told me that she had both changed and made their lives . . . In her short life she influenced more people than I have ever done over twice as many years. . . . There was another difference between Laura and me: she felt sad when she refused the men who proposed to her; I pitied no man who loved me.[40]

The next marriage in the family was of Frank, Charles' second surviving son, to a beautiful girl called Anne Redmayne, whose family lived near Durham. Anne was always carefully chaperoned and so on one occasion when Frank wanted to take her to Durham Cathedral, Laura and Doll Liddell had to accompany them. Mr Redmayne disapproved of the Tennant girls' unconventional ways. 'When they were in the drawing-room with Mr Redmayne Laura said, "I hear you like music, Mr. Redmayne?". He answered in the affirmative, and she sat down and played the piano quite beautifully to him for half an hour. He was quite bewitched, and captivated by her charm, nothing he could do was too much for her. She had neuralgia and he insisted upon going down into his cellar and opening a very very old bottle of port of which he had only a few bottles left, which were kept for most special people, to give to her.'[41] Frank and Annie lived at Hynford House in North Berwick and later at Innes near Elgin.

The Tennant family circle and their always interesting

and often distinguished friends became so conspicuous in London that in the late eighties they were given a name. At a dinner party given by Lady Brownlow, Lord Charles Beresford exclaimed: 'You are always talking about your souls . . . I shall call you the Souls.' (Other 'Souls', apart from the Tennants, included George Curzon, George Wyndham, Harry Cust, Godfrey Webb, Lady Horner, Lady Wemyss, Lady Desborough, Lord Pembroke, Lady Granby, St John Brodrick and Lady Brownlow.) This description stuck to them, but was nearly always used only by those who were not Souls. Arthur Balfour, who was the 'King' of the Souls, explained: 'To me the name of "Souls" seemed always meaningless and slightly ludicrous. It seems to imply some kind of organisation and purpose, where no organisation or purpose was dreamed of. It seems to suggest a process of selection, possibly even rejection, by a group which, in so far as it had any separate existence, was a spontaneous and natural growth, born of casual friendship and unpremeditated sympathy.'(42)

Doll Liddell wrote of the Souls that: 'These gatherings were the origin of the Souls who a few years later were talked of in society as if they were a definite organised association. In reality they were nothing more than a set of friends, the nucleus of which had been brought together by the social gifts of the Tennant family. Even as a set they had no definite limits, as some of them were, so to speak, only occasional Souls, though there was a certain group who were generally found together.'(43)

George Curzon gave a famous dinner party at the Bachelors' Club on 10 July 1889, when he invited about fifty Souls and each was greeted with a printed set of verses about themselves. About the Tennants he wrote:

Here a trio we meet
Whom you never will beat,
Tho' wide you may wander and far go;
From that wonderful art
Of that Gallant Old Bart
Sprang CHARTY, and LUCY and MARGOT?

To LUCY he gave
The wiles that enslave,
Heart and tongue of an angel to CHARTY;
To MARGOT the wit
And the wielding of it,
That make her the joy of the party.

Lord TOMMY is proud
That to CHARTY he vowed
The graces and gifts of a true man.
And proud are the friends
Of ALFRED, who blends
The athlete, the hero, the woman!

George Curzon gave a repeat dinner party on 9 July 1890, for which he also composed some verses.

Thanks to the Souls it was no longer smart to be exclusive or fashionable to be dull. They revived the art of conversation, which in Victorian days had fallen into a decline.

The Souls were the first people to entertain political opponents. Sometimes these meetings even helped to resolve political differences. On one occasion, when temperatures were running high over the question of Home Rule, the intrepid Margot gave a luncheon party at 40 Grosvenor Square to which she invited both Gladstone and Lord Randolph Churchill. Despite the fact that the Grand Old Man had been virulently attacked in public by Lord Randolph, when the two men met at her house they talked fluently and amicably, and the news of their friendly meeting became the talk of the town.

Jack was the next member of the family to marry. On 1 October 1889 he married Helen Gordon-Duff, the sister of Thomas Gordon-Duff who married Charles's eldest daughter, Posie. Margot described Helen: 'Jack's fiancée whom we like very much has brains of crystal and a heart of gold, Jack *is* lucky.'[44] One of Helen's bridesmaids, Joan Gordon-Duff (Lindsay), wrote this account of the wedding: 'Helen had lovely auburn hair and was brilliant. I can just remember her giving me rides "pick-a-back" on her "bustle" and I was bridesmaid at her wedding to Jack Tennant, my mother's youngest brother, in 1889. It took place in the drawingroom on account of my grandfather's health, Randall Davidson [later Archbishop of Canterbury] officiating. He had been my father's greatest friend at Harrow and Oxford, and was my godfather and was also one of the frequent visitors.'[45]

Their happiness was short-lived and Helen and Jack's life together was sadly reminiscent of their respective brother and sister, Tom and Posie. Helen died of tuberculosis in 1892. Four years later Jack married May Abrahams, who was the first woman factory inspector. (She was later made a Companion of Honour.) Henry Asquith as Home Secretary made this appointment in 1893. Jack Tennant, who was Asquith's private secretary for many years, was Liberal M.P. for Berwickshire from 1894–1918. He was under secretary at the Board of Trade, and under secretary at the War Office from 1914–1915, and Secretary of State for Scotland 1915.

On 12 December 1889 Margot went to stay for the first time at Hawarden with Mr and Mrs Gladstone, and wrote an amusing description of her conversation with Mr Gladstone on books, people and politics. She described in detail 'The Temple of Peace', the library where he worked, and how he allowed her to sit reading while he wrote letters.[46] Her visit must have been a success. Philip Magnus writes:

> As Gladstone grew older, the repressions of a lifetime were lifted a little, and he found it possible to relax simply and naturally in the presence of young, pretty and vivacious women. Margot Tennant for example, left Hawarden just before Parnell arrived for his one visit. After she had left Gladstone sent her a poem, which in quality is well above his average as a versifier:
>
> When Parliament ceases and comes the recess,
> And we seek in the Country, rest after distress,
> As a rule upon visitors place an embargo,
> But make an exception in favour of Margot.

For she brings such a treasure of movement and life,
Fun, spirit, and stir, to folk weary with strife,
Though young and though fair, who can hold such a cargo
Of all the good qualities going, as Margot?

Uphill and down dale, 'tis a capital name
To blossom in friendship, to sparkle in fame.
There's but one objection can light upon Margot,
Its likeness in rhyming, not meaning, to Argot.'

Never mind, never mind, we will give it the slip,
'Tis not Argot the language, but Argo the ship,
And, by sea or by land, I will swear you may far go
Before you can hit on a double for Margot.

December 17, 1889 W.E.G.[47]

In November 1890 Mr and Mrs Gladstone came to stay for three days at Glen. Sir Charles and members of his family awaited the train's arrival at Innerleithen station where a red carpet was laid out and a special step erected at the edge of the platform. Despite the thin drizzle of rain a crowd had assembled to cheer the Grand Old Man. When the honoured guest arrived he was driven to Glen in an open carriage with Charles and his two daughters Charty and Margot. The gateway was garlanded with ivy and evergreens in which the word *Welcome* was spelt out, and the courtyard was gay with flags. Lady Tennant received the guests on the front steps. The next day Mr Gladstone planted a sapling in the grounds, and inspected the orchids in the greenhouses; the following day he cut down a fully-grown oak with a specially procured 5 lb. axe. At dinner the old man talked incessantly on all manner of subjects ranging from Disraeli's novels to the splendours of Queen Elizabeth's reign. When they got on to the topic of confiscations Mr Gladstone said: 'You might as well disendow Sir Charles Tennant of the Glen—what would you call that?' 'A Radical measure' was Margot's lightning answer which received

20. A shooting party at Glen, August 1899. *(back row)* H. J. Tennant, Alfred Lyttelton, E. P. Tennant, Captain Leigh Winsloe; *(second row)* Miss Anne Tennant, Sir Charles, Marguerite (the second Lady Tennant), Mrs E. P. Tennant, Edith Lyttelton (Alfred's second wife), Miss Hill; *(front row)* F. J. Tennant, Captain A. Wolfe-Murray.

21. Group at Glen, 1895. *(back row, l. to r.)* Unknown, H. J. Tennant, Mrs E. P. Tennant, Edward P. Tennant *(front row, l. to r.)* Lucy Graham-Smith, H. H. Asquith, Margot Asquith, Unknown.

22. Sir Charles Tennant by J. S. Sargent, 1901. The portrait is an excellent likeness and Sargent wrote to the second Lady Tennant '. . . . I am sure that it has caught something at a favourable moment. . . .'

23. Marguerite, Lady Tennant, and her three daughters, Katharine, Nancy and Peggy, by J. J. Shannon, 1908. (detail) The daughters became Baroness Elliot of Harwood, Lady Crathorne and Dame Margaret Wakehurst. This work was enthusiastically received at the 1908 Royal Academy Summer Exhibition.

much applause. On the third day the guests were driven down to Innerleithen station, where their special train, a saloon, a brake-van and a composite carriage, awaited them.[48]

Margot adored riding and was absolutely without fear on the hunting field. Winston Churchill, reviewing her *Autobiography* in the *Daily Mail* in 1920, described her beautifully: 'Few there were in the gay, hard-riding crowd which frequented Melton Mowbray or followed the Duke of Beaufort's hounds in the 'nineties able to surpass this feather-weight daredevil, mounted upon enormous horses, who with faultless nerve and thrust and inexhaustible energy, spurred by love of chase and desire to excel, came sometimes to grief but always to the fore.'[49]

She had several riding accidents, the worst of which spoilt the shape of her nose. On at least one occasion Margot took her horse indoors.

> One day, when I was mounted to ride in the Row, my papa kept me waiting so long at the door of 40 Grosvenor Square that I thought I would ride Tatts into the front hall and give him a call; it only meant going up one step from the pavement to the porch and another through the double doors held open by the footmen. Unluckily, after a somewhat cautious approach by Tatts up the last step into the marble hall, he caught his reflection in a mirror. At this he instantly stood erect upon his hind legs, crashing my tall hat into the crystal chandelier. His four legs all gave way on the polished floor and down we went with a noise like thunder, the pony on top of me, the chandelier on the top of him and my father and the footmen helpless spectators. I was up and on Tatts' head in a moment, but not before he had kicked a fine old English chest into a jelly. This misadventure upset my father's temper and my pony's nerve, as well as preventing me from dancing for several days.[50]

There is a story that Charles' comment was: 'Really, Margot! You know I don't like you riding your horse in the house.'

Margot's short, unsatisfactory engagement, after a long

love affair, with Peter Flower, came about through their mutual passion for riding and hunting. He appealed to the out-of-doors side of her nature, but he cared very little for books or politics and was uncomfortable in the society of men of intellect. In her *Autobiography* she tells of an occasion when he was present, which reflects charmingly on her father.

> We had not been talking on the sofa for more than five minutes when I heard a shuffle of feet outside the library-door. I got up with lightning rapidity and put out the two candles on the writing-table with the palms of my hands, returning noiselessly to Peter's side on the sofa, where we sat in black darkness. The door opened and my father came in holding a bedroom candle in his hand; he proceeded to walk stealthily round the room, looking at his pictures. The sofa on which we were sitting was in the window and had nothing behind it but the curtains. He held his candle high and close to every picture in turn and, putting his head forward scanned them with tenderness and love. I saw Peter's idiotic hat and stick under the Gainsborough and could not resist nudging him as 'The Ladies Erne and Dillon' were slowly approached. A candle held near one's face is the most blinding of all things and, after inspecting the sloping shoulders and anaemic features of the Gainsborough ladies, my father, quietly humming to himself, returned to his bed.[(51)]

In the summer of 1891 Emma expressed a desire to go to Egypt with Charles and Margot. Her unspoken reasons were first to give Charles the rest which his doctors had recommended and second to remove Margot from her Leicestershire hunting life. Charles, who disliked travelling abroad, was only persuaded to go because it might prevent his daughter from marrying a hunting man. He did not look forward to the trip and when Arthur Balfour asked him shortly before leaving how he felt about it he replied: 'As well as a man going to be executed can feel.'[(52)]

The three set off on 13 November for their two-and-a-half-month tour, which turned out to be a tremendous success. Margot's diary of the journey contains illuminating insights into Charles' and Emma's personalities. She describes how, when they were visiting Milan cathedral, 'Papa spoke at the top of his voice while all the people were praying. I have come to the conclusion that he has really immense moral sentiment, a good deal of artistic sentiment and no religious sentiment whatever; awe is unknown to him'.[53] Later he irritated her still more: 'Papa tries me very highly with lunch in the train, and at meals; he is so hasty and drops his pear on the railway floor and on his clothes, and lets the "baba au rhum" clean the seats, etc. He eats everything, except what he doesn't like and then says "I am obliged to be a little careful, you see" (when rejecting some continental contrivance of rice and indiarubber mushrooms)'[54]. Other entries, however, testify to Margot's admiration and love of her parents.

> 1st December. I felt in watching my parents what a wonderful cross they made. As a family we ought to be more remarkable. The refinement and gentle unworldliness—mixed with originality—of Mama; her sensitive shrinking from moral responsibility and decisions of any kind; her social diffidence, unselfishness, and reserve—all fit and modify Papa's abundant vitality and fearlessness; his push, un-selfconsciousness, and unreflecting remarks are too simple to offend. He has the sweetest and most generous temper, and the finest kind of nature—incapable of hurting anyone's feelings, too busy, too healthy, too fond, and full of life to feel anything morbidly. His activities have through circumstances developed sides of which his children know nothing; but we are all more like him than Mama in our energy and geniality to strangers and servants. The boys have more of Mama's self-effacing reserve, but we have Papa's confidence and hope; I regret to say we have missed the beauty of my mother's family, and I cannot share her view that this is a good thing as—'it protects one from temptation'.[55]
>
> 18th December—Papa and I rode donkeys, and had a nice *tête-à-tête* talk; he is well, and happy, exchanging reminiscences with Mr. Harris on old Bath days and early actors—Helen Faucit, Macready, and Malibran. He has

a wonderful memory, and knows Byron, the Ingoldsby Legends, Shakespeare, Milton, and Tommy Moore, by the yard. He told me that one day in Bath—when he was about eighteen—while looking through a tobacconist's window, he saw a very pretty girl behind the counter, upon which he walked into the shop, and straight up to her, kissed her, saying as an excuse to her: 'It is all your fault for being so pretty!'(56)

Earlier in the year Margot had met Henry Asquith at a dinner party given by Lord Battersea. He wrote to her regularly while she was abroad on what he called her 'flight into Egypt' and he never wavered in his devotion to her. 'You tell me not to stop loving you as if you thought I had done, or would or could do so . . . We have a trying time before us: at least I have: but before it begins I entreat you never to doubt that, locked and buried though it may be, your place is always sacred and always your own.'(57) Asquith could hardly have realised just how trying a time he was going to have, as it was to be another two-and-a-half years before Margot, who was already twenty-eight years old, decided she could marry him. It seems surprising that someone who recorded 'I had always prophesied I would marry a Prime Minister and live in high political circles,'(58) should have hesitated so long to marry a man destined to fill that office. However she had reasons for her hesitation; the Asquith and Tennant temperaments were very different. 'The Tennants', she said, 'believed in appealing to the hearts of men', whereas 'the Asquiths—without mental flurry and with perfect self mastery—believed in the free application of intellect to every human emotion.'(59)

One daunting consideration for Margot was that she would become responsible for the five children of Asquith's first marriage. She also knew that her extravagances could scarcely be supported by Asquith's earnings either at the Bar or as a minister; nor did she like the idea of giving up hunting or a leading role in London society. To help her resolve these problems she talked to her friends. Gladstone reassured her: 'My dear Margot, I think you would make an excellent wife to any politician—even a Prime Minister!'[60] Benjamin Jowett, the famous Master of Balliol, warned her: 'It is not possible to be a leader of fashion and to do your duty to the five children.'[61]

There was a great deal of speculation in the press about whom Margot was to marry. Amongst the many names linked with hers were those of Lord Rosebery and Arthur Balfour. Margot's father advised her that to deny the Rosebery rumour publicly would only draw attention to it; but Rosebery took a different view and for a time this caused a rift. Arthur Balfour, when asked whether he was engaged to Margot, answered: 'No, that is not so. I rather think of having a career of my own.'[62]

Sir Henry Ponsonby, perhaps Queen Victoria's most trusted adviser, wrote in a letter to Algernon West on 14 October 1893, 'Does Miss Margot contradict her reported marriage? I think she has been married by newspaper report to all the bachelors and widowers in the two governments.'[63]

Margot's critics were gratified by the publication in 1893 of a novel by E. F. Benson, son of the Archbishop of Canterbury, called *Dodo*. The heroine, who was modelled on the most superficial part of Margot's character, provided ammunition for those who wanted to dissuade Asquith from marrying her. Rosebery meeting Asquith in Rotten Row suggested: 'My dear Asquith, I advise you to read *Dodo* . . . there is a great deal of truth in it.'[64]

Asquith, when *Dodo* was left prominently beside his bed in the house of a friend, in a very unAsquithian gesture hurled the book out of the window.

When her engagement to Henry Asquith was at last announced on 19 February 1894 it came as a surprise to no one. As Lady Frances Balfour said: 'It was an event for which society was prepared, as one partner in the happy event had taken all and sundry into her confidence.'[65]

Queen Victoria however was amazed that so cautious a politician should choose to marry such a seemingly frivolous woman. Asquith, who was not familiar with Court procedure, wrote to Sir Henry Ponsonby to ask if Royal consent was required, and the Queen noted on the back of his letter, 'How curious . . . *that he* shd. ask if my consent is required to his marriage. If this *was* required the Queen wd. not give it as she thinks she is most unfit for a C. Minister's wife. V.R.I.'[66]

The Cabinet postponed its meeting so as not to clash with the wedding, which took place on 10 May 1894. Excited crowds lined the pavements from Grosvenor Square to St George's, Hanover Square. Margot's old nurse at the entrance to the church was offered £10 and then 'anything you like' for her ticket by a man who said, 'I must see Margot Tennant married.'[67]

Even Margot could not have prophesied that four Prime Ministers would sign the marriage register. Gladstone represented the past, Rosebery the present and Balfour and the bridegroom the future.

The last marriage in Charles's first family was that of his eldest son, Edward Priaulx Tennant, to Pamela Wyndham on 11 July 1895. She was one of the three lovely sisters immortalised in Sargent's 'The Three Graces', which hangs in the Metropolitan Museum of Art in New York. The other two sisters were Mary, Countess of Wemyss and Mrs Adeane.

Edward was Liberal Member of Parliament for Salisbury from 1906 to 1910. He built Wilsford House in Wiltshire, where he and Pamela lived for many years. After his father died he inherited The Glen. He was a keen fisherman and a good shot. He loved Glen and did much in forestry there. In 1911 he was made Lord High Commissioner to the General Assembly of the Church of Scotland, and was created Baron Glenconner. He died in 1920.

On 21 January 1895, the year of Edward's marriage, Emma died. Margot wrote: 'Mama is dead. She died this morning and Glen is not my home any more: I feel as if I should be "received" here in future instead of finding my own darling, tender little mother, who wanted arranging for and caring for, and to whom my gossipy trivialities were precious and all my love stories a trust.'[68]

Emma, in the tradition of the Victorian family, had borne twelve children, and as so often happened, only eight had survived childhood; but these eight had all brought into their mother's life at Glen and in Grosvenor Square an astonishing number of brilliant people. She was rather shy and often lacking in self-confidence, but she managed to fulfil her role as Charles's wife and as hostess to many different people very happily. Margot wrote 'Her twelve children, who took up all her time, accounted for some of her "à quoi bon" attitude towards life, but she had little or no concentration, and a feminine mind both in its purity and inconsequence; she was the least self-centred and self-scanned of human beings, unworldly and uncomplaining.'[69]

In the *Peebles Advertiser and County Newspaper*, 1895, there is an account of the funeral at Traquair Church which was attended by Charles, his sons and their wives, his daughters and sons-in-law, Lord and Lady Ribblesdale, Mr and Mrs Asquith, Mr and Mrs H. J. Tennant M.P., and a great company of people from Innerleithen and Peebles, who had known and loved Emma. She was one of the oldest members of this little church, having attended the services there for forty years. There is a memorial to her in this church and in the churchyard are the gravestones of many of the Tennant family.

CHAPTER TWELVE

Sir Charles Tennant, second marriage

THERE is a signature in the visitors' book at Glen which appears for the first time on 28 September 1898. 'Marguerite A. Miles'. How the thirty-year-old Miss Miles met and married Charles, now a seventy-five-year-old widower, is the last chapter in this history of the Tennant family.

Four miles from Easton Grey, where Lucy and her husband Tom Graham-Smith lived, and where Charty and Tommy Ribblesdale used to keep their horses and hunt with the Beaufort Hounds, is the ancient and beautiful town of Malmesbury. Colonel Charles William Miles and his wife Maria lived on its outskirts in the large Victorian manor house of Burtonhill (now a Shaftesbury Home for Physically Handicapped Children). Peter, as he was always known, was the ninth child of Philip John Miles, perhaps Bristol's most respected and successful merchant prince, who formed a superb collection of Old Master paintings at his home at Leigh Court. Peter's elder brother William was created a baronet in 1859. Maria Miles was the third child of Jeremiah and Frances Hill of Henbury, Bristol. Her maternal grandfather had been Thomas Daniel, a famous Lord Mayor of Bristol.

Maria was unusually talented in those skills that the Victorians spent so much time in cultivating. She always travelled with a small bag containing a water-colour-paint box, a silver water container, an ivory palette, pencils, brushes and a sketch-book. She made quick and beautiful sketches of the places she visited. She wrote frequently to her mother and sometimes painted the view from her window on the envelope, often skilfully incorporating the Penny Red stamp into her design. Some Victorian envelopes were printed with designs, but hand-painted envelopes were uncommon and Maria's form a remarkable and rare collection. She was also an accomplished performer on the piano and the violin and she had a lovely singing voice.

Peter had the reputation of being the hardest heavy-weight rider of his day. He hunted four or five days a week and was the Honorary Secrctary of the Beaufort Hunt. Marguerite nearly always drove her father to the meet in their American waggon which seated eight people. She was very fond of driving and said that she had inherited good hands from her father and that most horses went well with her.

W. H. Bromley in 1852 wrote a long and entertaining poem 'A legend of the Quorn Countrie' which describes a confrontation between Miles and Gilmour, another famous heavy-weight horseman:

'Twas in November's dreary sky
Strange meteors were seen to fly;
And rumour spread throughout the land
That some convulsion was at hand,
And presently the fact was known,
That one who weighed near seventeen stone,
Light of hand and firm of seat
Arrived at Quorn was hard to beat
Well! all men deemed the fact absurd,
And Gilmour laughed at what he heard;
And not until he saw the man,
The sinking in his boots began.
....

'My name he said is Peter Miles,
'And there is none like me
'From Land's End to Northumberland,
'And all the North Countrie.
'You Melton men, you Leicester knaves
'Come ride with me, say I
'Five minutes over Skeffington,
'And then lie down and die
....
But he who was not wont to brook
A hasty word an angry look,
Now with a meek submissive face
Yielded the trophies of the chase,
Without a blow resigned his sway,
And Miles triumphant leads the way.
....
And none with him dispute the right
To lead the field from morn to night,
But though among the thrusting train,
You seek for Gilmour's face in vain;
Wait till the second horsemen pass,
And see a form—'tis his alas!
The heavy-weight who funks the stiles,
And trembles at the name of Miles.[1]

Colonel Miles became the Conservative Member of Parliament for Malmesbury in 1880. He was a very popular man and after the result was announced he and Mrs Miles were drawn back to Burtonhill in a landau by the people, amidst tremendous cheering and shouting. Charles Tennant, the new member for Peebles and Selkirk, who sat on the opposite benches, would one day become his son-in-law.

On non-hunting days neighbours came over to Burtonhill to play tennis. It was a happy house which always bustled with activity. There were large house-parties, particularly during the hunting season. The Mileses arranged many events to raise money for local charities. There were *tableaux vivants*, amateur dramatics, musical evenings and impromptu dances. Sometimes, almost on the spur of the moment, the young people would organise fancy dress dances, designing for themselves the most remarkable costumes. Among the visitors to Burtonhill were the Graham-Smiths, the Ribblesdales and Margot Tennant. Later, when she looked back to those days, Marguerite always said that she would not have believed it if someone had told her that she would marry their father.

In the summer the Miles family moved to London, which Marguerite did not enjoy. But she was interested in Parliament and records that her mother used to take her to the House of Commons. She was present when John Bright resigned and Mr Gladstone spoke in reply: 'The scene impressed itself on my memory, looking down through the grille from the Ladies' Gallery, and seeing these two fine old gentlemen below me, speaking in very measured tones.[2]

Marguerite became one of the best women golfers of her day. In the winter of 1885 the family moved to Pau in the South of France to enable her father to recuperate from a severe congestion of the lungs. Here she was taught by a Dutchman, Bobby Boreel, and she was such an apt pupil that she won the Gold Medal on the Ladies' Links. In 1894 and 1895 she competed successfully in the Ladies' Golf Championships at Westward Ho and at Gullane in East Lothian. She was also good at lawn tennis and at billiards.

After her father's death in 1892 Marguerite with her mother and sister went to live with her ninety-one-year-old grandmother, Frances Hill, at Henbury House near Bristol. When she died they moved to a small house, Woodhill, at Gerrards Cross, where in 1897 Mrs Miles herself died.

Marguerite first met Sir Charles Tennant on 10 June 1898 at one of Lord Burnham's house parties at Hall Barn near Gerrards Cross. She records:

> Sir Charles Tennant and Lucy Graham-Smith came to stay. From the moment I was introduced to him he never took his eyes off me. We played golf on Sunday, and on Monday morning he made plans that I should dine in Grosvenor Square at two of his big dinner parties. I stayed

a good deal with a friend who had a flat in South Audley Street that summer, and often before he went to the city he would pop in to see me. . . . He made me promise that I would stay at Glen in August.

With characteristic impatience, Charles conducted a whirlwind romance which took his children completely by surprise. As a result Marguerite's initial reception by her future stepchildren was tearful and melodramatic. Margot said she would travel to Glen to say good-bye to it and all the people there; this, she proclaimed, was the end for her of the place she loved so dearly. All Charles's children were older than Marguerite and she herself was forty-five years younger than Charles. In mid-October he was still addressing her as 'My dear Miss Miles' but on 25 October Marguerite noted in her diary:

'Sir C. came at five and dashed in after dinner. All arranged.'

Determined as he was, Charles must have been worried about the reactions of his family and friends. Writing to Marguerite on 28 October he said: 'All have received our news affectionately and lovingly so that any little misgivings of mine have vanished and you will be welcomed as my bride by all.' No doubt the difference in age seemed smaller than it really was, for he was physically extremely fit and his mind was still like quicksilver. The day after the engagement was announced his son-in-law Henry Asquith wrote:

Brooks's
Oct. 26, 1898

My dear Sir Charles,

I dined here tonight with Haldane and Tweedmouth and I availed myself of the permission you gave me when we parted, I told them the news.

Both were full of congratulations and good wishes for the future.

I hope you will have a comfortable journey, and I am sure you will receive at home, from those whom I have endeavoured to prepare for the new situation, the warmest and most affectionate of welcomes.

Yrs. ev. affly.
H. H. Asquith

I am going to tell Rosebery tomorrow morning.

Marguerite, unlike Charles and his first wife Emma, kept letters she received from her husband and members of his first family. There are several hundred and some are quoted in this chapter. They are in the possession of the family.

From Lord Rosebery:

Dalmeny Park
Edinburgh
Nov. 2. '98

My dear Tennant,

I could not stop to speak to you yesterday, being in charge of an incognito Empress. But I wanted to wish you joy of your marriage. You have, I doubt not, made a wise choice, and must have carefully considered the comfort and happiness that it will impart to your life. May all that comfort and happiness be yours. This is the sincerest wish of one who may now claim to call himself a very old friend.

Other letters of congratulation poured in. R. B. Haldane wrote:

You know how intimate I am with Asquith. It was not unnatural that last night he should tell me *in confidence* the news that is interesting him so much. The same thing struck us both—that your life for several years past has been a very lonely one, & that this event will bring a new and very great interest into it. The Glen & Grosvenor Square must often have seemed solitary places of late & now all this will be changed.

You and your bride will have the best and warmest wishes for your happiness from an unusually great circle of friends, & I wish to be one of the first of these to write to congratulate you.

William Gladstone's widow wrote shakily on black-edged notepaper on 12 November: 'It was most kind of you to write and tell me of your marriage rather than tell me by any one else & most sincerely do I hope that you may have every blessing. I well know your very kind heart from everything we have received from you.'

Margot's earlier worries about the marriage had clearly been dispelled before the ceremony. In November she wrote to her father: 'No father, not the Duke of Westminster or any rich man has been such an angel of generosity to their children as you've been & there is nothing we would not do for you. I can think of nothing but you & pray for your happiness. I am particularly fond of Marguerite and feel grateful for her feeling for me & all of us & am sure you will be happy.'

Charles made the wedding arrangements and took a great interest in his bride's trousseau. On one occasion he wired her about some fur for a new coat which he feared might be of poor quality, saying he 'would rather pay more and have it handsome'.

The marriage took place at 2.30 on Friday, 25 November 1898 in the Church of St Saviour, Walton Place, London. Marguerite was given away by her eldest brother Colonel Napier Miles, who commanded the First Life Guards. Godfrey Webb, one of the Souls, was best man. This choice must have pleased Charles' children as Webb was a frequent visitor to Glen and godfather to Margot's daughter. Afterwards a reception was held at 13 Chesham Place, home of Colonel and Mrs Miles, where some of the ninety-five presents were displayed.

Charles and Marguerite returned to Glen the following day. Writing to his eldest son Edward, Charles says:

> We are happy here. She has made the acquaintance of everyone and they are all delighted with her, both in the house and outside. We were received with a cheer at the Galashiels station, with a perfect ovation at Innerleithen, and here the courtyard was a blaze of light and every man, woman and child in the place—a lovely clear night. She thanked them all gracefully for their welcome, and I said

a few words, and they gave us ringing cheers which we will not soon forget. To-day it is blowing a gale, but she has driven the ponies up to see Mrs Dalgleish [a shepherd's wife] whom she had not called on. They were so pleased with her visit. She is a beautiful whip and can give us all lessons in the art—her father made her always drive him and she is very fond of it. Last night she played and sang to the guitar, a beautiful instrument which was made for the Queen of Spain and was given to her by a relation of her mother who had been in Spain. She has a charming voice which she has not cultivated as much as she ought, the violin having been her great attraction. You will be astonished with what she does on that. She goes through the Greenhouses every day, Mr McIntyre [the head gardener] feels that he has got someone to look after them now, as she had charge of her father's gardens and knows a great deal. She does the flowers in the rooms and is never idle, so you see we have rather a new life here.

Half-way through their first meal together at Glen, as Charles sat at the head of the table with Marguerite beside him, he took out a leather case and opened it. Inside was a magnificent necklace of emeralds and diamonds which he lovingly presented to his young wife.

Charles' second marriage transformed him. Violet Bonham-Carter, Margot's step-daughter, remembered how when she was staying at Glen he appeared calm and fulfilled and had lost all his old feverish restlessness.(3) This was the effect Marguerite was to have on him for the rest of his life. His second marriage in no way slowed down his busy career. He was still often away from home and he expected a line from Marguerite every day, responding by sending her a daily bulletin himself.

Marguerite's new life cannot have been easy. Never could she have imagined that she would become the stepmother of men and women older than herself. Furthermore she was not Scottish and she had been brought up in a Tory household. Her father had sat in Parliament in opposition to the Tennant family's friends and hero, Mr Gladstone. Yet she seems to have surmounted many of these difficulties, as letters from her new stepsons and stepdaughters testify. Margot wrote to her: 'I heard by letter from Papa to R [Lord Ribblesdale] how *very very* happy he is and what a welcome they have all given you.'

Alfred Lyttelton wrote:

> This is just a line which you must not trouble to answer to say how deeply we enjoyed our visit to Glen and to thank you for the very large share which you contributed to our enjoyment. Naturally I have a feeling for Glen which is quite separate and apart from anything else. For many years it has been the home of my most dear memories. I do think it is a triumph of delicate kindness that you shd. have made me feel no change, except the delightful change in the happiness and well-being of the Bart, & that involved in the addition which your own many gifts have made to him and to all of us. It was an hourly pleasure to see the happiness which you have brought to the Bart.

Charty's feelings were similar in her letter of 8 September:

> I have been so busy since I returned with my house full that I have never had a second to write and Tell you how tremendously I enjoyed my week with you. I have never loved any place so much as Glen, nor do I ever feel so well as there, every outline of it is dear to me, & you were so sweet to me & to everybody that you made us all happy.
>
> I told Miss Hill that I never knew anybody so sweet under such trying circumstances, you were never irritable as I should have been. I think you showed the most lovely self-control & I felt you an example to us all. I like seeing you and Papa together though he is sometimes rather naughty in his chaff, but he enjoys it so much, poor darling, that you are so wise not to mind it,—as I know I should.

All this must surely have been made possible only by the complete fulfilment that Marguerite found in her marriage.

On 9 April Margot wrote to Lord Curzon: 'She is expecting a baby in October which is a great feat. Eddy and Jack are in the same proud position and Frank's wife had a little son 10 days ago—the 3 sons and the father *en même temps*, our race does not look like dying out yet!'

24. Sir Charles Tennant was throughout his life a very keen golfer, who practised his game at every opportunity and in the most surprising places.

25. The thirty-year-old Marguerite Miles married the seventy-five year old Sir Charles Tennant in 1898, and bore him four more children. She is sitting beneath 'The Frankland Sisters' by John Hoppner which was one of the many superb paintings at 40 Grosvenor Square. It is now in the National Gallery, Washington, D.C.

26. Tennant's Stalk from Sighthill Cemetery looking south, photographed in 1900. The chimney was finally demolished with the aid of high explosives in 1922.

27. Sir Charles' second family in 1904. Nannie Skinner (who was 65 years with the Tennant family and died in her 90th year in 1958) holds Nancy (Crathorne); Katharine (Elliot of Harwood) is in the pram and Peggy (Wakehurst) is on the right.

There were great rejoicings at Glen when Marguerite gave birth to a daughter at 12.30 a.m. on 4 November, the day Charles had been born seventy-six years earlier. She was christened Margaret, but was always known as Peggy. Two days later Charty Ribblesdale wrote from Gisburne Park, Clitheroe to her father:

> I must send you true words of love and congratulation on the arrival of my little sister. Laura says she must write a letter from the niece of 7 years old to the one-day-old aunt! It seems odd to have the niece much older than the aunt! I have written to tell Marguerite how pleased I am that she is out of her troubles and that she has got a dear little companion for life, which a son wd. not have been.
>
> Is the daughter like you or Marguerite? I hope she is like you & girls often take after their father more than their mother. . . .
>
> Bless you, darling, I am sure your new daughter will be a delicious plaything for you.
>
> Your loving child,
> Charty.

Shortly after Peggy's birth Marguerite started another child. Margot, who was also pregnant, wrote to her on 20 April 1900:

> Thanks for a very tender and darling letter. You May trust me not to tell a *soul* of yr. affairs at all times. I think 2 babies together are delicious & am glad you are going to have another. I don't think I want you to have a large family but I think 2 or 3 is heavenly. Lucy *is* brave but low about herself & her hands are a crushing blow to me, also when tired she is fearfully lame my heart aches for her when I see her eyes filling with tears watching baby and me picking primroses. She is going to be *here* [Easton Grey] most of the season and with me when she is in London. The kindest thing you cd. do for her is to ask her to yr. opera box & pleasant dinners occasionally, its very dear of you to feel so full of compassion for her. Her life has been simply taken away & I worship the ground she treads on. The R's [Ribblesdales] & she go to Paris for Xhibition 15th May.

> We, H. [Henry Asquith] & I go we think for Whitsuntide though I shall be big and ugly I expect then. I'm marvellously tiny now but it won't last.

Because of her pregnancy Marguerite was unable to travel to Paris with Charles in September to see the International Exhibition. The Prince of Wales, who had shown a strong interest in it, had asked Charles if he would lend some of his paintings by Reynolds, Constable, Bonington and Morland. The exhibits were mainly eighteenth-century paintings, but there were also some works by Burne-Jones, whose paintings the Prince of Wales particularly admired. The British pavilion, designed by Lutyens, was a curious mixture of styles, one façade being a direct copy of a Jacobean house at Bradford-on-Avon. The library was fitted and furnished by the Corporation of the City of Bath.

A letter from Mr Robson, of Messrs Radley, Robson & Mackay, written to Charles says: 'I am sure whoever hung the pictures favoured yours, and you would have been delighted to have heard the acclamations of pleasure made by the people who were visiting the collection, mostly French people, and they had a keen appreciation for the Reynolds and Constables.'

Charles' comments are contained in the following letter to Marguerite, dated 27 September:

> I have just come in from a long tour in the Rue des Nations, very interesting but very fatiguing, on one's legs for about three hours. I will tell you all about it when we meet. The weather is divine and adds a charm to the scene. The exterior is even more striking than the interiors, many of the latter are like big shops which you can see anywhere.
>
> I am glad to get yrs. of Tuesday. The English Pavilion but for the pictures would be a failure; it is not well done. My pictures are by far the most striking, but they really looked better at home; the backgrounds of mixed red and white paper are very bad and ought not to have been allowed.

In November 1900 a second daughter, Jean, was born at Glen—an attractive child with dark curly hair. Marguerite always thought she must have sustained some injury at birth as she never developed normally and died in 1910.

Charles's political views were now undergoing a change much to the consternation of his family and to Margot in particular. He had been against Harcourt's introduction of death duties in 1894 and in the election of 1900 at the height of the Boer War he supported the Conservatives for reasons which he explained in two letters to Marguerite:

> Elections going as expected. I said Glasgow would not return a single opponent of the Govt. and the result has confirmed my prophecy. It is not a question of Tory and Liberal—it is a question of supporting the Govt. of the Country in a national crisis and this is the cause of the large Unionist majorities.

and later the same day:

> I have just come in to find yours and Margot's telegrams. You know that my sympathies are with the Govt. at this crisis. Eddy, as you know, stood without consulting me at all. I will, however, send a telegram to Mr Henry Ballantyne, his Chairman, tomorrow, expressing a sincere hope that their efforts to send my son to Parliament as their representative will be crowned with success. I could not attend the meeting without speaking and I could not conceal my views. It wd. in my opinion amount to a calamity for the Empire if Lord Salisbury was turned out of power at this moment.

The Liberals did badly in the Election and Margot wrote to Marguerite on 2 November assessing the new Conservative Cabinet. About her husband she said: 'I can't help aching a little inside when I see my Henry so head and shoulders above these young men, in the prime of his life and intellectual powers, waiting on C.-B. [Campbell-Bannerman] and loyally serving our quarrelsome badly led lot, without a thought for himself in this world. I believe in taking the chance when it is offered—poor old boy he feels it all tho' he says little.'

Margot was clearly beginning to regret the decision she and Henry had taken the previous year when the question of the leadership of the Liberal Party had been discussed. As she explained to Lord Curzon in a letter dated 9 April 1899:

> our house was thronged with whips etc. all wanting Henry to succeed Harcourt but after a long talk with Henry we agreed it was too heavy a loss of income & that if C.B. took it & H. did all he cd. for him we cd. work the thing fairly well till the next Gen. Election, when with a great deal of economizing & care we sd. have put by some of H's earnings at the Bar & start fresh. C.B. is not young or very strong & is not likely to prove a formidable rival, he is devoted to H. & is a dear old thing & was quite delightful about it all & so it was fixed up and you know the rest.

Later in the same letter she says

> Papa's marriage has made it clear that we can't hope for anything more from him. He has been a very splendid father to all of us & is as happy & well as he can be.

Nevertheless Henry entrusted Lord Haldane with the delicate task of asking Lord Rosebery and A. J. Balfour to put in a good word with Charles to encourage him to increase his daughter's allowance.[(4)] In spite of his changing political views 'The Bart' relieved Asquith of his financial worries by settling the substantial sum of £5000 a year on Margot, and on 20 October 1901 Henry wrote from Duncombe Park, Helmsley: 'The question of gradually giving up the Bar, so as to be able to devote my whole time and strength to public life has been occupying my thoughts a great deal since your generous kindness made it possible to put pecuniary considerations in the second place.'

Margot had underestimated not only her husband's skill but also her father's extraordinary generosity.

One of the chief political issues at this time was the controversy of Free Trade versus Protection. The Liberal Party had always upheld Free Trade and Asquith was their ablest spokesman on the subject. The Unionists were split, with Balfour rather weakly upholding the traditional Tory position and Joseph Chamberlain coming out firmly in favour of Protection. Both Asquith and Chamberlain toured the country making fiery speeches and the exchange became something of a gladiatorial contest.

It was a great blow to Margot when Charles, who had been a Free Trader all his life, joined Joseph Chamberlain's Tariff Reform committee in 1903. She and her father seldom discussed political questions in writing but she often wrote to Marguerite, who had now become a confidante for her stepchildren. Several letters contain requests such as: 'I want you to use your influence with Papa.'

Margot wrote to Marguerite on 24 June 1903: 'I have always been quite open with you dearest & I must tell you Henry has been a little hurt by Papa's deserting him at a critical moment in his life,' and the following December: 'Dear Papa, I long to see him and put my arms round his neck and tell him that nothing makes any difference between us, but of course I cd. sob when I think that he and I for the first time (except on Home Rule—I was *never* a Home Ruler) in our lives disagree on a subject wh. will be the making or marring of my husband's life.'

Family unity was clearly preserved as in the same letter Margot writes: 'The whole hunting-field congratulated me on papa's dividend in Champion Reefs, 165 per cent—its too splendid! I told them it was entirely papa who had done it.'

Margot was clearly still hoping to alter her father's opinion when she wrote to Marguerite:

> I am sorry Papa is not a Free Trader but he and I have differed over politics often and it makes no difference to us, *we never* quarrel. It may interest him however to hear that public opinion of the *best* kind is against him and Joe. It is quite true that some of our things go to the wall but you must sacrifice the smaller for the greater. Our trade returns are better this year than they have ever been. We are *immensely* rich, the war has hardly been felt. We are not going to risk being poor and dislocating *all* our trade and upsetting the Colonies between themselves & offending everyone to please a minority led by Joe [the Rt. Hon.

Joseph Chamberlain M.P.]. He is a wonderful *administrator* & a big man but he has never legislated one successful thing from three acres and a cow when he was a radical, his German alliance, his old age pensions & now this. Sir R. Finlay who is here told Frances Balfour [Lady Frances Balfour, daughter of the Duke of Argyll], 'Joe has gone mad.' Arthur Balfour is here and looks worn and ill. We don't speak of home politics only foreign affairs, books and golf. It makes one smile (if it did not make me cry for Arthur's sake whom I *love*) to think that Tuesday, Chaplin brings in his amendment to reimpose the duty on corn (wh. as you know the Govt. took off in their Budget) & that it will be beaten by a large majority—all of us and all the big men on the Govt. front bench. It will be beaten by a Gov. committed to Protection, but I fancy he will be asked to withdraw his amendment as the situation would be grotesque. Lady Frances says at Hatfield they are all wild with Joe for launching all this in his wild speech without half the Cabinet even knowing. Old Free Traders like Lansdowne, Devonshire, Selborne are naturally upset. Anyhow it will be very exciting—and I will read IX Century [sic]—we are flooded with literature on both sides. Strachey of Spectator dined with us & spoke almost with tears of this gigantic blunder.

Protection was brought in by the Government in 1900 and Lady Violet Bonham-Carter remembered that Margot hid *The Scotsman*, which was in favour of Protection, in the lining of the curtains at Glen so that Charles, who had become a Protectionist, could not read it!

Charles's energy remained amazing. Something of his powerful presence can be seen in the impressive portrait of him by Sargent, painted in 1901. (See Plate 22). It is an excellent likeness and, as the artist himself said, he had 'caught something at a favourable moment'. He was still attending innumerable board meetings in London and elsewhere and travelling incessantly. By 1900 his connections with Glasgow had lessened. He therefore sold 195 West George Street and bought a large house called Broadoaks in Byfleet, thirty miles from London (now part of the Ministry of Defence). Here he was able to indulge once more in one of his favourite pursuits, that of the amateur landscape architect. At Glen he had had half a century in which to see his ideas materialise and his home bears evidence of his excellent eye and skill in the creation of sweeping curves and beautifully placed clumps of trees and shrubs. At Broadoaks he could start again. First he supervised every detail of the building alterations, which included the addition of a large stable block. By 1902 he was able to concentrate on the gardens. Writing to Marguerite on 4 March of that year, he describes his annoyance that:

> Trees ordered have not arrived and the time for planting is fast passing away and this delay has been entirely unnecessary.
>
> House very well on indeed—looks well though larger than I expected. Stables up to the height of walls—they too look very large—must plant them out with Scotch Firs & oaks & hollies—poplars of no use—Robinson quite wrong to have planted so many—I don't like them at all, and Ashdown says they are 'really of no use'. I wish you would write to Robinson not to order any more trees abroad. He was astonished at the hollies I had got from Waterers—the fact is, he does not know their nursery and does not go there. I will get all the trees now myself and from the local nurseries which it is my wish and duty to encourage. What we require for our large Belt are oaks, Beech, Birch and Hollies—and purple Beech, I will not have any Poplars.

With remarkable speed an azalea garden, a rock garden, a rose garden and a Dutch garden were created and after Charles's death the magazine *Garden Life* commented 'among modern gardens in Surrey those of Broadoaks take the first place in point of beauty and variety'.

Charles and Marguerite came to love Broadoaks and spent a considerable amount of time there. Soon the large house was filled with fine mezzotints, Chinese porcelain and paintings—all the things with which Charles liked to surround himself.

In 1902 he bought another property which he called Glenconner. This was in North Berwick, which was a very fashionable golfing resort at that time. Glenconner was an attractive small Scottish baronial house which was decorated in Georgian style, and as usual Charles filled its rooms with works of art, including prints by Fragonard and Turner. (Glenconner is now lived in by Charles's granddaughter, the Hon. Mrs John Reader-Harris and her family.) He and Marguerite both loved golf and they had been drawn to North Berwick for this reason. Frank and Annie Tennant who lived near them at Hynford House wrote: 'This place is simply crowded and people sit on the grass in crowds round the tee waiting for their turn. It took Miss Choate an hour and ten minutes to do two holes. Frank goes to Muirfield every day as you cannot really golf here.'

Charles liked to practise his golf strokes whenever he possibly could, which would sometimes mean at the strangest possible times. When he was staying in Biarritz in 1904 his hotel room was immediately above that of Baron von Eckhardstein, who noted: 'All night long I heard "Ping, Ping, Ping" over my head, on making enquiries I found that the old gentleman had been playing golf and practising mashie shots into his chamber pot all night.'[5] Marguerite wrote after his death: 'Never a day passed that he did not hit a golf ball and I would often find him swinging his clubs indoors. His energy and application were unceasing and his vitality amazing. . . . Billiards was just the same. In everything he always aimed at the highest pitch of excellence,' Grosvenor Square was also a favourite practice ground where flower beds and groups of shrubs made ideal obstacles for Charles's mashie shots.

On 17 January 1903 the *Morning Post* records 'Lady Tennant gave birth to a daughter on 15th—at 40 Grosvenor Square—Both are doing well.' This was Katharine's arrival —Charles's fifteenth child and the third by the second marriage. As has been recorded earlier in this book one of the characteristics of his family was that his children alternately had fair and dark, curly and straight hair. Katharine's was curly and fair and of the variety which has been known as Tennant hair—very curly indeed.

A year later on 20 August Marguerite's fourth and last child by Charles, Nancy, was born at Glen, fifty-four years after her eldest half-sister Janet, when her father was eighty-one. The story goes that one day the new baby was brought in to Charles by the nanny as he was showing a friend his paintings in 40 Grosvenor Square. 'Another work by an old master!' the friend aptly remarked.

Charles and Marguerite entertained lavishly at 40 Grosvenor Square and one particularly happy occasion was the dance they gave in May 1905 for Margot's step-daughter Violet Asquith and Charles's grandchild Frances Tennant. On the day of the ball Charles sent them each a diamond necklace. Violet recalls how conspicuous they felt as it was the custom for young girls to wear pearls, not diamonds.(6)

The *Onlooker* of 3 June said: 'The whole thing was quite delightful. . . . Lady Tennant is such a splendid hostess, and though this is the only dance she is giving this season, she will probably give a number of her smart dinners. . . . The house is a gorgeous one, and the immense double drawing-room which was cleared for dancing, was all done in pink roses, which with the wonderful collection of pictures, made a brilliant display.' The *Onlooker* also noticed the presence of amongst others, the Duchess of Wellington, Lady Gosford, the Duke of Marlborough and Lord Churchill, 'who literally danced the whole evening'.

When Peggy, Katharine and Nancy were born their step-sisters were very well known and the *Ladies' Field* of September 1904 remarked: 'It will be interesting in the future to note whether they attain anything like the position and reputation of their step-sisters'. As two of them are active in public and private life and the third is the part-author of this book, a short account of their lives is given in Appendix I.

In 1905 during the absence of Charles and Marguerite Glen was largely destroyed by fire. They had lent the house to Eddie, Pamela and their children, who mercifully were unharmed. The factor wrote that the damage was terrible.

The letter was received while Charles and his wife were playing golf at Biarritz and he characteristically insisted on finishing the game before digesting its contents. The pictures and *objets d'art* were saved but the structure was destroyed. The rebuilding of the house by Sir Robert Lorrimer in the style of the original architect was begun almost immediately.

Charles never saw Glen again. He became unwell at Biarritz in March 1906. The King who was staying in the same hotel visited him on several occasions and sent his doctor to attend him. Charles was able to return to London in May and he went immediately to Broadoaks. His condition weakened and on 4 June 1906 he died. His family travelled by train with his coffin to Innerleithen and thence they processed to the family burial ground at Traquair, one and a half miles from Glen.

Over one hundred newspapers carried obituaries, emphasising different aspects of his varied life. Of them all, that which gives the most vivid picture of the indomitable old man is one which appeared on 16 June. It is written by a friend with deep affection.

> If you happened to be walking along the Thames Embankment about eleven o'clock up to a few years ago and watched the steady stream of hansoms, motors, and broughams which flow along that splendid thoroughfare towards the City, you were sure to be attracted by a certain figure—always in a hansom, by the way, and never in the costlier and more private conveyance.
>
> I recall the face and figure as I saw it many a morning when my occupations brought me to an office close to the Embankment, and here is my recollection of it. A face long, thin, almost hatchet-shaped—the face that nearly always goes with grim resolution and doggedness of character; the whiskers white, thickish, not long, beautifully combed so that they formed as it were an aureole; the eyes grey, bright, tranquil, large and open; the mouth beautifully chiselled, the upper lip shaven and finely curved—a strong as well as handsome mouth; and the figure the exact complement, so to speak, of the face—that is to say, thin, alert, finely proportioned, and so beautifully fitted

into the clothes as almost to suggest that this carefully dressed and spick-and-span man wore in his old age the stays in which the young Prussian guardsman encases his person. Of course there were no stays, but the trimness of the figure and the clothes fitting with the closeness of a glove, suggested the idea to you.

This was how Sir Charles Tennant looked as he rode every morning to the City when he was in London. He looked exactly the same wherever you saw him—always perfectly dressed, always trim, always alert, always moving with the grace, the elasticity and the rapidity of a man who had an indomitable and restless spirit and the ease of one who had been trained in some great school of drill and gymnastics.

You might see him late at night at one of our London routs, and instead of the yawning, tired, bored creatures that most men and women are who burn the candle at both ends in the driving life of London, he was as alert, as interested in everything that went on, as ready to chat with you as if he were the young maid going through the ecstasy of her first season. If you followed him to that beautiful home of his in Scotland he was again the same; a perfect host, delighted to show you all the abounding art treasures of his house, the masterpieces of the ancient masters, or a beautiful little book picked up in Italy, or a Marie Stuart medallion.

It was indeed a full life. At one time he was director of no fewer than twenty companies; in Glasgow he had gigantic Chemical Works—the tall stack is one of the landmarks of the city; in far-off India he was one of the chief proprietors of one of the biggest of gold mines in the country. Cautious and yet daring he had made money in everything, and a gigantic income, most of which he could claim to have earned by his own indomitable industry, skill, foresight and courage.

By his first wife he had twelve children, and through his daughters he was associated with some of the remarkable men of his time—with Mr Asquith, with Mr Alfred Lyttelton, the late Colonial Secretary, with Lord Ribblesdale. Two of his sons, Edward his successor, and 'Jack'—as he is universally known—are members of Parliament.

Marrying when he was well advanced in life, he leaves a second family of four children and he died at the splendid age of eighty-three, alert, hopeful, and generous to the last.

Of the numberless stories told of his kindness of heart I just choose one from those I have seen. He was an ardent sportsman and on the sacred twelfth was always one of the first in the field. A guilty poacher was his natural born enemy, but when one was brought before him by his gamekeepers he simply reproved the rascal and then, as he looked hungry, told him to go round to the kitchen and have some food.

He belongs to that wondrous race of robust Scotsmen, who are the leaders in so many walks of life and who carry the robust physique of their native land that makes them young at eighty into the fevered life of towns.

The descendants of the Tennants recorded in this biography run into hundreds, perhaps thousands. They have spread out all over the world, to the United States, Canada, Australia and South Africa. A look at the genealogical tables shows that many of these descendants have held, or hold, positions of influence in politics, industry, the city and in every branch of the arts. Many of them have merited biographies of their own. This book records for the present generation the story of their forebears, and for others the example of an enterprising family.

Appendix I

Sir Charles Tennant's second family

Margaret (Peggy) was born in 1899 and married John de Vere Loder in 1920. During their fifty years of married life Peggy supported her husband devotedly in all his public work. She was particularly interested in mental health and founded the Northern Ireland Association for Mental Health. John was Conservative Member of Parliament from 1924–9 and from 1931–6. After the death of his father he became the 2nd Baron Wakehurst. In 1937 he went to New South Wales as Governor and he and his wife lived there until after the war. They returned home in 1945. In 1952 he was appointed Governor of Northern Ireland. He and Peggy took an active part in the life of the Province and retired in 1964. He was Lord Prior of the Order of St John, in 1962 he was made a Knight of the Garter. In 1965 she was made a D.B.E. and Hon. LL.D. of Queen's University, Belfast. In 1971 she was created a Dame Grand Cross of The Order of St John. John died in October 1970. They have four children—Henrietta, who married John Reader-Harris in 1953; Christopher, who married Inge Hess in 1956; David and Robert.

Katharine was born in 1903 and married the Rt Hon Walter Elliot, C.H., M.C., F.R.S., M.P., in 1934. He was awarded the M.C. and Bar in the First World War, and was a Conservative Member of Parliament for almost forty years. He held several Cabinet posts. After he died in 1958, Katharine fought a by-election in the Kelvingrove Division of Glasgow. She was not successful, but it was of interest that part of the constituency was the same as when Charles, her father, was returned for the Partick division of Glasgow in 1879 and in which the Tennant house in West George Street stood. Katharine inherited her father's energy, vitality and good health and has played a considerable part in national and international affairs throughout her life. She lives in Roxburghshire and farms at Harwood and is active on the county council. She also inherited her family's skill as a golfer and rider. In 1958 she was made D.B.E., and a Hon. LL.D. of Glasgow University. She and Peggy are the only two sisters who have ever been created D.B.E.s. In October 1958 she was one of the first women to be made a Life Peer, and in November of that year the first woman to make a speech in the House of Lords. She moved the loyal Address to the Queen in October 1962 at the opening of Parliament, the first time this had been done by a woman in the House of Lords. Seventy-eight years earlier, in Peebles in the General Election of 1880, Charles had said, in answer to a question, that he was not opposed to the then almost unheard-of idea of women in Parliament. In 1954–6–7 Katharine represented the United Kingdom as a Delegate to the United Nations. In 1969 she was a candidate in the Glasgow University Rectorial Election but was defeated by the Socialist, Lord Macleod of Fuinary. Things have changed since Margot wrote to Marguerite in 1902 saying 'Scotch Universities are as Tory as English are Liberal'!

Nancy, the sixteenth and youngest child, was born in 1904. She was like the fascinating Laura of her father's first family, lovely to look at, brilliant in conversation and a talented painter who exhibited works at the Royal Academy. She met Thomas Dugdale when he was Walter Elliot's best man at her sister's wedding and they married two years later in 1936. For thirty years he was Conservative Member of Parliament for Richmond, Yorkshire, and was in Winston Churchill's post-war Cabinet. In 1959 he was created 1st Baron Crathorne. Nancy greatly assisted her husband and became an excellent and entertaining speaker. She started and ran many youth and art activities in Yorkshire, for which she was awarded the O.B.E. in 1961. After her husband's retirement from active politics in 1959, she found a cause which fully exercised all her artistic interests and talents. In Richmond, Yorkshire, she restored the second oldest theatre in England, dating from 1788, which had been disused for a century. It was virtually a salvage-dump when Nancy started, but between 1960 and 1963, almost single-handed, she formed a trust and raised enough money to restore the building to its original form.

Since the inaugural performance in 1963 in which both Dames Sybil Thorndike and Edith Evans took part, the Georgian Theatre has presented drama, music and one-man shows of a high order. Nancy's taste in all these matters never failed. Rupert Hart-Davis wrote of her after her death in *The Times*, 20 May 1969: 'Ideally happy in her marriage and in the love of her two sons [James and David], she was a rare life-enhancer, inspiring by her infectious energy and warm affection, an almost universal devotion, of which she was innocently unaware . . . she was a life-giver, a benefactor and a blessing.'

Marguerite married Geoffrey Lubbock in 1908 and they had two sons Peter and David.

Appendix II

The Leblanc Process

Because of the importance of the Leblanc process to three generations of the Tennant family an understanding of its basic operation is relevant. The following plan and explanation, quoted from W. A. Campbell's *The Chemical Industry*, pp. 25–9, describes the process in its earliest and simplest form:

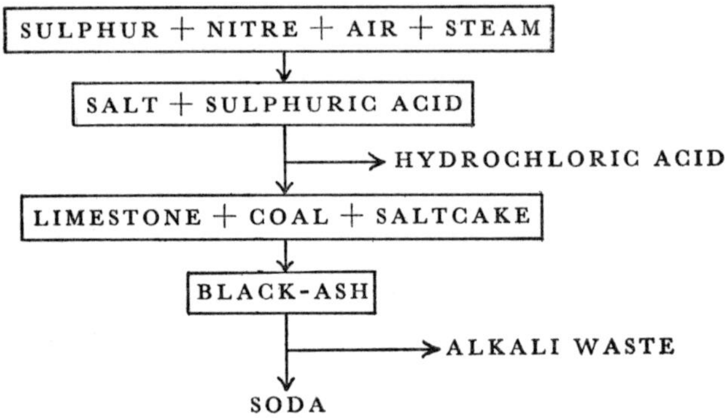

> In stage two of the process
>
> salt was decomposed with sulphuric acid with the formation of sodium sulphate (saltcake) and the consequent liberation of hydrochloric acid gas. In this operation the semi-liquid mass was heated in a reverberatory furnace with periodic raking to assist the escape of the hydrochloric acid gas. This section of the works was always marked by the presence of a tall chimney which drew the fire and helped to dissipate the acid fumes into the upper air. The hot mixture of sulphuric acid and salt was extremely corrosive, so that the iron pans and brick linings of

the furnaces needed frequent renewal, as did the implements used for raking. . . . The saltcake was trundled in barrows to the black-ash section where it was heated with coal and limestone: at first this was carried out in furnaces similar to those used in making saltcake, but later the famous 'revolvers' (mechanical furnaces for mixing the ingredients while they were being heated) were introduced. The black-ash was run into bogies, square iron boxes on wheels, and then allowed to cool. The cold lumps of cuboid form were by some curious logic termed 'balls', and the building in which they were collected was known as the 'ball-house'. . . . The crude ball soda was extracted with water in lixiviating (water extraction) tanks; hence the soda passed into solution and the calcium sulphide and coal ash were left behind. Waste heat from one or other of the furnaces was employed in evaporating the soda solution (tank-liquor) to give the product 'soda ash' or anhydrous sodium carbonate. The solid residue (tank waste) was either tipped on a heap outside the factory or taken out to sea in barges.

The outward form of an early Leblanc soda works would thus present itself as a collection of long low buildings to house the furnaces, overlooked by the lofty rectangular pile of the acid chambers and dominated by the tall chimney from which clouds of acrid fumes would issue at intervals of a few hours. Outside the walls, and gradually attaining an eminence of its own, would be the waste heap, a dark grey running eyesore at all times and in wet weather the source of a foetid sulphide smell.

Appendix III

Tennant's Stalk

This description, published in *The Mirror* of 4 December 1841, appeared while the chimney was being erected:

> The chimney is founded on a bed of solid sandstone rock, twenty feet below the surface of the ground. The diameter of this outer chimney is fifty feet at its foundation, forty feet diameter at the surface of the ground, and will diminish in an unbroken curved line of batter to a diameter of fourteen feet six inches when it will have attained an altitude of from 424 to 430 feet. The inner chimney is a cylinder of sixteen feet in diameter, rising perpendicularly to a height of 260 feet. The inner chimney is unconnected with the outer one, but comes very nearly in contact at its termination, allowing only for expansion arising from the temperature. The flues from the extensive works are introduced into the inner chimney through four circular apertures, each seven feet six inches in diameter; both chimneys are built with brick; between the sandstone rock and the brick footings there is a layer of concrete, four feet thick, composed of small broken whinstone and cement.
>
> The bricks used are from the Heathfield Brickworks and are of a very superior description, being a composition of common clay and fire clay, containing a small portion of iron ore. The Top of the chimney will be coped with granite.
>
> The chimney when completed will be elevated upwards of 600 feet above high water level at the Broomielaw; and will be an object of magnificent simplicity, and present to the traveller a landmark of colossal dimensions. The Stalk when completed will be about the height of the Great Pyramid of Egypt.

The chimney was completed on 28 June 1842, and at 435½ feet was then the highest in the world, remaining one of the chief land-marks of Glasgow for the next eighty years. It was used to take the products of combustion from about 120 tons of coal each day.

Appendix IV

St Rollox in 1858

J. D. Burn *Commercial Enterprise*, London 1858 p. 114–19

St Rollox Chemical Works

If there were no other manufacturing or commercial establishment in Glasgow than the stupendous works of Charles Tennant & Co, it would be a place of commercial importance. This chemical laboratory stands alone in its greatness, not only in Great Britain, but there is nothing equal to it in the whole world. . . .

The interior of St Rollox works is certainly the most extraordinary labyrinth ever man put his foot in. We have no idea of the number of furnaces in operation for making the three principal articles—soda, soda-ash, and chloride of lime—but there must be some hundreds. The soap department is, itself, a large manufactory. In this place sixty tons are produced upon an average weekly. When the soap has undergone the process of making, the material, while in a liquid state, is put into iron-frame moulds five feet deep by fifteen inches. When the soap becomes solidified, it is cut into long blocks by a fine piece of wire; these again are cut up into wedges of a certain weight and built up into large stalks. A stranger in going into this warehouse would conceive he was being introduced into the society of an immense quantity of bricks of various colours.

The most extraordinary part of the works is that in which the sulphuric acid is made. In going into this place we pass between two mountains of sulphur, each of which contains 5,000 tons. We then enter a devils den, with an immense row of glowing furnaces on each side of us, and huge lead tubes above our heads and around us. After we have been half-roasted, and our lungs, struggling with the atmosphere, are loaded with sulphuric gas, our good Mentor takes us up a flight of narrow wooden steps until we ascend some hundred feet above the surrounding buildings. It would be utterly impossible to describe the surprising scene that meets the view. Immediately beneath us there are fifty-eight lead chambers for receiving the sulphurous gas, and converting it into vitriol; each of these immense aerial reservoirs holds 21,000 cubic feet of gas. These chambers are approached by many miles of wooden stages, from which, down to the south and west, the huge city forms a most glorious picture, with the Cathedral in the foreground, marked with the impress of 700 years. Looking to the west, beyond the town, the Firth of Clyde expands, and again steals away among the mountains of Argyleshire, with the Castle of Dumbarton resting, as it were, on the bosom of the water. Turn which way we will, a magnificent panorama meets the eye. In looking to the south-west, we take in Langside, where poor Mary lost her kingdom, and the ruin of Crookston Castle, beneath whose walls she rested in feverish anxiety while her sad fate was being sealed. Turning our eyes to the north-east, we are confronted with the mammoth stalk . . . This huge monster is continually pouring his sooty treasures into the region of the clouds. If we cast our eyes to the north, we take in the range of the Campsie Hills, and we can discover the valley in the intermediate space along which the indefatigable Romans built a wall, to keep the hardy mountaineers in their own bleak wilds . . .

We are once more on the solid earth, and much of it is melting in our presence. Men are moving about like spirits in the fitful glare of the fiery furnaces; some are breaking up the mountains of crystallised soda, others again are bearing immense loads of salt into furnaces. We may mention that this material is the basis of all the leading articles manufactured in the works, with the exception of vitriol.

We are now introduced to the company of a pair of stills, in which the sulphuric acid is reduced in bulk and raised in strength. These stills are made of platina, no other material will stand a fellowship of such intense heat with the corroding liquid that passes through them. Upon leaving the work, we pass between huge air-tight chambers in which the chloride of lime is made. Eighteen tons of lime, finely powdered, is put into one of these compartments, and after it has undergone the necessary process, it comes out twelve tons heavier than when it went in, having absorbed two-thirds its weight in chlorine while undergoing the change . . . This part of the St Rollox chemical works only occupies thirteen acres!!!

About a hundred yards to the east, we arrive at another large work which cannot occupy less than three acres. When we enter here, the first thing that takes our attention, after passing the porter's lodge, is an immense mountain of wood hoops; these are brought from Norway where they are contracted for. Passing onward, we enter a large brick building, where our ears are greeted with the noise of a large amount of machinery. This is the St Rollox cooperage. From 800 to 900 casks, large and small, are turned out of this place weekly on an average the year round. Seeing so large an amount of work is done, we will necessarily look for an army of coopers. In this, however, we will be disappointed. Every part of a cask is fashioned and made by machinery. In one place the staves are planed and shaped; in another, the heads and bottoms are cut and bevelled. The staves necessary to form a cask are set up by men for the purpose with a single iron hoop; the embryo cask is then placed in a steam-chamber, and when taken out is put in another chamber, where the two halves of a mould of the required size are made to enfold the staves by the powerful aid of a Bramah press. When the cask comes out of one of these machines, it is braced tight by four strong iron hoops. All that requires to be done to complete the work, is to put on the wooden hoops and fit in the ends. Some idea may be formed of the immense number of hoops required for this work when it is known that each cask is bound by sixteen; this will give 134,000 weekly, or 6,710,000 annually! The most of the manual labour done in this place is performed by boys.

For some time past the firm of Charles Tennant & Co., have had screw steam vessels plying between London and Glasgow, and another steamer carries the produce of their works to the various ports of the Baltic, and returns freighted with materials for their own consumption. Numerous coasting vessels are constantly employed in bringing limestone from Ireland, and sulphur from Italy. The firm have also coalmines of their own, with an iron-foundry to supply the machinery and other necessary fittings for their works. It may appear incredible to many of our readers when we state that 100,000 tons of coals are consumed on the premises annually! The average number of men employed in the works is 1000; the number of people, however, employed directly and indirectly, must exceed that by at least eight times. The following materials were consumed in the year ending 1854:

Coal	...	90,162 tons	(If we take into account the coal dross consumed on the premises, we believe the entire quantity exceeds two hundred thousand tons annually.)
Limestone	...	30,000 tons	
Salt ...	...	17,000 tons	
Sulphur	...	5,600 tons	
Manganese	...	4,500 tons	

The whole of the chemical works are laid in all directions with permanent railways for the transit of both raw and manufactured materials.

From the returns made by Messrs Charles Tennant to the Industrial Exhibition of Paris in 1854, the following quantities of the subjoined articles were manufactured by them during the previous year:

Soda-ash ...	...	12,000 tons
Soda-ash in crystals	...	7,000 tons
Bleaching powder	...	7,000 tons
Sulphuric acid	...	2,000 tons

In reference to the sulphuric acid, we may mention that the above quantity was what was made for sale only. We believe the quantity required for their own use amounts to at least 14,000 tons annually.

It may be supposed that the sulphuric department of these works was highly pernicious to the health of those engaged in it. From what we have been able to learn, the average health of the men employed is equal to that of any similar number of unskilled labourers engaged in any other business. These gentlemen have always evinced a humane regard for the well-being of the people in their employ. For many years they have retained the services of a medical gentleman, who had long been known in Glasgow for his philanthropic and public spirit. They also support a school upon their own premises for the free education of the children of their workpeople. When we were in Glasgow in the early part of 1858 the Messrs Tennant were then erecting a large building for a new schoolhouse calculated to hold two thousand pupils. [It is doubtful whether the number would have been so large. It is more likely to have been around 800.] This school will provide an improved system of education for the children, both male and female, such as will enable them to go into the world very differently prepared to perform their parts on its stage to that of their parents.

Glasgow may be justly proud of the many living monuments of her genius and enterprise; but we should say, that if she had only this single establishment to boast of, she would still have much to flatter her pride. When the present race of Tennants shall have passed away, they will have left their names indelibly stamped upon the history, not only of Glasgow, but upon that of the social progress of the nation. Mr John Tennant may feel justly proud of the Order of the Legion of Honour conferred upon him by the Emperor of the French; and we should say, if his own countrymen had the same estimate of high scientific and commercial merit, he would wear a ligature upon his right limb.

Appendix V

Artist	Title	Purchase date	Price[1] in £	Sale date
Gainsborough	Ladies Erne & Dillon	1882	approx. 4500	1927
Millais	Gladstone	1886	3150	1898
Reynolds	Fortune Tellers	1886	15,750	1923
Hogarth	Peg Woffington	1886	1000	1960
Romney	Countess of Derby	1887	3250	1923
Romney	Lady Hamilton	—	—	1923
Reynolds	Self-portrait	1888	450	1923
Morland	Boys Robbing an Orchard	1888	798	1923 }
Morland	Children playing at Soldiers	1889	735	1923 }
Hoppner	Mrs Gwynne	1889	2600	1927
Romney	Mrs Jordan	1889	6600	1967
Reynolds	Viscountess Crosbie	1890	9900	1923
Constable	Opening of Waterloo Bridge	1891	5000	1955
Reynolds	Boy with Grapes	1893	2300	1923
Turner	Van Tromp's Shallop	1893	6930	1923
Raeburn	Leslie Boy	1894	375	circa 1925
Bonington	Fish Market, Boulogne	1895	3465	1962
Reynolds	Collina (Lady Gertrude Fitzpatrick)	1896	14,000	1962
Reynolds	Miss Ridge	1897	5800	1923
Turner	Approach to Venice	1899	8250	1923
Hoppner	Frankland Sisters	1899	14,700	1923
Turner	Newark Abbey	1901	8800	1962
Stubbs	Greenland Falcon	1905	304	1961

1. These prices should be multiplied by ten for equivalent pound value today.

Price[2] in £	Purchaser	Present whereabouts
approx. 25,000	Howard Young Gallery	Private Collection
—	given National Gallery	National Portrait Gallery, London
27,000	Duveen	Henry E. Huntington Museum, California
3000	via Sotheby	Private Collection, England
25,000	Knoedler	Jules Bache Collection, Metropolitan Museum, New York
4000	Knoedler	Private Collection, U.S.A.
4000	Knoedler	Private Collection, Rochester, New York State
7000 the pair	Knoedler	Two Private Collections, England
4000	Howard Young Gallery	Private Collection, U.S.A.
600	Oscar and Peter Johnson	Private Collection, U.K.
55,000	Duveen	Henry E. Huntington Museum, California
63,000	via Leggatt	Private Collection, England
4000	Knoedler	Private Collection, U.S.A.
15,000	Knoedler	Ailsa Mellon Bruce Collection, National Gallery, Washington D.C.
15,000		Mary Hanna Collection, Cincinnati Museum, Ohio
—	via Agnew	Mr and Mrs Paul Mellon, Washington D.C.
—	via Agnew	Columbus Gallery of Fine Arts, Ohio
5000	Knoedler	Mary Hanna Collection, Cincinnati Museum, Ohio
20,000	Knoedler	Andrew Mellon Collection, National Gallery, Washington D.C.
40,000	Knoedler	Andrew Mellon Collection, National Gallery, Washington D.C.
—	via Agnew	Mr and Mrs Paul Mellon, Washington, D.C.
11,500	Colnaghis at Sothebys	Mr and Mrs Paul Mellon, Washington D.C.

2. The 1920s prices should be multiplied by five for equivalent pound value today.

TENNANT KNOX & CO. *circa* 1796

works started at Darnley and moved to St Rollox, Glasgow, 1799

Company in 1815 became CHARLES TENNANT & CO. of ST ROLLOX

London 1801

New company
C. Tennant
& Co. 1815

New company
C. Tennant Sons &
Co., 1834

Incorporated as a
limited company
C. Tennant Sons & Co. Ltd.
1907

Cocoa and sugar Estates in Trinidad
1957 owned by John and Charles Tennant
and run by C. Tennant Sons & Co.,
London

Incorporated as a limited company
in 1909 as Tennant Estates Ltd.
with branch offices at Port of Spain, Trinidad
and Bolivar, Venezuela

1928 Tennant Estates went into
voluntary liquidation and
immediately reformed with plantations
only as Tennant Estates (1928) Ltd.

Associated Companies—only those bearing name of 'C. Tennant Sons & Co.' listed

Cardiff 1872
Birmingham 1906
New York 1907
Tennant interest
sold in 1933 to
British Metal
Corporation Ltd.
Montreal 1912–16
Skandinavien 1916
France 1920–21
Canada 1932

1962 C. Tennant Sons & Co. Ltd. became a holding company enabling
its trading, finance and investment activities to be carried on by three
wholly owned subsidiaries, Tennant Trading Ltd., Tennant Guaranty,
Tennant Securities Ltd.

1963 Consolidated Goldfields Ltd. seeking well-established marketing
organisation acquired control of total company.

Belfast

Dublin

New company
formed in 1935
Charles Tennant
& Co. (Eire) Ltd.
Subsidiary of
Charles Tennant
& Co. Ltd.

Dundee *c.* 1814

Dalmuir 1832–50
Vitriol works

Renfrew 1833–70
Starch and logwood
works

Carnoustie 1836
sulphuric acid and
fertiliser works

New company
formed in 1892
Charles Tennant
& Co. of Carnoustie
(Ltd.)

1885 Charles Tennant & Co. of St Rollox formed into limited company, owning works at St Rollox, Hebburn, Carnoustie, Cochrane Street and offices in Belfast and Dublin

1890 United Alkali Company formed and bought St Rollox Hebburn, Haverton Hill works

1891 31 Dec. Charles Tennant & Co. Ltd of St. Rollox went into voluntary liquidation and reformed the following day as private company: Charles Tennant & Co.

1898 St. Rollox Soap Works, which did not become part of United Alkali, amalgamated with A. Ogston & Sons as Ogston & Tennants Ltd. a new company

1913 Charles Tennant again incorporated as limited liability company as Charles Tennant & Co. Ltd.

1931 Charles Tennant & Co. Ltd. acquired by the newly-formed Tennants Consolidated Ltd.

Hebburn 1865–90 Chemical works

Haverton Hill salt works 1887–90

Cochrane Street Glasgow, *c.* 1815? Drysalting

New company Tennants Clow & Co (Liverpool) 1830

New company Tennants Clow & Co. (Manchester) 1837

New company Tennant & Co. (Liverpool & Manchester) 1852

Incorporated as limited company Tennants (Lancashire) 1913

In 1930 Tennants Consolidated Ltd. was formed. It acquired the shares of Charles Tennant & Co. Ltd. in 1931. In 1936 it acquired the shares of Tennants (Lancashire) Ltd. Additional subsidiary companies of Tennants Consolidated Ltd. are: Charles Tennant & Co. (Northern Ireland) Ltd.; Charles Tennant & Co. (Canada) Ltd.; Tennants Group Investments Ltd.; Tennants Tar Distillers and Engineering Supplies Ltd.; Tennants Textile Colours Ltd.

Appendix VI

TENNANT COMPANIES

Factories and Offices

Appendix VII

Company Positions held by Sir Charles Tennant

President	The United Alkali Company
Chairman	Mysore Gold Mining Company (Ltd)
	Champion Reef Gold Mining Company of India (Ltd)
	Nine Reefs Company (Ltd)
	Coromandel Gold Mines of India (Ltd)
	Tharsis Sulphur & Copper Company
	Nobel Dynamite Trust Company
	North British Mercantile Insurance Co (Glasgow Board)
	The Steel Company of Scotland (Ltd)
	The Union Bank of Scotland (Ltd)
	Cassel Cyanide Co (Ltd)
	Charles Tennant & Co Ltd
	Charles Tennant & Co of St Rollox (Ltd)
	Charles Tennant & Co of Carnoustie (Ltd)
	Tennants (Lancashire) (Ltd)
Deputy Chairman	North British Railway Co
Vice-Chairman	Gold Fields of Mysore & General Exploration Co (Ltd)
Director	Balaghat Gold Mining Co (Ltd)
	Road Block Gold Mines of India (Ltd)
	Sudan Gold Fields (Ltd)
	Assam Oil Co (Ltd)
	Assam Railways & Trading Co (Ltd)
	British South African Explosives Co (Ltd)
	Oriental Gold Mining Companies of India (Ltd)
	Blane Valley Railway Co (Ltd)
	City of Glasgow Union Railway Co (Ltd)
Voting Trustee	New York, Pennsylvania & Ohio Railroad Co
London Finance Committee	Chicago Great Western Railway Co

Genealogies

I

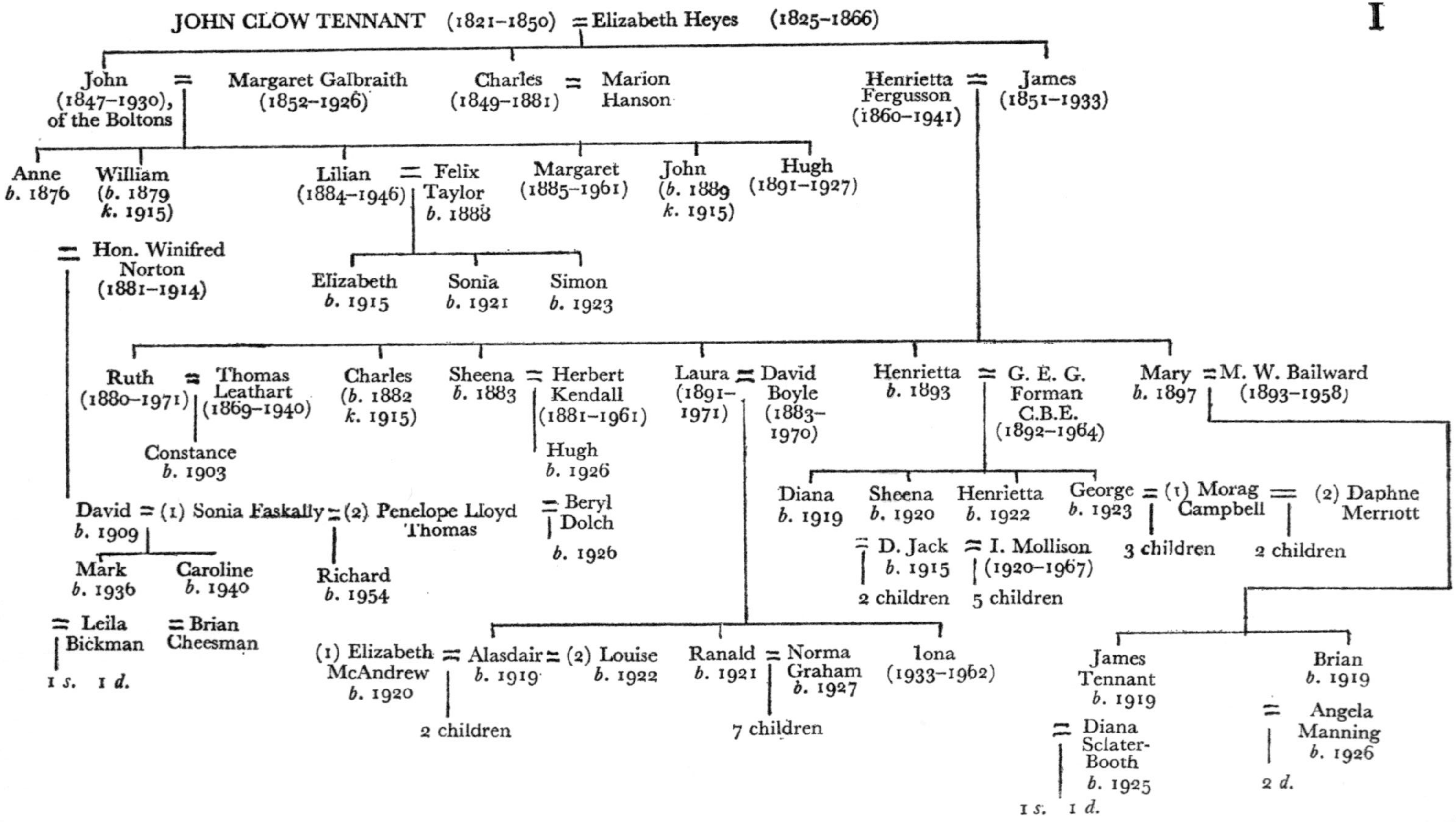
JOHN CLOW TENNANT (1821–1850) = Elizabeth Heyes (1825–1866)
John (1847–1930), of the Boltons = Margaret Galbraith (1852–1926)
Charles (1849–1881) = Marion Hanson
Henrietta Fergusson (1860–1941) = James (1851–1933)
Anne b. 1876
William (b. 1879 k. 1915)
= Hon. Winifred Norton (1881–1914)
Lilian (1884–1946) = Felix Taylor b. 1888
Margaret (1885–1961)
John (b. 1889 k. 1915)
Hugh (1891–1927)
Elizabeth b. 1915
Sonia b. 1921
Simon b. 1923
Ruth (1880–1971) = Thomas Leathart (1869–1940)
Constance b. 1903
Charles (b. 1882 k. 1915)
Sheena b. 1883 = Herbert Kendall (1881–1961)
Hugh b. 1926
= Beryl Dolch
b. 1926
Laura (1891–1971) = David Boyle (1883–1970)
Henrietta b. 1893 = G. E. G. Forman C.B.E. (1892–1964)
Mary b. 1897 = M. W. Bailward (1893–1958)
David b. 1909 = (1) Sonia Faskally = (2) Penelope Lloyd Thomas
Mark b. 1936
Caroline b. 1940
Richard b. 1954
= Leila Bickman
= Brian Cheesman
1 s. 1 d.
Diana b. 1919
Sheena b. 1920
Henrietta b. 1922
George b. 1923 = (1) Morag Campbell = (2) Daphne Merriott
= D. Jack b. 1915
= I. Mollison (1920–1967)
2 children
5 children
3 children
2 children
(1) Elizabeth McAndrew b. 1920 = Alasdair b. 1919 = (2) Louise b. 1922
2 children
Ranald b. 1921 = Norma Graham b. 1927
7 children
Iona (1933–1962)
James Tennant b. 1919
= Diana Sclater-Booth b. 1925
1 s. 1 d.
Brian b. 1919
= Angela Manning b. 1926
2 d.

11

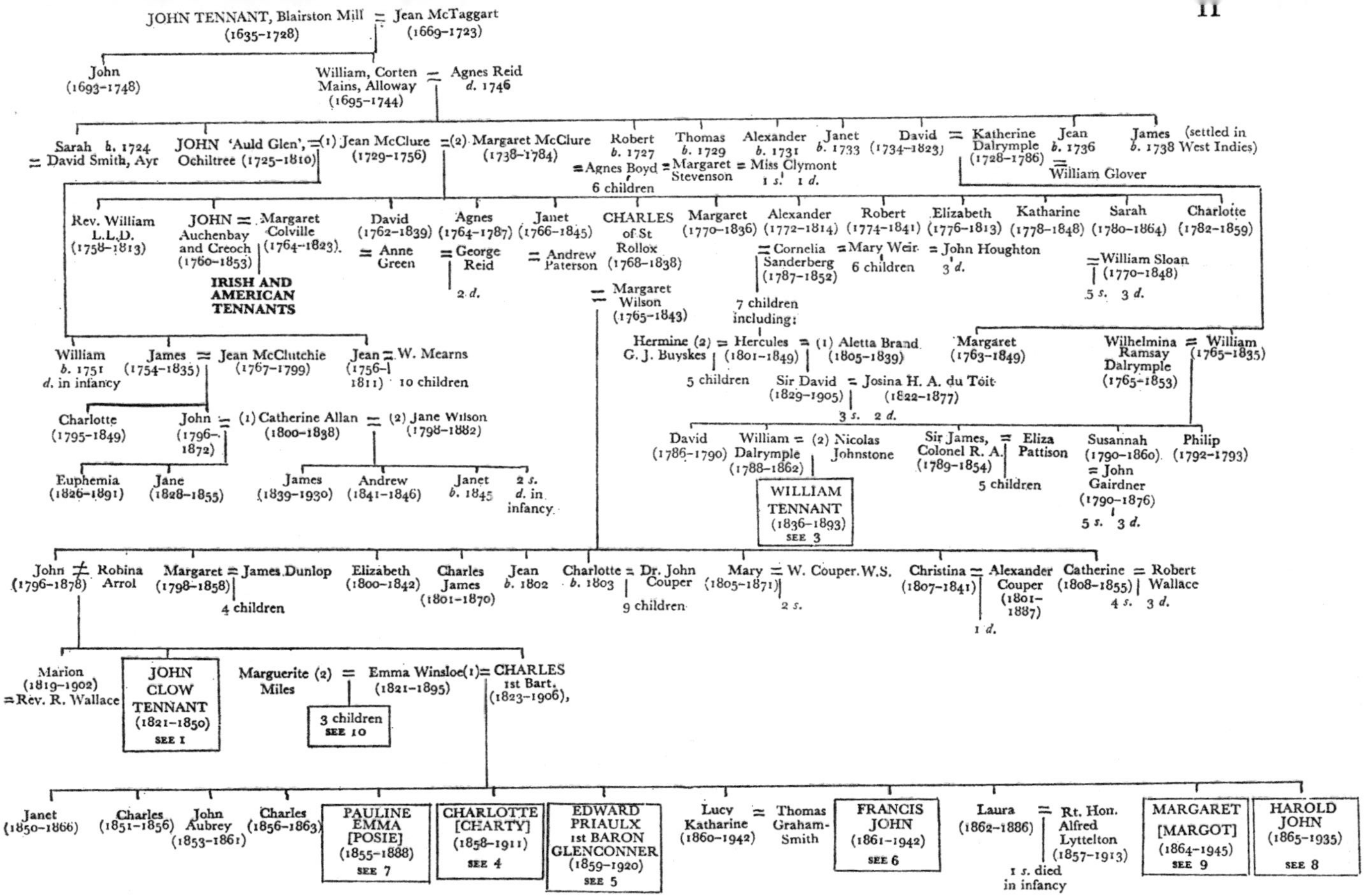

JOHN TENNANT, Blairston Mill = Jean McTaggart
(1635–1728) (1669–1723)
John (1693–1748)
William, Corten Mains, Alloway (1695–1744) = Agnes Reid d. 1746
Sarah b. 1724 = David Smith, Ayr
JOHN 'Auld Glen', Ochiltree (1725–1810) =(1) Jean McClure (1729–1756) =(2) Margaret McClure (1738–1784)
Robert b. 1727 = Agnes Boyd
6 children
Thomas b. 1729 = Margaret Stevenson
Alexander b. 1731 = Miss Clymont
1 s. 1 d.
Janet b. 1733
David (1734–1823) = Katherine Dalrymple (1728–1786)
Jean b. 1736 = William Glover
James b. 1738 (settled in West Indies)
Rev. William L.L.D. (1758–1813)
JOHN Auchenbay and Creoch (1760–1853) = Margaret Colville (1764–1823)
IRISH AND AMERICAN TENNANTS
David (1762–1839) = Anne Green
Agnes (1764–1787) = George Reid
2 d.
Janet (1766–1845) = Andrew Paterson
CHARLES of St Rollox (1768–1838) = Margaret Wilson (1765–1843)
Margaret (1770–1836)
Alexander (1772–1814) = Cornelia Sanderberg (1787–1852)
7 children including:
Robert (1774–1841) = Mary Weir
6 children
Elizabeth (1776–1813) = John Houghton
3 d.
Katharine (1778–1848)
Sarah (1780–1864) = William Sloan (1770–1848)
5 s. 3 d.
Charlotte (1782–1859)
William b. 1751 d. in infancy
James (1754–1835) = Jean McClutchie (1767–1799)
Jean (1756–1811) = W. Mearns
10 children
Hermine (2) = Hercules = (1) Aletta Brand
G. J. Buyskes (1801–1849) (1805–1839)
5 children
Sir David (1829–1905) = Josina H. A. du Toit (1822–1877)
3 s. 2 d.
Margaret (1763–1849)
Wilhelmina Ramsay Dalrymple (1765–1853) = William (1765–1835)
Charlotte (1795–1849)
John (1796–1872) = (1) Catherine Allan (1800–1838) = (2) Jane Wilson (1798–1882)
Euphemia (1826–1891)
Jane (1828–1855)
James (1839–1930)
Andrew (1841–1846)
Janet b. 1845
2 s. d. in infancy
David (1786–1790)
William Dalrymple (1788–1862) = (2) Nicolas Johnstone
WILLIAM TENNANT (1836–1893) SEE 3
Sir James, Colonel R. A. (1789–1854) = Eliza Pattison
5 children
Susannah (1790–1860) = John Gairdner (1790–1876)
5 s. 3 d.
Philip (1792–1793)
John (1796–1878) ≠ Robina Arrol
Margaret (1798–1858) = James Dunlop
4 children
Elizabeth (1800–1842)
Charles James (1801–1870)
Jean b. 1802
Charlotte b. 1803 = Dr. John Couper
9 children
Mary (1805–1871) = W. Couper. W.S.
2 s.
Christina (1807–1841) = Alexander Couper (1801–1887)
1 d.
Catherine (1808–1855) = Robert Wallace
4 s. 3 d.
Marion (1819–1902) = Rev. R. Wallace
JOHN CLOW TENNANT (1821–1850) SEE I
Marguerite (2) = Emma Winsloe (1) = CHARLES
Miles (1821–1895) 1st Bart. (1823–1906),
3 children SEE 10
Janet (1850–1866)
Charles (1851–1856)
John Aubrey (1853–1861)
Charles (1856–1863)
PAULINE EMMA [POSIE] (1855–1888) SEE 7
CHARLOTTE [CHARTY] (1858–1911) SEE 4
EDWARD PRIAULX 1st BARON GLENCONNER (1859–1920) SEE 5
Lucy Katharine (1860–1942) = Thomas Graham-Smith
FRANCIS JOHN (1861–1942) SEE 6
Laura (1862–1886) = Rt. Hon. Alfred Lyttelton (1857–1913)
1 s. died in infancy
MARGARET [MARGOT] (1864–1945) SEE 9
HAROLD JOHN (1865–1935) SEE 8

III

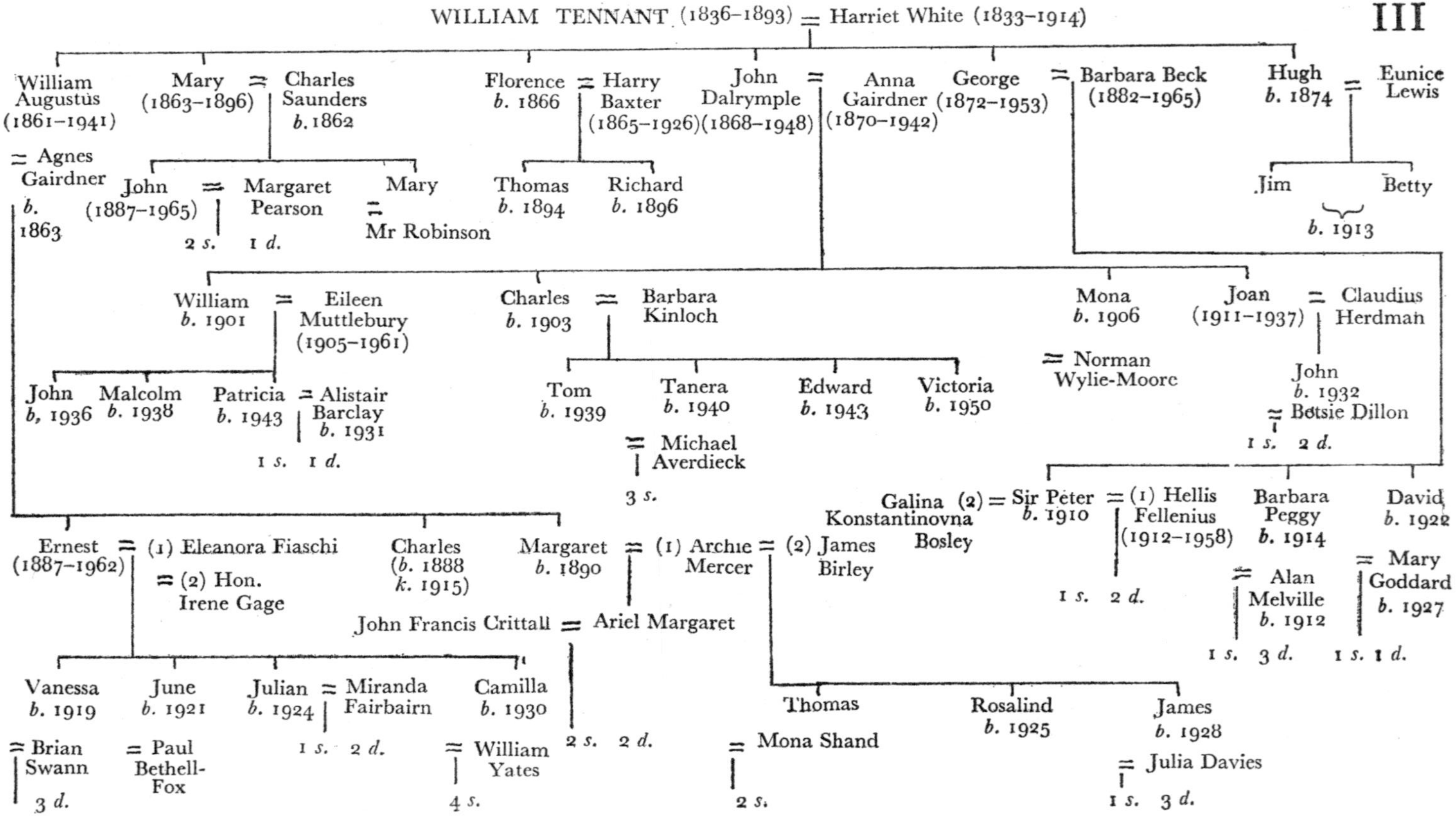
WILLIAM TENNANT (1836–1893) = Harriet White (1833–1914)
William Augustus (1861–1941)
= Agnes Gairdner b. 1863
Mary (1863–1896) = Charles Saunders b. 1862
John (1887–1965) = Margaret Pearson
2 s. 1 d.
Mary = Mr Robinson
Florence b. 1866 = Harry Baxter (1865–1926)
Thomas b. 1894
Richard b. 1896
John Dalrymple (1868–1948) = Anna Gairdner (1870–1942)
George (1872–1953) = Barbara Beck (1882–1965)
Hugh b. 1874 = Eunice Lewis
Jim
Betty
b. 1913
William b. 1901 = Eileen Muttlebury (1905–1961)
John b, 1936
Malcolm b. 1938
Patricia b. 1943 = Alistair Barclay b. 1931
1 s. 1 d.
Charles b. 1903 = Barbara Kinloch
Tom b. 1939
Tanera b. 1940
= Michael Averdieck
3 s.
Edward b. 1943
Victoria b. 1950
Mona b. 1906
= Norman Wylie-Moore
Joan (1911–1937) = Claudius Herdman
John b. 1932
= Betsie Dillon
1 s. 2 d.
Ernest (1887–1962) = (1) Eleanora Fiaschi
= (2) Hon. Irene Gage
Charles (b. 1888 k. 1915)
Margaret b. 1890 = (1) Archie Mercer = (2) James Birley
John Francis Crittall = Ariel Margaret
2 s. 2 d.
Galina Konstantinovna Bosley (2) = Sir Peter b. 1910 = (1) Hellis Fellenius (1912–1958)
1 s. 2 d.
Barbara Peggy b. 1914
= Alan Melville b. 1912
1 s. 3 d.
David b. 1922
= Mary Goddard b. 1927
1 s. 1 d.
Vanessa b. 1919
= Brian Swann
3 d.
June b. 1921
= Paul Bethell-Fox
Julian b. 1924 = Miranda Fairbairn
1 s. 2 d.
Camilla b. 1930
= William Yates
4 s.
Thomas
= Mona Shand
2 s.
Rosalind b. 1925
James b. 1928
= Julia Davies
1 s. 3 d.

IV

CHARLOTTE MONKTON [CHARTY] TENNANT (1852–1911) = Thomas Lister, 4th Baron Ribblesdale (1854–1926)

- Thomas (1878–1904)
- Barbara (1882–1943) = Sir Mathew Wilson, 4th Bart. (1875–1958)
  - Martin, 5th Bart. *b.* 1906
  - Margaret Motion *née* Holden (1) = Anthony *b.* 1908 =(2) Emily Lambert *née* Milliken
    - Mathew *b.* 1935
  - Peter *b.* 1913 = Helen Ranken
    - Thomas *b.* 1937 = Judith Jenkins
      - 2 *d.*
    - Alexandra Jellicoe *b.* 1944 = Philip *b.* 1940
- Charles (*b.* 1887 *k.* 1916)
- Laura (1892–1965) = Simon Fraser, 16th Baron Lovat (1871–1933)
  - Simon, 17th Baron Lovat *b.* 1911 = Rosamund Broughton
    - Simon Master of Lovat *b.* 1939
    - Fiona *b.* 1941
    - Annabel *b.* 1942 = Hugh Mackay, 14th Baron Reay *b.* 1937
      - 1 *s.* 1 *d.*
    - Kim *b.* 1946
    - Hugh *b.* 1947
    - Andrew *b.* 1952
  - Magdalen *b.* 1913 = John Scott, 4th Earl of Eldon *b.* 1899
    - Comtesse Claudine de Montjoye-Vaufrey et de la Roche = John, Viscount Encombe *b.* 1937
      - 1 *s.* 2 *d.*
    - Simon Peter *b.* 1939 = Isabel de Bertodano
  - Hugh *b.* 1918 = Lady Antonia Pakenham *b.* 1932.
    - 3 *s.* 3 *d.*
  - Veronica Nell *b.* 1920 = (1) Alan Phipps
    - 1 *s.* 1 *d.*
  - Veronica = (2) Sir Fitzroy Maclean, 1st Bart.
    - 2 *s.*
  - Mary Diana Rose (1926–1940)
- Diana *b.* 1893 = (1) Percy Wyndham = (2) Arthur Capel = (3) Vere [Burghie] Fane, 14th Earl of Westmorland (1893–1948)
  - (1) George Ward, 1st Viscount Ward of Witley *b.* 1907 = Anne *b.* 1919 = (2) Thurston Holland-Martin = (3) Peter Higgins
    - (by George Ward) 1 *s.* 1 *d.*
    - (by Thurston Holland-Martin) 2 *s.*
  - Franz Osborn (1) = June *b.* 1920 = (2) Jeremy Hutchinson Q.C.
    - 1 *s.*
  - David, 15th Earl of Westmorland *b.* 1924 = Jane Findlay *b.* 1928
    - 2 *s.* 1 *d.*
  - Julian *b.* 1927
  - Rose *b.* 1930 = John Macdonald-Buchanan *b.* 1920
    - 1 *s.* 2 *d.*

V

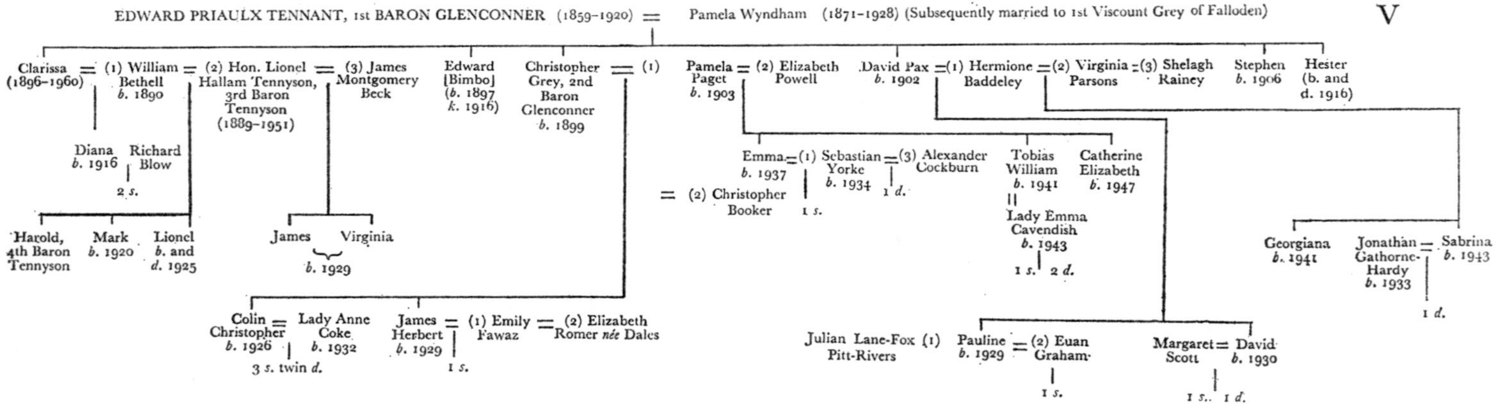
EDWARD PRIAULX TENNANT, 1st BARON GLENCONNER (1859–1920) = Pamela Wyndham (1871–1928) (Subsequently married to 1st Viscount Grey of Falloden)
Clarissa (1896–1960) = (1) William Bethell b. 1890 = (2) Hon. Lionel Hallam Tennyson, 3rd Baron Tennyson (1889–1951) = (3) James Montgomery Beck
Edward [Bimbo] (b. 1897 k. 1916)
Christopher Grey, 2nd Baron Glenconner b. 1899 = (1) Pamela Paget b. 1903 = (2) Elizabeth Powell
David Pax b. 1902 = (1) Hermione Baddeley = (2) Virginia Parsons = (3) Shelagh Rainey
Stephen b. 1906
Hester (b. and d. 1916)
Diana b. 1916
Richard Blow
2 s.
Harold, 4th Baron Tennyson
Mark b. 1920
Lionel b. and d. 1925
James
Virginia
b. 1929
Colin Christopher b. 1926 = Lady Anne Coke b. 1932
3 s. twin d.
James Herbert b. 1929 = (1) Emily Fawaz = (2) Elizabeth Romer née Dales
1 s.
Emma b. 1937 = (1) Sebastian Yorke b. 1934 = (3) Alexander Cockburn
= (2) Christopher Booker
1 s.
1 d.
Tobias William b. 1941 = Lady Emma Cavendish b. 1943
1 s. 2 d.
Catherine Elizabeth b. 1947
Julian Lane-Fox Pitt-Rivers (1) = Pauline b. 1929 = (2) Euan Graham
1 s.
Margaret Scott = David b. 1930
1 s. 1 d.
Georgiana b. 1941
Jonathan Gathorne-Hardy b. 1933 = Sabrina b. 1943
1 d.

VI

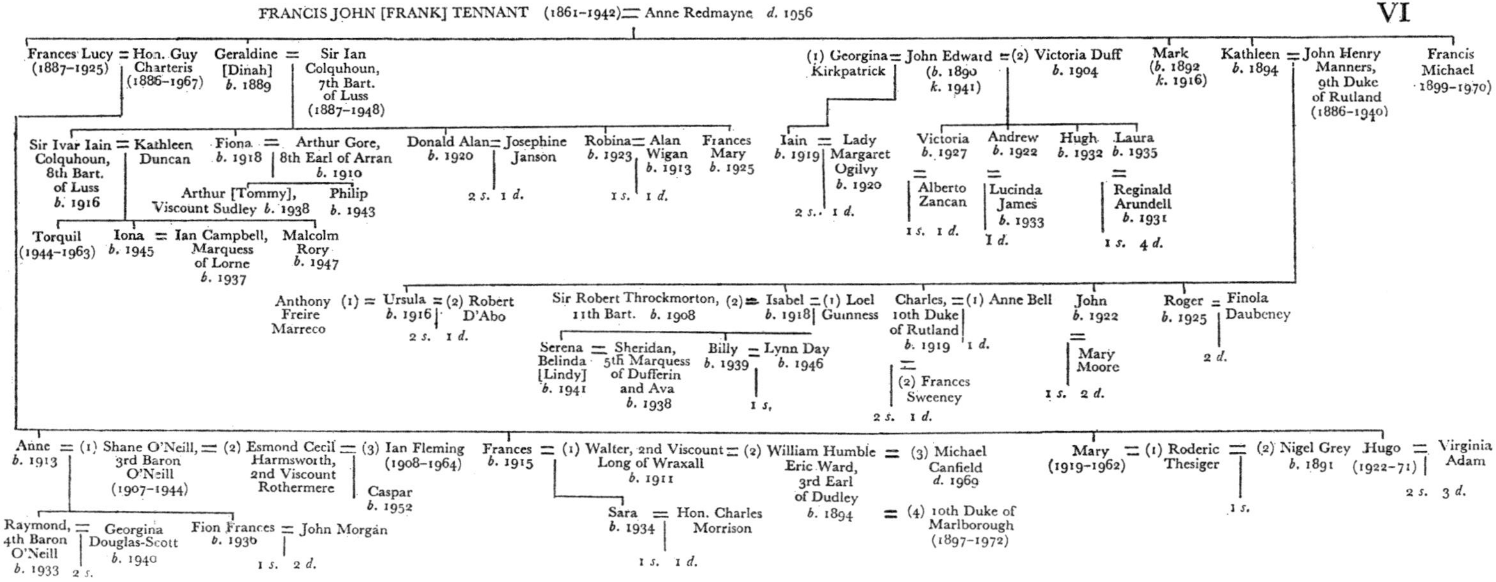
FRANCIS JOHN [FRANK] TENNANT (1861–1942) = Anne Redmayne d. 1956
Frances Lucy (1887–1925) = Hon. Guy Charteris (1886–1967)
Geraldine [Dinah] b. 1889 = Sir Ian Colquhoun, 7th Bart. of Luss (1887–1948)
(1) Georgina Kirkpatrick = John Edward (b. 1890 k. 1941) = (2) Victoria Duff b. 1904
Mark (b. 1892 k. 1916)
Kathleen b. 1894 = John Henry Manners, 9th Duke of Rutland (1886–1940)
Francis Michael 1899–1970)
Sir Ivar Iain Colquhoun, 8th Bart. of Luss b. 1916 = Kathleen Duncan
Fiona b. 1918 = Arthur Gore, 8th Earl of Arran b. 1910
Arthur [Tommy], Viscount Sudley b. 1938
Philip b. 1943
Donald Alan b. 1920 = Josephine Janson
2 s. 1 d.
Robina b. 1923 = Alan Wigan b. 1913
1 s. 1 d.
Frances Mary b. 1925
Iain b. 1919 = Lady Margaret Ogilvy b. 1920
2 s. 1 d.
Victoria b. 1927 = Alberto Zancan
1 s. 1 d.
Andrew b. 1922 = Lucinda James b. 1933
1 d.
Hugh b. 1932
Laura b. 1935 = Reginald Arundell b. 1931
1 s. 4 d.
Torquil (1944–1963)
Iona b. 1945 = Ian Campbell, Marquess of Lorne b. 1937
Malcolm Rory b. 1947
Anthony Freire Marreco (1) = Ursula b. 1916 = (2) Robert D'Abo
2 s. 1 d.
Sir Robert Throckmorton, 11th Bart. b. 1908 (2) = Isabel b. 1918 = (1) Loel Guinness
Serena Belinda [Lindy] b. 1941 = Sheridan, 5th Marquess of Dufferin and Ava b. 1938
Billy b. 1939 = Lynn Day b. 1946
1 s.
Charles, 10th Duke of Rutland b. 1919 = (1) Anne Bell
1 d.
= (2) Frances Sweeney
2 s. 1 d.
John b. 1922 = Mary Moore
1 s. 2 d.
Roger b. 1925 = Finola Daubeney
2 d.
Anne b. 1913 = (1) Shane O'Neill, 3rd Baron O'Neill (1907–1944) = (2) Esmond Cecil Harmsworth, 2nd Viscount Rothermere = (3) Ian Fleming (1908–1964)
Caspar b. 1952
Raymond, 4th Baron O'Neill b. 1933 = Georgina Douglas-Scott b. 1940
2 s.
Fion Frances b. 1930 = John Morgan
1 s. 2 d.
Frances b. 1915 = (1) Walter, 2nd Viscount Long of Wraxall b. 1911 = (2) William Humble Eric Ward, 3rd Earl of Dudley b. 1894 = (3) Michael Canfield d. 1969 = (4) 10th Duke of Marlborough (1897–1972)
Sara b. 1934 = Hon. Charles Morrison
1 s. 1 d.
Mary (1919–1962) = (1) Roderic Thesiger = (2) Nigel Grey b. 1891
1 s.
Hugo (1922–71) = Virginia Adam
2 s. 3 d.

VII

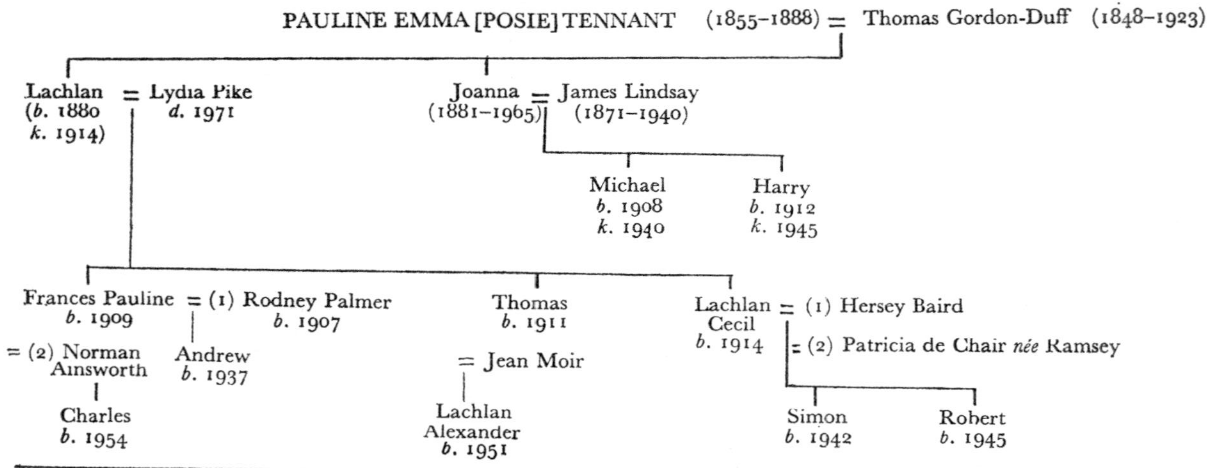
PAULINE EMMA [POSIE] TENNANT (1855–1888) = Thomas Gordon-Duff (1848–1923)
Lachlan (b. 1880 k. 1914) = Lydia Pike d. 1971
Joanna (1881–1965) = James Lindsay (1871–1940)
Michael b. 1908 k. 1940
Harry b. 1912 k. 1945
Frances Pauline b. 1909 = (1) Rodney Palmer b. 1907
= (2) Norman Ainsworth
Andrew b. 1937
Charles b. 1954
Thomas b. 1911
= Jean Moir
Lachlan Alexander b. 1951
Lachlan Cecil b. 1914 = (1) Hersey Baird
= (2) Patricia de Chair née Ramsey
Simon b. 1942
Robert b. 1945

VIII

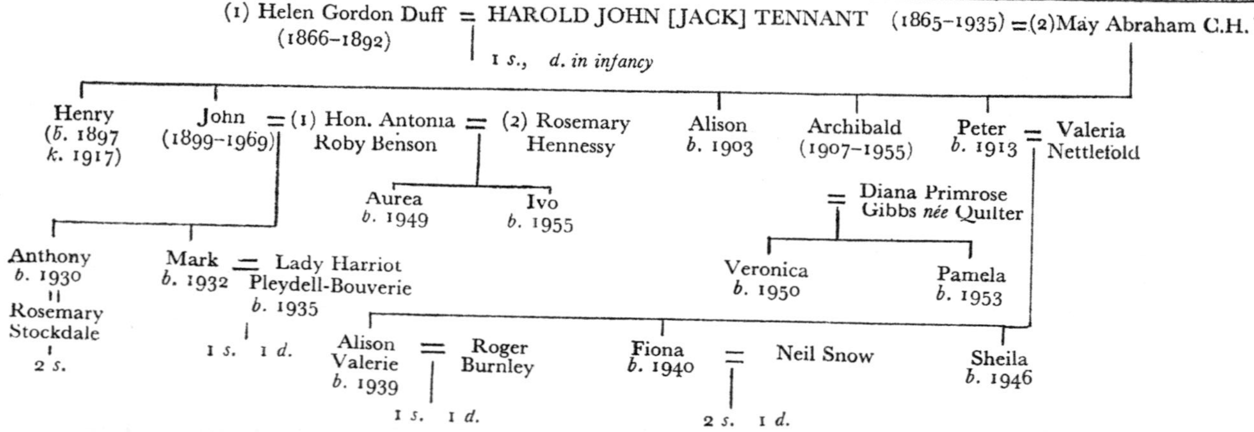
(1) Helen Gordon Duff (1866–1892) = HAROLD JOHN [JACK] TENNANT (1865–1935) = (2) May Abraham C.H.
1 s., d. in infancy
Henry (b. 1897 k. 1917)
John (1899–1969) = (1) Hon. Antonia Roby Benson = (2) Rosemary Hennessy
Alison b. 1903
Archibald (1907–1955)
Peter b. 1913 = Valeria Nettlefold
Aurea b. 1949
Ivo b. 1955
= Diana Primrose Gibbs née Quilter
Anthony b. 1930 = Rosemary Stockdale
2 s.
Mark b. 1932 = Lady Harriot Pleydell-Bouverie b. 1935
1 s. 1 d.
Veronica b. 1950
Pamela b. 1953
Alison Valerie b. 1939 = Roger Burnley
1 s. 1 d.
Fiona b. 1940 = Neil Snow
2 s. 1 d.
Sheila b. 1946

IX

MARGARET EMMA ALICE [MARGOT] TENNANT (1864–1945) = Rt. Hon. H. H. Asquith, 1st Earl of Oxford and Asquith. (1852–1928). Previously married to Helen Melland by whom he had 5 children, Violet (Bonham-Carter), Raymond, Herbert, Arthur and Cyril.

- Elizabeth (1897–1943) = Prince Antoine Bibesco *d.* 1951
  - Princess Priscilla *b.* 1920
- Anthony [Puffin] (1902–1968)

X

CHARLES TENNANT, 1st Bart. (1823–1906) = (2) Marguerite Miles (1868–1943)

- Margaret [Peggy] D.B.E. *b.* 1899 = John de Vere Loder, 2nd Baron Wakehurst (1895–1970)
  - Henrietta *b.* 1922 = John Reader-Harris *b.* 1914
    - 1 *s.* 1 *d.*
  - Christopher, 3rd Baron Wakehurst *b.* 1925 = Ingeborg Krumbholz-Hess *b.* 1931
    - 1 *s.* 1 *d.*
  - David James *b.* 1928
  - Robert Beauclerk *b.* 1934
- Katharine, Baroness Elliot of Harwood D.B.E. *b.* 1903 = Rt. Hon. Walter Elliot (1888–1958)
- Nancy (1904–1969) = Thomas Lionel Dugdale, 1st Baron Crathorne *b.* 1897
  - James *b.* 1939 = Sylvia Montgomery *b.* 1942
    - 1 *d.*
  - David *b.* 1942 = Susan Powell *b.* 1947

Select Bibliography

Agnew, C. Morland, *Catalogue of Sir Charles Tennant's Pictures*, privately printed, 1896.
Alexander, Sir William, 'Charles Tennant', *Chemistry and Industry*, October 1943.
Allen, J. Fenwick, *Some Founders of the Chemical Industry*, Manchester, Vol. I 1907.
Asquith, Margot, *Autobiography*, Thornton Butterworth, Vol. I 1920, Vol. I 1922.
Asquith, Margot, *More Memories*, Cassell, 1933.
Asquith, Margot, *Places and Persons*, Thornton Butterworth, 1925.
Asquith, Margot, 'My visit to Hawarden', *Cornhill*, Nov., 1915.
Asquith, Margot, ed., *Myself When Young*, Muller, 1938.
'Ayr Academy and Burgh School, 1233–1895', *Ayrshire Post*, 1895.

Bailey, H. W., *Chronicle of the Family of Gairdner*, privately printed 1947.
Bailey, John, ed., *The Diary of Lady Frederick Cavendish*, Murray, 1927.
Balfour, A. J., *Chapters of Autobiography*, Cassell, 1930.
Balfour, Lady Frances, *Ne Obliviscaris*, Hodder & Stoughton, 1930.
Bancroft, R. M. and F. J. *Tall Chimney Construction*, Calvert, 1885.
Benson, E. F., *Dodo*, Methuen, 1893.
Berthollet, C. L., *Essay on the New Method of Bleaching*, trans. Robert Kerr, Edinburgh, 1791.
Blunt, Wilfrid Scawen, *My Diaries 1888–1914*, Secker, 1932.
Bonham-Carter, Mark, Introduction to Margot Asquith's *Autobiography*, Eyre & Spottiswoode, new edition, 1962.
Bonham-Carter, Lady Violet, 'The Souls', *Listener*, 30 October 1947.
Brown, Andrew, *History of Glasgow*, Glasgow, 1715.
Brown, George Douglas, *The House with the Green Shutters*, Nelson, 1908.
Brown, P. Hume, *History of Scotland*, Vol. 3, Cambridge, 1911.

Buchanan, George, *An Account of Railways in Lanarkshire*, Edinburgh, 1832.
Burn, J. D., *Commercial Enterprise*, London, 1858.
Butt, John E., *The Industrial Archaeology of Scotland*, Newton Abbot, 1967.

Campbell, W. A., *The Chemical Industry*, Longman, 1971.
Carswell, Catherine, *The Life of Robert Burns*, Chatto & Windus, 2nd ed., 1951.
Catalogue of Pictures in the Tennant Gallery, London, n.d.
Chambers, Robert, *The Life and Works of Robert Burns*, Edinburgh, 1891.
Chandos, Viscount, *From Peace to War: A Study in Contrast 1857–1918*, Bodley Head, 1968.
Checkland, S. G., *The Mines of Tharsis*, George Allen & Unwin, 1967.
Clow, A. and N. L., *The Chemical Revolution*, Batchworth Press, 1952.
Crathorne, Nancy, 'From Farm to Factory and High Finance in Four Generations', *Chemistry and Industry*, 13 February 1965.
Cunningham, Allan, *The Works of Robert Burns with His Life*, Cochrane & McCrone, 1834.
Currie, J., ed., *The Works of Robert Burns with an Account of his Life*, Liverpool, 1800.

Daiches, David, *Robert Burns*, Bell, 1952.
Dodd, George, *The Land we live in*, vol. II, London, 1847.
Dugdale, James, 'Sir Charles Tennant, The Story of a Victorian Collector', *Connoisseur*, September 1971.

Elliot, Walter, 'Glasgow University 1451–1951', *History Today*, August 1951.
Enterprise, An account of the activities and aims of the Tennant companies, Adprint, 1945.

Ferguson, J. de Lancey, ed., *The Letters of Robert Burns*, Clarendon Press, 1931.
Fleck, Alexander, 'The British Sulphuric Acid Industry', *Chemistry and Industry*, 1952.

Gairdner, Charles Dalrymple, *Autobiography* privately reprinted from the *Kilmarnock Standard* 1861.

Galt, John, *Annals of the Parish*, London, 1821.
Graham, H. G., *The Social Life of Scotland in the Eighteenth Century*, Black, 1899.

Haber, L. F., *The Chemical Industry during the Nineteenth Century*, Oxford University Press, 1958.
Hamilton, Henry, *The Industrial Revolution in Scotland*, Oxford, 1932.
Hardie, D. W. F., 'The Macintoshes and the Origins of the Chemical Industry', *Chemistry and Industry*, 28 June 1952.
Harvey, Francis, *First States and Proofs of Rare Engravings forming the Collection of Sir Charles Tennant*, privately printed 1898.
Henderson, G. G., *Industries of Glasgow and the West Coast of Scotland*, Glasgow, 1901.
Higgins, S. H., *A History of Bleaching*, London, 1924.
Higgins, William, *The Theory and Practice of Bleaching*, Dublin Society, 1799.
Home, Dr Francis, *Experiments on Bleaching*, Edinburgh, 1756.
Home, H., *Gentleman Farmer*, Edinburgh, 5th ed., 1802.
Horner, Francis, *Time Remembered*, Heinemann, 1933.
Hume, John R., 'The St Rollox Chemical Works, 1799–1964', *Journal of Industrial Archaeology*, August, 1966.
'Hundred and Fifty Years of St. Rollox', *I.C.I. Magazine*, September 1947.
Hutchinson, H. G., *Portrait of the Eighties*, T. Fisher Unwin, 1920.
Hutchinson, Horace, ed., *The Private Diaries of Sir Algernon West*, Murray, 1922.
Hutchison, H., 'The brave days of St. Rollox', *I.C.I. Magazine*, August, 1964.

Jenkins, Roy, *Asquith*, Collins, 1964.
Johnston, Thomas, *History of the Working Classes in Scotland*, Glasgow, n.d.

Killin, T., 'Burns and The Tennants of Glenconner', *Annual Burns Chronicle and Club Directory*, no. xv, January 1960.
Kingzett, C. T., *History, Products and Processes of the Alkali Trade*, London, 1877.
Knowles, L. C. A., *The Industrial and Commercial Revolutions in Great Britain in the Nineteenth Century*, Routledge, 1921.

Liddell, A. G. C., *Notes from the Life of an Ordinary Mortal*, Murray, 1911.
Lister, Beatrix, ed., *Emma, Lady Ribblesdale, Letters and Diaries*, privately printed, 1930.
Lyttelton, Edith, *Alfred Lyttelton*, Longmans, 1917.

Mackenzie, Peter, *Reminiscences of Glasgow and the West of Scotland*, Glasgow, 1865–8.
Macintosh, George, *Biographical Memoirs of the late Charles Macintosh F.R.S. of Campsie and Dunchattan*, privately printed, 1847.
MacTear, James, 'On the Regeneration of Sulphur, as conducted at St. Rollox by the "MacTear' process", *Chemical News*, vol. 36, no. 943, 21 Dec 1877.
MacTear, James, 'On the Growth of the Alkali and Bleaching Manufacture in the Glasgow district', *Chemical News*, vol. 35, no. 893, 5 Jan 1877.
McUre, John, *A View of the City of Glasgow*, Glasgow, 1736.
Magnus, Philip, *Gladstone*, Murray, 1954.
Maitland, William, *History and Survey of London from its foundations to the present day*, London, 1756.
Masterman, Lucy, ed., *Mary Gladstone (Mrs Drew): her diaries and letters*, Methuen, 1930.
Memorials of Ochiltree, privately printed, Glasgow, 1879.
Miall, S., *A History of the British Chemical Industry*, Benn, 1931.
Mitchell, J. O., *Old Glasgow Essays*, Glasgow, 1905.
Murdoch, A., *Ochiltree, its History and Reminiscences*, Gardner, *c.* 1911.
Muspratt, Sheridan, *Chemistry as Applied to Arts and Manufactures*, London, 1860.

Parkes, Samual, *Chemical Essays*, London, 1815.
Phillips, Lisle March, Chisholm, Bertram, eds., *Some Hawarden Letters, 1878–1913, written to Mrs. Drew*, Nisbit, 1917.

Rait, Robert S., *The History of the Union Bank of Scotland*, Glasgow, 1930.
Reader, W. J., *Imperial Chemical Industries*, Volume I, *The Forerunners 1870–1926*, Oxford University Press, 1970.
Ribblesdale, Lord, *Impressions and Memories*, Cassell, 1927.
Rose, Kenneth, *Superior Person, a portrait of Curzon and his Circle*, Weidenfeld & Nicolson, 1969.

Spender, J. A., Asquith, Cyril, *Life of Lord Oxford and Asquith*, Hutchinson, 1932.
Stewart, George, *Curiosities of Glasgow Citizenship*, Glasgow, 1881.
Strang, John, *Glasgow and its Clubs*, Glasgow, 1864.
Strawhorn, J., and Boyd, W., *Ayrshire, The Third Statistical Account of Scotland*, Oliver & Boyd, 1951.

Tennant, E. W. D., *One Hundred and Forty Years of the Tennant Companies 1797–1937*, privately printed, 1937.
Tennant, E. W. D., 'One Hundred and Seventy-five Years of the Tennant Companies', unpublished MS.
Tennant, E. W. D., *True Account*, Max Parrish, 1957.
Tennant, E. W. D., 'The Early History of the St Rollox Chemical Works', *Chemistry and Industry*, 1947.
Tennant, H. J., *Sir Charles Tennant*, privately printed, 1932.
Tennant, Lady P., *The Children and the Pictures*, Heinemann, 1908.
Thom, Wm., *Rhymes and Recollections of a Handloom weaver*, Paisley, 1880.
Toovey, C. J., *The Library of Sir Charles Tennant*, privately printed, 1896.
Tuckman, Barbara, *The Proud Tower*, Macmillan, 1966.

Walker, William, *Memoirs of the Distinguished Men of Science of Great Britain living in the years 1807–1808*, London, 1862.
Wallace, William, ed., *Poetical Works of Robert Burns*, Chambers, reprinted, 1948.
West, Sir Algernon, *Recollections 1832–1886*, vol. 2, Smith Elder, 1899.
Wolfe Murray, George, *The Tweedale Shooting Club*, privately printed, Edinburgh, 1940.

Notes and References

In these references, works listed in the bibliography have been cited as briefly as possible.

Part I: Prologue

1 *pleasant and odiferous smell.* McUre, p. 144.

Chapter I: First Beginnings on the Land

1 *the blood and name.*' Quoted in Frances Walker, excerpt from *Kilmarnock Standard*, 'History of Ochiltree', p. 20 in typed copy in family archives.
2 *is spiritual.* Communication to Katharine Elliot from Sir James Fergusson.
3 *Ayrshire farmer* Murdoch, p. 242.
4 *a cuff on the lug.* Murdoch, p. 93.

Chapter II: Auld Glen 1726–1810

1 *sumptuous 'down sitting'.* The accounts of James Macrae's travels and of his cousin's marriage are recorded in *Memorials of Ochiltree.*
2 *than an English wedding'.* Graham, p. 54.
3 *the corn's to shear.* Carswell, p. 39.
4 *Knowledge of Agriculture.* This society is referred to in Graham, p. 263.
5 *board me by turns.* Daiches, p. 37.
6 *an aid to learning . . .* Carswell, p. 47.
7 *hereby discharge. J. Tennant. Memorials of Ochiltree,* p. 49.
8 *for his improvement.* Daiches, p. 41.
9 *between 1794 and 1796. History of the Burgh School of Ayr* (privately printed for the Academy Bazaar, 1895) p. 45.
10 *the birchen rod'.* Murdoch, p. 145.
11 *at the funeral.*' Killin, p. 84.
12 *yours Sincerely, (Robt Burns)* Ferguson, I 20.
13 *as their president.* Original Members—Hugh Reid, Robert and Gilbert Burns, Alexander Brown, Walter Mitchell, Thomas Wright, William McTavin. Quotations about the Tarbolton Bachelors' Club come from Daiches, pp. 56–9.

14 *in braid daylight:' Memorials of Ochiltree*, p. 45.
15 *Edinburgh literary circles.* Carswell, p. 222.
16 *sense appealing*, Adam Smith's *Theory of the Moral Sentiments* was published in 1759; Thomas Reid's *Inquiry into the Human Mind, on the Principles of Common Sense*, in 1764.
17 *Brown and Boston.* Bunyan's *Pilgrim's Progress*, *The Self-interpreting Bible* of the Rev. John Brown of Haddington (1722–87) and *The Fourfold State* of the Rev. Thomas Boston of Ettrick (1676–1732) used to be found in every pious Scottish household.
18 *he's a parent*, Supporters of the view that the 'Epistle' was written at Mossgiel find further confirmation in these two lines, which they maintain were written in anticipation of the birth (15 May 1786) of John Tennant's first child, Jane. The report goes that when Burns was engaged on its composition he heard that a messenger had arrived at Mauchline from Auchenbay, which was three miles distant, for a midwife.
19 *Robt. Burns.* Ferguson, vol. I, p. 281.
20 *Robt. Burns.* Ferguson, II 55.
21 *Robt. Burns.* Ferguson, I 182. The original letter is at Glen.
22 *pleased with them.* Ferguson, I 197.
23 *a good deal* . . . Ibid. 198.
24 *to accept it'.* Ibid. 199.
25 *live by it.'* Ibid. 207.
26 *to your Country.* Ferguson, II 37.
27 *looked for another.' Memorials*, p. 44.
28 *auld Glenconner gane'.* From *Poems and Songs* by Robert Hetrick, Dalmellington (privately printed, Ayr, 1826), pp. 94, 95.

Chapter III

1 *second mother tongue'.* 'Ayr Academy', p. 26.
2 *their next meal.* Ibid. p. 38.
3 *England and France.* Ibid. p. 58.
4 *have an assistant'.* Ibid. p. 61.
5 *sore it is'* Gairdner, p. 6.
6 *went headlong'*, Chambers Vol. IV, p. 285–6.

Chapter IV

1 *gradually on Wednesday.'* Thom, p. 3.

2 *at its owner's enterprise.* Stewart, p. 43.
3 *of milk sours.*' Dr F. Home, pp. 90–2.
4 *untamed element Chlorine*'. Elliot in *History Today.* August, 1951.
5 *under Watt's direction*'. Higgins, p. 75.
6 *to be expected.*' Ibid. p. 78.
7 *for bleaching purposes.*) Kingzett, p. 178.
8 *Mr. Alexander Dunlop.*' Macintosh, p. 37.
9 *from chlorine liquor.* Ibid. p. xv.
10 *fourteen years later.* Draft of co-partnership document is in City Archives, Glasgow (ref. T-MJ 409).
11 *liquor and powder.* City Archives, Glasgow, *Minute Book of the Register of Sasines for the Regality of Glasgow* the disposition being recorded on 5 May 1800 (refs to Minute Book B/10/5/10, Register B 10/2/73).
12 *£8 10s a ton.* MacTear, 'On the Growth of the Alkali and Bleaching Manufacture'.
13 *knowledge of chemistry.* The Report was produced by Mr Inspector General Duffin. This and the following extracts come from the minutes of the Trustees of the Linen and Hempen Manufacturers of Ireland.
14 *of official honesty.*' Macintosh, p. 42.
15 *in several Wards.*' Maitland, vol. II, book II, p. 1031.
16 *James Knox.* Letters from Knox to Macintosh, Macintosh, pp. 42–4.
17 *the Kings Bench.* Case is dealt with in Higgins, pp. 80–9.
18 *the Lancashire bleachers. Glasgow Courier*, 9 June 1804.
19 *two or three.* MacTear, 'On the Growth of the Alkali and Bleaching Manufacture', p. 16.
20 *of alkali making.* ibid.
21 *the actual results.*' Macintosh, p. xv.
22 *£12 per ton.* MacTear, 'On the Growth', p. 4.
23 *to the bleachers.* Haber, p. 11.
24 *to make alkali.* See Appendix II for an explanation of this process.
25 *at St Rollox.* MacTear, 'On the Growth', p. 25.
26 *and committed suicide.* Allen, p. 78.
27 *be briefly dismissed.* Haber, pp. 15 and 16.
28 in *The Antiquary.* Published 1816. See ch. 15.

Chapter V

1 *importance in Glasgow.* P. Hume Brown. III p. 309.

3 *great man's gate*'. Brown. III p. 307.
4 *in any trial.* Mackenzie, I p. 426.
5 '*to the people*'. Gairdner, p. 101.
6 *old circus behind*'. Mackenzie, I p. 197.
7 *on the Magistrates*'. Ibid. p. 306.
8 *said the Bailie.* Ibid. p. 306.
9 *the present discontent.* Ibid. p. 308.
10 *presence and Councils*'. Ibid. p. 310.
11 *say, perfectly unparalleled.* Mackenzie, II p. 246–8.
12 *night for Glasgow.*' Ibid. p. 249–50.
13 *the differ o't.* Ibid. p. 244.
14 *in the city*'. Strang, p. 457.

Chapter VI

1 *of man*', Buchanan, p. 8.
2 *at his post.* E. W. D. Tennant, '175 years of the Tennant Companies', unpublished MS., pp. 18–20.

Chapter VII

1 *of bleaching powder.* E. W. D. Tennant, *140 Years*, p. 17.
2 *to his support*'. Stewart. p. 43.
3 *very forcible*', H. J. Tennant, p. 13.
4 *was Andrew Thomson.* Bancroft, p. 37.
5 *pyramid of Egypt*'. See Appendix III.
6 *place—THE Chimney.* Dodd, p. 320. Another colourful account of St Rollox appeared in 1858 in J. D. Burn. See Appendix IV.
7 *those dung heaps*'. Government Report of 1842.
8 *deceive even experts*'. *I.C.I. Magazine*, Sep 1947.
9 *coal were consumed.* Haber, p. 157.
10 *friends and relatives. The Scotsman*, April, 1878.

Chapter VIII

1 *fortune on it.*' Asquith, *Autobiography*, I p. 6.
2 *a single mistake.* For an account of the Club, of which several Tennants were members, see Wolfe Murray.
3 *at the office.* E. W. D. Tennant, *140 Years*, p. 37.
4 *sheer and adventurous.*' Asquith, *Autobiography*, p. 10.
5 *reason and wisdom.*' H. J. Tennant, p. 19.
6 *round the sun*'. Letter to George Curzon, 1887.
7 *up 50 tomorrow.* Rosebery Papers.
8 *to, almost touching.*' Ibid.

9 *his granddaughter, Clare:* Lady P. Tennant, pp. 8 and 9.
10 *at any period.'* Ruskin, *Modern Painters*, I p. 136.
11 information about Sir Charles' collection is based on Dugdale.
12 *our fervid agreement.'* H. J. Tennant, pp. 46, 47.

Chapter IX

1 *the Tharsis Company.* Checkland. *passim.*
2 *mine in Sicily.* Campbell, p. 17.
3 *Spanish pyrites mine.* Checkland, p. 16.
4 *in ore treatment.'* Ibid. p. 105.
5 *patents in existence.'* Ibid. p. 111.
6 *concern another chance.'* Supplement to *The Mining World and Engineering Record*, 22 March 1902, p. 510.
7 *know what would.'* Supplement, *The Mining World and Engineering Record*, 22 Mar 1902, p. 512.
8 *by-products, fought back.'* Checkland, p. 145.
9 *of soft soap.'* Reader, p. 101.
10 *greatly improved upon*, MacTear, 'On the Regeneration'.
11 *five other firms.* Reader, pp. 105, 106.
12 *was often impossible.* E.W.D.Tennant, '175 Years', pp. 54-6.

Chapter X

1 *thereby be served'* Magnus, p. 150.
2 *the nineteenth century.* N. Wilding and P. Laundy, *Encyclopaedia of Parliament* (Cassell 1958).
3 *be a DICTATOR.'* Magnus, pp. 270–5.
4 *amounted to genius'.* Asquith, *Autobiography*, I p. 9.
5 *of Magna Carta.* Lister, p. 54.

Chapter XI

1 *is so impressionable.'* Asquith, *More Memories*, p. 13.
2 *I was sixteen.'* Ibid. p. 12.
3 *lions than sisters.'* Asquith, *Autobiography*, I p. 3.
4 *into the sky.'* Letter to George Curzon from Laura, 1884.
5 *my Glen background.'* Asquith, *More Memories*, pp. 19 and 20.
6 *white linen curtains.* Asquith, Diary, 20 Oct 1893, pp. 78–94.
7 *the same . . . Glen.'* Asquith, *Autobiography*, I, p. 5.
8 *I ever met.'* John Tennant, 'Some memories of the past', an unpublished typescript.
9 *multitude of friends.'* H. J. Tennant, p. 21.

10 *a perpetual joy*'. Asquith, *Autobiography*, I p. 1.
11 '*No, thank God!*' Ibid. p. 8.
12 *London shop windows.*' Ibid. p. 2.
13 *see them together*'. H. J. Tennant, p. 51.
14 *shown me gratitude*'. Asquith, *Autobiography*, I p. 8.
15 *would ever achieve.*' Tuckman, p. 15.
16 *delicacy of mind*'. Asquith, *Autobiography*, I p. 2.
17 *the Tennant family.*' Lady F. Balfour, pp. 391, 392.
18 *almost universal interest.*' Asquith, unpublished diaries.
19 *with Mr Gladstone.* Asquith, 'Myself when Young', p. 27.
20 *ball and party.*' Asquith, *More Memories*, p. 222.
21 *of their society.*' Lady F. Balfour, p. 393.
22 *Gerald, 'Doll' Liddell*, 'Doll' Liddell's relationship with Laura has been fully written about in Chandos, pp. 25–41, and in his own autobiography, A. G. C. Liddell.
23 *and crying together.* Asquith, unpublished diaries.
24 *of the dance.* Liddell, p. 227.
25 *originality and charm.* Mary Gladstone in Masterman, p. 268.
26 *seemed to escape. Laura* by Mary Gladstone, unpublished typescript.
27 *she was in his arms.* Lyttelton, p. 130. In this account of Alfred's life by his second wife there is a chapter about Laura (pp. 123–48) which recounts beautifully their short life together.
28 *an Englishman.* Asquith *Autobiography*, I p. 37
29 *if possible, attain.* Lyttelton, p. 408.
30 *cannot enter in. Laura*, op. cit.
31 *prospect of happiness.* Rosebery papers.
32 *noblest in us.*' *Laura* op. cit.
33 *you will not forget.* Asquith *Autobiography*, p. 40.
34 *all is spirit.* Lyttelton, p. 147, 148.
35 *love for her sister.* Phillips etc., p. 184.
36 *one in a hundred.* Rosebery papers.
37 *to the end.* Phillips, p. 181.
38 *each other's company.* Rose p. 163.
39 *my broken life.* Lyttelton, p. 369.
40 *who loved me.* Asquith *Autobiography*, I p. 28–9.
41 *to give to her.* Anne Tennant—personal communication to Nancy Crathorne, 1951.
42 *unpremeditated sympathy.* Balfour, p. 232.

43 *generally found together*. A. G. C. Liddell, p. 212.
44 *Jack is lucky*. Letter to Lord Curzon, 14 September 1889.
45 *frequent visitors*. Unpublished papers of Joan Lindsay.
46 *he wrote letters*: Asquith, 'My visit to Hawarden', p. 577–94.
47 *W.E.G.*: Magnus, pp. 382 and 383.
48 *awaited them*: This account is taken from Jack and Helen Tennant's unpublished typescript. 'Mr and Mrs Gladstone's visit to Glen.'
49 *to the fore*. Mark Bonham-Carter, p. xx.
50 *several days*. Ibid. p. 86.
51 *to his bed*. Ibid. p. 245.
52 *executed can feel*. Asquith *Places and Persons*, p. 13.
53 *unknown to him*. Margot Asquith 'A Little Journey in the Winter of 1891' (unpublished passage excluded from *Places and Persons*).
54 *mushrooms*. Ibid.
55 *from temptation*. Asquith *Places and Persons*, p. 38, 39.
56 *being so pretty*. Ibid. p. 60.
57 *always your own*. Jenkins, p. 75.
58 *political circles*. Asquith *Autobiography*, p. 145.
59 *human emotion*. Ibid. p. 269.
60 *even a Prime Minister*. Asquith *More Memories*, p. 16.
61 *to the five children*. Spender and Asquith, p. 96.
62 *career of my own*. Asquith *Autobiography*, p. 162.
63 *the two governments*. Horace G. Hutchinson, p. 203.
64 *truth in it*. Asquith *More Memories*, p. 129.
65 *into her confidence*. Lady Frances Balfour, II, p. 229.
66 *Minister's wife, V.R.I.* Rose, p. 171.
67 *Margot Tennant married*. Asquith *Autobiography*, I p. 267–8.
68 *stories a trust*. Ibid. p. 13.
69 *unworldly and uncomplaining*. Ibid. p. 13.

Chapter XII

1 *at the name of Miles*. Lawrence Ridge, *Lays of the Belvoir Hunt*, p. 68–80. Peter Miles was also the hero of Bromley's book *Sport*.
2 *measured tones*. Marguerite left some autobiographical notes amongst her papers from which her quotations are taken.

3 *feverish restlessness*: Personal communication from Lady Violet Bonham-Carter to Nancy Crathorne, Nov 23 1965.

4 *daughter's allowance*. Letter from Haldane to Balfour, 18 December 1898, Balfour Papers, mentioned in Stephen Koss' *Haldane* (Columbia University Press, 1969) p. 28.

5 *pot all night*' E. W. D. Tennant *True Account*, p. 101.

6 *not diamonds*. Personal communication from Lady Violet Bonham-Carter to Nancy Crathorne, op. cit.

INDEX

Abrahams, May (Mrs Harold John Tennant), 189
Agnew, William, 126, 127, 128
Aiken, Andrew, 50
Aiken, Robert, 46, 51
Ainsworth, Henry, 97
Alexander, Kenneth, 90
Alexander, Thomas, 90
Alexander, William, 89
Alexander, Sir William, 90
Alloway, 4, 18–19, 25, 44
Antiquary, The (Scott), 77
Arrol, Robina, 99–100, 101
Asquith, Herbert Henry, 181, 189, 194–6, 203, 209–11
Asquith, Mrs H. H. – *see* Tennant, Margaret ('Margot')
Ayr, 3, 10, 12, 13, 18, 23–4, 45–9, 118

Balfour, Arthur, 157, 173, 187, 192, 195, 210, 212
Balfour, Lady Frances, 171, 173, 195, 212
Balfour, Gerald, 173, 180
Ballikinrain, 100, 102
Belfast, 66, 75
Benson, E. F., 195
Beresford, Lord Charles, 187
Berthollet, Comte, 58, 59
Biarritz, 214, 216
Blair, John Hunter, 138
Blairston Mill, 4, 5, 17, 44
Bleaching Salt Company, 64–6
Bonham-Carter, Lady Violet, 205, 212, 215
Braxfield, Lord, 79
Brigend of Doon, 6
Bright, John, 157, 201
Broadoaks, Byfleet, 212–13, 216
Bromley, W. H., 199
Brown, George, 111
Brown, Mrs George (Jane Tennant), 111
Browning, Rev Archibald, 118–19
Brunner, Sir John, 120, 142
Brunner, John, 119
Brunner, Mond and Co., 120, 142, 144, 145
Burne-Jones, Edward, 184, 208
Burnes, William, 17, 18, 25–6, 47
Burns, Robert, 6, 12, 16, 21, 22, 25, 41, 50, 79; birth, 17; friendship with Auld Glen's family, 19, 23, 26, 28, 30, 32, 38–40, 126; early schooling, 18–19; 'propensity to fall in love', 26–8; as freemason, 28–9; reads early poems to Auld Glen and family, 31; early fame, 31–2, 37; rhyming epistle to James T., 32–5, 37; whisky transactions, 35–6; ride to Edinburgh, 37–8; farming schemes, 38–40; and Dalrymple family, 47–8, 51

Caroline, Queen, 83–5
Cassel, Henry Renner, 139
Cassel Cyanide Company, 140, 145
Cassel Gold Extracting Company, 139–40
Chamberlain, Joseph, 157, 158, 211
Churchill, Lord Randolph, 158–9, 188
Churchill, Winston, 191
Claudet, Frederich, 138
Couper, Mrs Alexander (Christine Tennant), 60
Couper, Mrs John (Charlotte Tennant), 60
Couper, Mrs W. (Mary Tennant), 60
Couper, Dr William, 60, 61, 111
Crathorne, Thomas Dugdale, 1st Baron, 220
Crathorne, Lady (Nancy Tennant), 215, 220
Curzon, Lord, 173, 182, 187–8, 206, 210

Dalrymple, Charles, 50
Dalrymple, Mrs Charles (Macrae M'Guire), 50
Dalrymple, James, 51

Dalrymple, Katherine (Mrs David Tennant), 46, 47
Dalrymple, Rev. Dr. William, 17, 23, 44, 47–9, 51
Darnley bleachfield, Eastwood, 56–7, 60–1, 63
Dodd, George, 108
Dundas, Henry, Viscount Melville, 78
Dundee, 75, 77
Dunlop, Alexander, 60, 61, 98, 111
Dunlop, Charles Tennant, 60, 75, 100, 111
Dunlop, James, 60

Eastwood, Glasgow, 56, 99
Edward VII, 216; as Prince of Wales, 136, 137, 138, 172, 208
Elliot, Rt Hon. Walter, 219, 220
Elliot of Harwood, Baroness – *see* Tennant Katharine

Flower, Peter, 192
Forth Bridge, 136–8

Gairdner, Charles D. 46, 81
Galbraith, William, 111
Garnkirk and Glasgow Railway, 90, 91–5, 104
Gladstone, Herbert, 156
Gladstone, Mary, 174–5, 177–8, 181, 182, 184
Gladstone, William Ewart, 149, 151–2, 154, 155, 156, 157, 158, 159, 160, 161, 162, 172, 177, 178, 179, 183–4, 189–90, 194, 196, 201
Gladstone, Mrs W. E., 177, 189, 190, 204
Glasgow, 61–3, 104; Chamber of Commerce, 68–71; drysaltery business at, 77; Reform movement in, 80, 82, 85–8, 103, 118; 'Radical Wet Wednesday', 82–3; support for Queen Caroline, 83–85; Crow Club, 87; Tennant house at 195 West George Street, 96, 97, 101, 103, 212; Sir Charles T. as MP for Partick division, 148–9, 161–3
Glen, The, Innerleithen, 124–5, 126, 153–4, 155, 166–8, 173, 174–7, 180, 185, 190, 196, 202, 204–7, 215–16
Glencairn, William, 13th Earl of, 13, 25, 31
Glencairn, Elizabeth M'Guire, Countess of, 13–14, 20, 22, 24, 25, 31, 41
Glenconner, Edward Tennant, 1st Baron – *see* Tennant, Edward
Glenconner, Christopher Tennant, 2nd Baron, 147
Glenconner farm, Ochiltree, 20–2, 24–5, 29, 31, 40, 55
Glenconner, North Berwick, 214
Gordon, Professor L. D. B., 107
Gordon-Duff, Helen (Mrs Harold John Tennant), 188–9
Gordon-Duff, Thomas, 168–9, 188
Gordon-Duff, Mrs Thomas – *see* Tennant, Pauline
Graham-Smith, Thomas, 171
Graham-Smith, Mrs Thomas – *see* Tennant, Lucy Katharine
Grainger, Thomas, 90–4

Haldane, Viscount, 202, 203, 210
Hebburn-upon-Tyne, 77, 105–6
Hetrick, Robert, 42
Holland, Henry Scott, 185
Humphreys, Edward, 131, 132
Humphreys, Tennant & Co., 131–2

Imperial Chemical Industries, 145
Innerleithen, 151, 152–3, 190, 191, 204, 216

Knox, James, 60, 61, 63, 65–6, 67, 69–70
Knox, John, 3–4, 14

Laigh Corton, Ayr, 12, 15, 20, 55
Leblanc, Nicolas, 74, 222–3
Liddell, 'Doll', 173–4, 180, 186, 187
Liverpool and Manchester Railway, 93
Lubbock, Geoffrey, 221
Lyttelton, Alfred, 177, 180–3, 185, 206
Lyttelton, Mrs Alfred – *see* Tennant, Laura
Lyttelton, Alfred Christopher, 185

McClure, Jean (Mrs John Tennant), 14–15
McClure, Margaret (Mrs John Tennant), 15, 24, 26
McClutchie, Jean (Mrs James Tennant), 34
M'Guire, Bell, 13
M'Guire, Elizabeth – *see* Glencairn, Countess of
M'Guire, Hugh, 13, 15, 50
M'Guire, Macrae (Mrs Charles Dalrymple), 50
Macintosh, Charles, 60–1, 69, 73
McIntyre, Duglad Campbell, 107–8
Macrae, Bell, 12
Macrae, Hon. James, 12–13, 50
MacTear, James, 75, 109, 111, 141, 143
McWilliam, Jean (Mrs John Tennant), 40–1
Mains Farm, Brigend of Doon, 6–11, 44
Malahide, 64–6
Manchester, 66, 67, 75
Maybole, 3, 4, 6
Merry, James, 104
Miles, Colonel Charles William ('Peter'), 198–201
Miles, Mrs (Maria Hill), 198–9, 201
Miles, Marguerite A. – *see* Tennant, Lady
Mond, Ludwig, 141, 142
Monkland and Kirkintilloch Railway, 91, 104
Monkton, Charlotte (Mrs Richard Winsloe), 122
Montgomery, Sir Graham, 149, 150, 153
Morison, Alexander, 111
Muir, Thomas, 79
Murdoch, John, 18–19, 22–4, 47
Murray, John A., 96
Muspratt, James, 75, 133
Mylne, Professor James, 80, 83
Mysore Gold Mining Company Ltd, 138–41

Nevett, William, 119, 120
Nobel Dynamite Trust Company, 141
Nobel's Explosives Co. Ltd, 96, 141
North British Railway Company, 136

Ochiltree, 3, 14, 20, 22, 24, 30, 42, 55
Oswald, James, 84, 87, 103

Parnell, Charles Stewart, 156, 157, 160
Peel, Sir Robert, 69
Perochon, Joseph, 66
Pollock, Jane (Mrs Charles James Tennant), 100
Ponsonby, Sir Henry, 154, 195

Rankine, Professor W. J. Mcquorn, 107
Redmayne, Anne (Mrs Francis John Tennant), 186, 206, 214
Reid, Agnes – *see* Tennant, Mrs William
Reid, George, 29, 37–8
Reid, Mrs George (Agnes Tennant), 29, 31, 37, 38
Reid, Rev George, 24, 29
Ribblesdale, Thomas Lister, 4th Baron, 125, 169–70, 185
Ribblesdale, Lady – *see* Tennant, Charlotte
Ribblesdale, Emma, Lady, 155
Rose, Kenneth, 185
Rosebery, Lord, 125, 137, 181, 184, 195, 196, 203, 210
Russell, Lord John, 85, 96, 97

St. Rollox: building of factory at, 61–3, 66; size of factory, 74–5; the 'Stalk', 75, 107–9, 224; expansion, 89, 95, 98, 106–10; transport problems, 89–92; school, 105, 228–9; waste and drainage problems, 109–10; decline of, 141–4; described in 1858, 225–9
St Rollox Shipping Company, 95
Salisbury, Lord, 155, 157
Scheele, Carl Wilhelm, 58
Secretan, Hyacinthe, 144
Siemens, Sir William, 135
Simson, William, 24, 25
Sloan, William, 94–5

Solvay, Ernest, 141, 142
'Souls', the, 187–8
Steel Company of Scotland, 135, 136, 145
Stephenson, George, 90, 92
Stevenson, William, 111

Tate, Agnes (Mrs George Reid), 29, 31, 37, 38
Tennant, Sir Charles (1823–1906), 20, 90, 101, 102; has idea of 'Stalk', 107; his life and achievement, 117, 131; education, 118–19; phenomenal memory, 119; early business life, 119–20; in London office of C. Tennant & Co., 120; business *coups* and foundation of fortune, 120, 121; appearance, 121; marriage to Emma Winsloe, 122; character, 122, 125, 155, 193; first London home, 123; buys Glen, 124–5; as sportsman, 125–6, 214; his library, 126; his art collection, 126–30; 161, 230; expert handling of company formation, 131; partner in Glasgow and London branches, 131; interest in sulphur sources and Tharsis Company, 132–5; and steel age in Scotland, 135–6; and Forth Bridge, 136–8; mining activities, 138–41, 144–5; and fight with Brunner-Mond, 142–4; elected Liberal MP for Glasgow (Partick), 148; elected for Peebles and Selkirk, 149–54, 156–7; baronetcy, 154; defeat in 1886 election, 159–61; defeat in 1892, 161–3; family life, 164–97; life at Glen, 167–8, 175–7; London home at 40 Grosvenor Square, 171, 215; Egyptian tour, 192–4; death of wife, 196–7; courtship of Marguerite Miles, 201–4; marriage, 204–5; second family, 206–7; 209, 214–15, 219–21; at International Exhibition (Paris 1900), 208; changing political views, 209, 210; generosity to Asquith, 210; desertion of Free Trade, 211; purchase of Broadoaks, 212–13; and Glenconner, 214; death, 216–18; company positions held by, 234
Tennant, Lady (Emma Winsloe, first w. of Sir Charles), 164, 173, 182; early married life, 122, 123, 124; character, 122, 123–4, 165, 193, 197; Egyptian tour, 192–4; death, 196–7
Tennant, Lady (Marguerite A. Miles, second w. of Sir Charles): family background, 198–201; first meeting with Sir Charles 201; engagement, 202–4; marriage, 204; life at Glen, 205–7; birth of children, 206–7, 209, 214–15; Margot's letters to, 207, 209, 211–12; second marriage, 221
Tennant, Charles (1768–1838), 21, 67; as 'Wabster Charlie', 33, 37, 55; apprentice weaver, 55–6; starts Darnley bleachfield, 56–7; marriage, 57; production of 'chlorine liquor' for bleaching, 59, 60; in partnership, 60–1; and 'bleaching salt', 61; purchase of St Rollox, 61; attempt to protect bleaching process, 68–71; purchase of company, 73; adoption of Leblanc process, 74; and Reform movement, 78, 80, 82–7; rail and waterway projects, 89–95; mansion in Glasgow, 96; refusal of knighthood, 97; death, 97–8
Tennant, Mrs Charles (Margaret Wilson), 57
Tennant, Charles (1851–6), 164
Tennant, Charles (1856–63), 165
Tennant, Charles James, 77, 85, 87, 99, 100, 102
Tennant, Mrs Charles James (Jane Pollock), 100
Tennant, Charlotte (Mrs John Couper), 60
Tennant, Charlotte ('Charty') (Lady Ribblesdale), 165, 174, 177, 185,

187, 188, 190; marriage, 169–70; and stepmother, 206, 207
Tennant, Christine (Mrs Alexander Couper), 60
Tennant, Christopher Grey, 2nd Baron Glenconner, 147
Tennant, Colin, 32, 38, 147
Tennant, David (1734–1823): 10, 18, 44–7
Tennant, Mrs David (Katherine Dalrymple), 46, 47
Tennant, David (1762–1839), 34, 96
Tennant, Edward Priaulx, 1st Baron Glenconner, 145, 154, 159, 165, 196, 204, 206, 215; at Eton, 166; and Glen, 167, 175–7, 196
Tennant, Mrs Edward (later Lady Glenconner) (Pamela Wyndham) 128, 196, 215
Tennant, Ernest Dalrymple, 112
Tennant, Francis John, 125, 165, 168, 186, 214
Tennant, Mrs Francis John (Anne Redmayne), 186, 206, 214
Tennant, Harold John ('Jack'), 106, 123, 129, 164, 165, 169, 170, 206; at Cambridge, 166; on Laura's death, 184–5; marriage and later career, 188–9
Tennant, Mrs Harold John I (Helen Gordon-Duff), 188–9
Tennant, Mrs Harold John II (May Abrahams), 189
Tennant, James (1754–1835), 15, 18, 25; friendship with Robert Burns, 19, 26, 30, 32, 34; as freemason, 28; Burns' rhyming epistle to, 32–5, 37; later life, 34
Tennant, Mrs James (Jean McClutchie), 34
Tennant, Jane (Mrs George Brown), 111
Tennant, Janet, 164, 165
Tennant, Jean (1756–1811), 15, 18
Tennant, Jean, 209
Tennant, John (1635–1723), 4–6
Tennant, John (s. of above), 5, 6
Tennant, John ('Auld Glen') (1726–1810), 10, 44; at Laigh Corton farm, 12, 20; first marriage, 14; second marriage, 15; his families, 15, 24, 26, 29, 34–7; leader in agrarian revolution, 16, 41; friendship with Burnes family, 17–20, 25–6; factor of Ochiltree, 20–22, 25; at Glenconner, 20–22, 29, 40; Burns' letter to, 38, 39; third marriage, 40–1; death, 42–3
Tennant, Mrs John I (Jean McClure), 14–15
Tennant, Mrs John II (Margaret McClure), 15, 24, 26
Tennant, Mrs John III (Jean McWilliam), 40–1
Tennant, John (1760–1853), 23, 29, 35–7
Tennant, Mrs John (Margaret Colville), 29
Tennant, John (1796–1878), 83, 87, 99–113, 122, 168; and Reform, 82, 85, 103; education 99; managing director at St Rollox, 99; life with Robina Arrol, 99–100, 101; character and way of life, 100–4, 105–6; family, 101, 102; benefactions, 103–4; varied interests, 104–5; builds St Rollox school, 105; and company's progress, 106, 111, 112, 131; welfare of employees, 110; death, 112–13; and his sons' careers, 119, 120, 124, 131; and Tharsis negotiations, 133
Tennant, John (1821–50), 101, 102, 120
Tennant, John Aubrey, 124, 164–5
Tennant, Julian, 112, 147
Tennant, Katharine (Baroness Elliot of Harwood), 138, 155, 214–15, 219–20
Tennant, Laura (Mrs Alfred Lyttelton), 165; and Glen, 166, 173, 174; in London society, 171, 172–3; character and appearance, 174, 177–80, 185, 186; cruise on *Pembroke Castle*, 177–9; engagement to Alfred Lyttelton, 180–2; marriage,

182; death in childbirth, 182–5; Margot on, 186
Tennant, Lucy Katharine (Mrs Thomas Graham-Smith), 165, 170–1, 174, 187, 188, 201; ill health, 171, 207; and Glen, 175, 176
Tennant, Margaret ('Margot') (Mrs H. H. Asquith) 117, 157, 165, 169, 170, 183, 188; and the Glen, 124, 166–7, 173, 174, 175–7; in London society, 171, 172–3; and Laura's engagement and marriage, 180–1, 182; character, 186; visit to Gladstone, 189–90; riding accidents, 191; brief engagement to Peter Flower, 191–2; Egyptian tour, 192–4; marriage to Asquith, 194–196; on mother's death, 196, 197; and stepmother, 202, 204, 206, 207, 209, 211–12; and Asquith's political life, 210–211; on father's support of Tariff Reform, 211–12
Tennant Margaret ('Peggy') (Lady Wakehurst), 207, 219
Tennant, Marion (Mrs Wallace), 100, 101, 102, 120, 122, 168
Tennant, Mary (Mrs W. Couper), 60
Tennant, Nancy (Lady Crathorne), 215, 220
Tennant, Pauline Emma ('Posie') (Mrs Thomas Gordon-Duff), 154, 165, 168–9, 182; marriage, 168; in South Africa, 169; ill health and death, 189
Tennant, Robert, 37, 63–5
Tennant, William (1695–1744), 6–11, 24
Tennant, Mrs William (Agnes Reid), 6, 7, 9, 11, 12, 24
Tennant, Rev. William, 34
Tennant, William, 145–7
Tennant, William Augustus, 112
Tennant, William Dalrymple, 112
Tennant, Charles, & Co, 73, 99, 131; expansion of, 74–7, 89, 95, 98; London office, 75, 99, 100, 106, 112, 120, 131, 145–7; welfare of workers, 105, 110, 228–9; changes in composition of, 111–12; production figures, 112
Tennant, Charles, Sons & Co, Ltd 77, 147
Tennant, C. & Sons and Co of New York, 77
Tennant, Clow, & Co, 120
Tennant, Knox & Co, 60–1, 62, 63–73
Tennant Estates (1928) Ltd, 147
Tennants Consolidated, 90
Tennants Lancashire Ltd, 120
Tennyson, Lord, 177, 178, 179
Tharsis Sulphur and Copper Company Ltd, 132–5, 138, 142, 143, 144, 145, 147
Thomson, Andrew, 107
Thomson, Thomas, 99
Thorburn, Walter, 149, 157, 159, 160
Tillicoultry, 118
Traquair, 197, 216
Trinidad, 132, 145
United Alkali Company, 143–4, 145
Victoria, Queen, 150, 154, 158, 195–6
Wakehurst, 2nd Baron, 219
Wakehurst, Lady (Margaret Tennant), 207, 219
Wallace, Rev Robert, 102
Wallace, Mrs Robert – *see* Tennant, Marion
Walter, Catherine (Mrs Richard Winsloe), 122
Watt, James, 58, 62
Webb, Godfrey, 175, 204
Wilson, Margaret (Mrs Charles Tennant), 57
Wilson, William, 57, 73
Winsloe, Mrs 122, 123
Winsloe, Emma – *see* Tennant, Lady
Winsloe, Rev. Richard, 122
Winsloe, Mrs Richard 122
Winsloe, Richard (son of above), 122
Winsloe, Mrs Richard (Charlotte Monkton), 122
Wishaw and Coltness Railway, 92, 93, 104
Wyndham, Pamela (Lady Glenconner), 128, 196, 215
Young, James, 75

St. Rollox
CHARLES
Manufa
Soaps,
CHLORIDE OF LIME OR BLEACHING POWDE
J & J. Johnstone
AGENT for the UNITED STA